RADIO for
EDUCATION and DEVELOPMENT

▓▓▓ PEOPLE AND COMMUNICATION ▓▓▓

Series Editors: F. GERALD KLINE   *Department of Journalism*
PETER CLARKE   *University of Michigan*

Volumes in this series: ▓▓▓▓▓▓▓▓▓▓▓▓▓▓▓▓▓▓▓▓▓▓▓▓▓▓▓▓

RADIO
for EDUCATION
and
DEVELOPMENT

DEAN T. JAMISON
EMILE G. McANANY

 SAGE PUBLICATIONS   Beverly Hills/London

For information address:

SAGE Publications, Inc.
275 South Beverly Drive
Beverly Hills, California 90212

SAGE Publications Ltd
28 Banner Street
London EC1Y 8QE

Printed in the United States of America

Library of Congress Cataloging in Publication Data

Jamison, Dean.
  Radio for education and development.

  (People and communication; vol. 4)
  1. Radio in education. I. McAnany, Emile G.,
joint author. II. Title.
LB1044.5.J35   371.33'31   77-28472
ISBN 0-8039-0865-2
ISBN 0-8039-0866-0 pbk.

FIRST PRINTING

Contents

Preface

In 1975 the Education Department of the World Bank initiated a study designed to improve its information base on the role of radio in education and development communication. The study had two parts. The purpose of the first part was to bring into one place, in a common format, a number of recently completed case studies of radio's use for in-school education, for formal education out-of-school, for nonformal education, and for interactive development communication. The World Bank recently published these case studies,[1] and Appendix A of this volume lists the titles of the studies and their authors' affiliations.

The purpose of the second part of the radio study was to synthesize, from the case studies and other sources, an overview of what is now known about radio's potential in education and development communication. In this volume Dean T. Jamison and Emile G. McAnany provide that synthesis.

The World Bank is indebted to the authors of the case studies for the effort they put into their preparation; the present volume draws heavily on their work. In addition, a number of individuals provided Jamison and McAnany with valuable comments on drafts of this work, and we would like to express here our warm appreciation to the following: Miren Etchevery, Shigenari Futagami, Jennie Hay, Mats Hultin, Steven Klees, Joanne Leslie, Henry Levin, William Rivers, Barbara Searle, Peter Spain, and Stuart Wells. Wilbur Schramm, too, through his writing and his personal influence, has helped to shape this book.

Although the World Bank provided financial support for the preparation of this volume, the conclusions it draws and opinions it expresses should not necessarily be considered to represent the Bank's views or policies.

—Aklilu Habte
Director
Education Department
The World Bank

NOTE

1. The case studies appear in P. Spain, D. Jamison, and E. McAnany (Eds.), *Radio for education and development: Case studies,* Volumes 1 and 2, World Bank Staff Working Paper No. 266, May, 1977.

chapter 1

Introduction

The rapid and extensive technological changes in man's ability to communicate and transfer information have quite rightly been called a revolution. We have just celebrated the first century of the telephone with a series of reflections on the economic and social consequences of this invention, and television pervades the lives of citizens in high-income countries. But on a worldwide scale it is the medium of radio that has been man's most potent communication innovation since the development of writing.[1] The large-scale manufacture of cheap, battery-operated transistor radios has been the breakthrough responsible for putting most of the world's people into an international communication network.

Two observations provide the context within which we develop the themes of this book. First, we believe the evidence suggests that, although continued technological innovation will make television broadcasting increasingly available to audiences in low-income countries, the constraints of cost and technical training for the television medium will leave radio dominant in these countries for at least another decade, and probably through the end of the century. Second, we believe that education and communication will play increasingly important roles in the development plans of many low-income countries, particularly in rural areas. Most rural people are physically isolated, illiterate, and poor. They read no newspapers, they have little hope of seeing a film in the course of a year, and television remains a rare experience even in the big cities. But a growing number of people in almost every village, no matter how small or how isolated, do listen regularly to radio. Governments concerned to communicate with more of their populations than their urban elites will be concerned with the effective use of radio.

Our purpose in this book is to provide an analytical summary of how radio has been and can be used in efforts to improve the lives of people, especially in low-income countries.[2] However, we should begin by putting this work into context by sketching what we conceive to be the elements of a national communication system.[3] A nation's communication system can be conceived as providing four major services: formal education, development communication, interactive communication, and entertainment. Table 1.1 lists the basic *objectives* of each service and the alternative *delivery systems* for supplying them. This book examines radio's role as a delivery system for formal education and development communication; it also briefly discusses (in the chapter on development communication) the quite limited role radio can play in providing interactive communication. Though radio's value in providing entertainment may well exceed its value for education and development communication, discussion of radio's entertainment role falls outside the scope of this book.

In the remainder of the Introduction we outline our major themes and overview the structure of the rest of the volume.

TABLE 1.1
Services of A National Communication System

	I FORMAL EDUCATION	II DEVELOPMENT COMMUNICATION	III INTERACTIVE COMMUNICATION	IV ENTERTAINMENT
OBJECTIVES				
Demand for Service	1. Basic Education (reading and language skills, mathematics, basic science, socialization) 2. Vocational Education (impartation of specific work skills—e.g., typing accountancy, surgery)	1. To motivate population 2. To inform population (e.g., local news, weather) 3. To teach adults (limited basic education, improved consumption and production efficiency) 4. To change behavior (family planning, etc.)	To allow exchange of information, agreements, and directives for: 1. Industry and commerce 2. Public administration 3. Security 4. Financial intermediation and banking 5. Personal use (direct consumption)	Direct consumption
DELIVERY SYSTEMS **Supply of Service**	**Locale** 1. In-school 2. Distance learning (at home) 3. Apprenticeship (at work) **Media** 1. Face-to-face instruction 2. Books 3. Other printed materials 4. Radio 5. Television 6. Recorded audio-visuals	1. Extension systems 2. Adult schools and listening groups (e.g., radio-phonic schools of Latin America, farm forums of India and Africa) 3. Campaigns (intensive efforts of limited duration, like the Tanzanian health campaign) 4. Spot announcements in the mass media	1. Telephony and telegraphy 2. Mail 3. Couriers (an important function of road, rail, and air systems is to transport couriers and mail) 4. Two-way radio	1. Press (including books) 2. Radio 3. Television 4. Films 5. Recorded audio-visuals

1.1 RADIO FOR EDUCATION

Almost from the time radio was invented there has been interest in its potential educational role, and by the late 1920s and 1930s a number of educational institutions in Europe, America, and elsewhere were making extensive use of radio. The coming of television and (in the United States) adverse regulatory decisions shifted interest away from radio; only recently have considerations of cost, outreach, and equity stimulated a renascense of interest in radio for education.

Uses for radio in education fall naturally into three broad categories: improving educational quality and relevance; lowering educational costs (or the rate of increase of costs); and improving access to education, particularly in rural areas. In the remainder of this section we briefly discuss reasons to believe that increased use of radio has the *potential* to improve education in each of these three ways. We also provide some comparative information on the experience with television.

QUALITY IMPROVEMENT

Early developers of educational radio were perhaps most strongly motivated by the potential they believed to exist for radio to improve educational quality. Results almost uniformly disappointed those who sought this goal. Reports of research on the instructional effectiveness of all media tended overwhelmingly to conclude that there were "no significant differences" between, for example, student performance in a class taught by an instructor, on the one hand, or, on the other, by that same instructor on radio, television, or audiotape. A number of comprehensive surveys exist (Chu and Schramm, 1967; Jamison, Suppes, and Wells, 1974; Schramm, 1977) on this point, and we quote the conclusions of Jamison, Suppes, and Wells (1974: 56).

Though there is a substantial past history in the use of instructional radio, few studies of its effectiveness exist. A number that do exist were, however, carefully done and they indicate that instructional radio, supplemented with appropriate printed material, is about as effective as traditional instruction. Despite this potential, the extent to which instructional radio can be substituted for traditional instruction remains to be tested. There is a much more extensive research literature on the effectiveness of instructional television, and excellent surveys of that literature already exist. There is strong evidence that instructional television, used in a way that closely simulates traditional instruction, is as effective, on the average, as traditional instruction for all grade levels and subject matters. There is very little evidence concerning the effectiveness of instructional television, used in ways that utilize the unique capabilities of the medium. A number of students and teachers have an initially unfavorable attitude toward instructional television, although the incidence of unfavorable attitudes tends to diminish as institutions gain experience with the medium. After such experience a majority of students have neutral or favorable attitudes toward instructional television.

While these findings of equal effectiveness disappointed those hoping for dramatic breakthroughs in instructional technique, they have, nonetheless, two important policy implications. First, as will be discussed in the next subsection, the finding of equal effectiveness opens the possibility of reducing costs, which may be particularly important if there is a substantial unmet social demand for education. Second, because radio is effective, its availability makes possible the provision of instruction in curriculum areas deemed important, but in which existing teachers are untrained. Perhaps the most dramatic such use is in language instruction; examples of this include using radio to teach English in Thailand, the Philippines, and the People's Republic of China. Other curriculum areas in which existing teachers may be untrained include natural science and mathematics, agricultural practices, and hygiene and public health. Thus even though radio in many cases may do no better than a competent teacher, there may be, nonetheless, a valuable role for it to play where competent teachers are scarce for the population to be served.

Despite the general finding of no significant difference, there are, nonetheless, occasional examples in which various media have outperformed traditional instructional practices. A number of these examples come from low-income countries where, presumably in part because of the poor quality of traditional instruction, achievement test scores tend to lag far behind those of high-income countries.[4] Three well-documented examples in which technology is improving quality are in El Salvador, Mexico, and Nicaragua. El Salvador makes heavy use of television in grades 7 through 9; an extensive evaluation of that project (Mayo, Hornik, and McAnany, 1976) found students using TV to be learning somewhat more than those having no access to it. The Mexican *Telesecundaria* provides beginning level secondary instruction to students in rural areas; the *Telesecundaria* may be of principal interest because it provided access to school to hitherto excluded rural groups, but evaluation of it (Mayo, McAnany, and Klees, 1975; Klees, 1974) also suggested that television improved students' test scores. Perhaps the most promising application of technology to improve quality, however, involves radio rather than television. Nicaragua's Radio Mathematics Project uses radio to carry the principal burden of instruction in mathematics for early elementary school students. Great effort is put into programming the radio lessons to maximize the children's interest and involvement, and in the course of each of the daily 30-minute radio broadcasts, each child is required to make close to 100 active responses to questions posed in the radio broadcast. Early evaluation results found strong achievement gains from radio instruction over traditional instruction, and evidence that radio indirectly reduced repetition rates; Chapter 2 discusses this project more fully.

Part of the reason that so many comparisons between media and traditional instruction have found them to be equally effective may be that many researchers hold notions of scientific adequacy that an outsider finds perplexing. These researchers seem to feel that to be scientifically adequate a comparison of radio with traditional instruction, say, should hold everything constant except the medium, i.e., one should have the same lecturer lecturing in the same way to the same sorts of students in the same environment. Under these circumstances it should cause little surprise to find no difference in outcomes. As an increasing number of projects begin to explore fully the potential of radio (as the Nicaraguan project already has), we would predict an increasing number of findings of quality improvement.

COST REDUCTION

Historical experience over the last two decades has shown rapidly rising educational system costs for both low- and high-income nations. One reason for the observed increase in expenditures on education has been enrollment expansion, especially in low-income countries. However, also of major importance in many countries is that, over time, it is becoming more expensive to educate each child in the system. It is likely that the future will bring increased traditional system costs (through rising real teacher costs) relative to instructional technology system costs (through reduction in or maintenance of the real costs of various technological alternatives), and thus the incentive to introduce these latter, more capital-intensive techniques will be increased. However, whatever potential radio and other technologies may have for reducing the cost of in-school education remains to be realized.

In the shorter term, the potential for use of technology to reduce costs per student per year is probably strongest at the secondary and post-secondary levels. At those levels the use of radio (and perhaps television) with correspondence for "distance learning" has demonstrated a capacity to reduce costs dramatically. The Open University of the United King-dom is perhaps the best known distance-learning system, but others are in operation in Botswana, the Dominican Republic, France, Germany, Japan, Kenya, and elsewhere (Schramm, 1977; MacKenzie, Postgate, and Scupham, 1975). Distance-learning systems realize their substantial cost advantages by requiring that students meet with teachers only occasionally—for two weeks in the summer, say, or at a monthly tutorial meeting.

IMPROVING ACCESS

A final potential use for instructional radio is to improve access to schooling for rural or urban disadvantaged groups. There are two broad approaches through which technology has been used in this way—distance learning and what might be labeled "extended schools."

The first, distance learning, was mentioned as being much less costly than more traditional forms of secondary and post-secondary instruction. Simply because of its lower cost, distance learning can improve access since, for any given budget level, more individuals can be reached with a distance-learning system than with a traditional one. Perhaps more important in terms of access, though, is that distance-learning systems can dissolve barriers of both distance and time to access to schooling. Traditionally, schools at higher levels exist principally in population centers because large total numbers of students are required to make such schools eco-nomically viable. Thus students from rural areas are either denied secondary schooling, or have to bear large travel or subsistence costs. This is far less of a problem with distance-learning systems. Since traditional schools typically meet at fixed hours during the day, finding time to attend is also frequently a problem for the poor who must work during the day to maintain their incomes. Distance study allows shifting the time for learning to the evening, thereby aiding a potential student in finding the time to continue his education. These points reflect the attractive side of distance-learning systems; important problems—of organization, program preparation, management, accreditation, and political acceptance—still remain. In those cases where these problems have been overcome, distance learning has achieved marked success.

A second way in which technologies have been used to improve access is through allowing the creation of relatively small but, nonetheless, self-sufficient schools in rural areas. An excellent example of this is the Mexican *Telesecundaria,* which was mentioned earlier. A number of rural towns in the states of Central Mexico equipped churches, community centers, or other unused space with a television receiver and benches; the Ministry of Education provided these schools with a primary teacher and the TV programs. Because the television carried the burden of instruction, trained secondary teachers were unnecessary. Tens of thousands of students completed the first cycle of secondary school at relatively low cost and with relatively high achievement (Mayo, McAnany, and Klees, 1975). Arena, Jamison, Oliveira, and Orivel (1977) describe a similar use of television in Brazil. Spain (1977) and Schmelkes (1977) describe more limited efforts using radio for this purpose, efforts that had much less success than those using television. The creation of small, self-sufficient schools is a more costly approach to extending access than is distance learning, but closer in structure to traditional schooling.

1.2 RADIO FOR DEVELOPMENT COMMUNICATION

Development communication is, in a sense, a residual category. It consists of all those other uses, besides formal education and entertainment, for which a country may wish to use its radio broadcasting. The variety of ways of classifying the purposes of development communication is wide indeed (McAnany, 1973); for this discussion we divide the purposes into four broad categories: to motivate, to inform, to teach, and to change behavior. These goals constitute one dimension along which radio's uses for development communication can be classified; a second dimension is that of strategies or ways of using radio. Before turning to the strategies it may be of use to discuss the purposes further.

Radio's use to *motivate* concerns arousing people to think about and, hopefully, ultimately to act on something. Radio programs on political themes often seek to motivate people to national patriotism; programs about the environment seek to motivate people to be more conscious of their ecology; and religious programs seek to inspire hope, love of neighbor, or inner peace.

Radio's use to *inform* would include, for example, programs on local, national, or international news; farm news; weather; and information about social activities and services available to listeners. Advertising can serve both to motivate and to inform.

Under the broad heading of using radio to *teach* we include acquisition of those more generalized cognitive skills that cut across many activities, most commonly literacy and numeracy, but also general skills for seeking information, like the ability to use a dictionary, a phone book, or other types of stored information. The teaching of these skills is often best achieved in formal schooling but can also be taught to adults, school dropouts, or others in a nonformal setting outside the school accreditation system and often in such informal ways as in radio soap operas. Also important is teaching of work skills. Radio programs that teach mothers how to prepare more nutritious meals for their families, farmers how to plant a better crop of corn, or people how to apply first aid in case of accidents, are imparting work skills. Using radio to teach for nonformal education is probably its most important development communication purpose.

Finally, using radio to *change behavior* refers to types of programs advising people of a specific activity without trying to explain much about it. Learning is at a minimum and people are asked simply to follow certain directions. Radio has been used to tell people the mechanics of how to get a vaccination, how to vote, how to register children for school, and so forth.

The second dimension for considering radio's role in development communication concerns strategies for radio's use. By strategy we refer to the way in which radio and other resources are organized to achieve the purposes discussed. Basically we have reduced these strategies to three main categories: open broadcasting, campaigns, and regular listening groups. We add to these a telecommunications category that, with two-way radio, makes radio a medium for interactive communication, much like telephone conference calls. *Open broadcasting* encompasses all of those radio uses that concentrate on producing and broadcasting the radio messages, but do nothing to organize or send supporting material to audiences. *Regular listening groups* refers to the uses of radio that call for the organization, supervision, and support of local listening groups that meet regularly to discuss and often act upon the radio messages. *Campaigns* combine many of the features of the other two categories, but extend over a short period of time (3 to 6 months), focus on a specific topic, and have only a limited set of objectives.

Table 1.2 lists a number of examples in which the different radio strategies are used to attain the goals listed. The reader will notice in reading the goals from left to right that they increase in order of specificity of learning from the generally more vague area of motivation (e.g., nation building, consciousness raising) to the quite specific direction of behavior change (e.g., to receive a vaccination for your child against cholera come to clinic X from 7 A.M. to 6 P.M. all next week beginning Monday). The strategies vary in the degree to which resources other than radio are involved. The last "strategy,"

TABLE 1.2

Goals and Strategies of Radio for Development Communication

Radio Strategies	Purposes of Use				
			To Teach (Nonformal Education)		To Change Behavior
	To Motivate	To Inform	Cognitive Skills	Work Skills	
Open Broadcasting	Kenya, health program (Unicef, 1975)	Guatemala, farm program (AED, 1976)	China, second language study (N.Y. Times)	Philippines, food preparation (Manoff, 1975)	How to get vaccinated
Radio Campaigns	Tanzania, Campaigns 1,2,3 (Hall, Dodds, 1977)	Botswana, Campaign 1 (Colclough, Crowley, 1974)	Tanzania Campaign 4 (Barrett, 1976)	Village accountancy courses (Dodds, 1972)	Ecuador, nutrition campaign (Manoff, 1975)
Listening Groups	Brazil, radio education movement MEB (de Kadt, 1970)	Colombia, radio schools, ACPO (Gomez, Gutirerrez, 1970)	Honduras, radio schools, ACPH (White, 1977b)	Ghana, farm forums (Coleman et al, 1968)	Guatemala, farm program (AED, 1976)
Telecommunications (Two-way radio)	Kewatin, Canada, community radio (Hudson, 1977)	Northern Ontario, two-way radio (Hudson, 1977)	Alaska, satellite two-way radio for health care (Kreimer, 1977)	Alaska, satellite two-way radio for health care (Kreimer, 1977)	Alaska, satellite two-way radio for health care (Kreimer, 1977)

telecommunication, is included with development communication strategies, rather than separately, as on Table 1.2, because the limited extent to which radio can be expected to play a role in interactive communications is insufficient to justify its being treated separately.

1.3 ORGANIZATION OF THE BOOK

In attempting to analyze the results of a large number of radio projects around the world, it is useful to adopt a framework within which the relative success or failure of these strategies might be judged. McAnany (1975) suggested several criteria in reviewing the work of radio schools, and in this volume we adapt these criteria to formulate five questions about radio for development communication. (1) Is the strategy effective, or does it work? (2) Does the strategy reach a large enough audience to make a significant impact on the solution of the problem? (3) What does the strategy cost? (4) What are the alternatives to using radio to achieve the same goal? (5) How easy or difficult is the implementation of the strategy, and can a strategy successfully used in one place be transferred to another? Obviously there will be different answers to these questions for different strategies. We quantify a few of the answers, but, more often, in reviewing the available evidence, we simply attempt to draw qualitative conclusions about the relative merits of each strategy in conjunction with different development goals.

The remainder of this book reflects this analytical framework. Chapter 2 reviews the available evidence on radio concerning questions one and two—radio's effectiveness and coverage—in the area of formal education. Chapter 3 does the same for the radio strategies of development communication. Chapter 4 reviews what we know about costs, responding to question three. Chapter 5, in addressing question five, discusses the various constraints (political, administrative, and technical) on the implementation of the different strategies. Question four, on alternatives or cost-effectiveness, is implicit or explicit throughout all of the chapters, but in the conclusion, Chapter 6, we summarize our findings and make recommendations about the strategies of radio use that we find most promising in terms of their relative effectiveness and cost. The book concludes with three appendices: Appendix A lists the case studies from which this book is in part drawn; Appendix B provides information on the radio transmission and reception infrastructure of countries around the world; and Appendix C, prepared by Peter L. Spain, contains an annotated bibliography on radio for education and development.

NOTES

1. Goody and Watt (1968) provide a valuable overview of studies of the impact of the invention of writing and spread of literacy on economic and social development.

2. We thus conceive this book to be a natural sequel to those portions of the International Institute for Educational Planning's *The New Educational Media: Memo to Educational Planners* (Schramm, Coombs, Kahnert, and Lyle, 1967) that dealt with radio. We are in this volume able to examine a number of important new projects and to draw conclusions about radio's potential in light of their experience. Schramm's (1964) work on mass communication and national development was a major influence on our current work, and remains a valuable source of information and ideas on these matters even though alternative conceptual paradigms (Rogers, 1976) now tend to place less emphasis on the importance of communication per se.

3. Though informal, interpersonal information networks (Bowman, 1976) and the prices of goods, services, and labor carry information, our concern in this volume is limited to more structured communication services.

4. Inkeles (1977: 157), in a review of the findings of the 19-country, 9-volume "International Evaluation of Educational Achievement," concludes as follows: "What was distinctive about the less developed countries was the extremely poor showing they made on the tests, at all ages and largely without regard to the subject tested on the mode of testing." Inkeles attributes this more to "lack of enrichment" in the environment of children from low-income countries than to poor quality of instruction; we would, however, be inclined to place greater weight on insufficient instructional quality.

chapter 2

Radio for
Formal
Education

The formal educational systems of low-income countries around the world share many or all of the following well-known problems: (1) they have rising unit costs, (2) they provide relatively poor access for rural children, (3) they provide a low quality of instruction, with the frequent result that students from these countries acquire less cognitive knowledge than do children of the same age in high-income countries, (4) they exhibit slow response in providing education relevant to development goals, and (5) their distributional impact is regressive, often highly regressive. The very difficulties that formal educational systems are facing have generated searches not only for ways in which these systems can be improved, but also for alternatives to formal education for meeting the instructional and informational needs of populations. In the next chapter, on radio's role in development communication, we discuss the uses and potential of radio in helping to create viable alternatives and complements to formal schooling. Our purpose in this chapter is to bring together information on the extent to which radio can be expected to improve the internal responses of formal educational systems to the problems they face.

Two sections constitute the remainder of this chapter. The first of these discusses alternatives for formal schooling and the role of radio among those alternatives. The second gives a more concrete sense of the range of uses to which radio has been put by reviewing the case studies in Spain, Jamison, and McAnany (1977) that deal with radio's use for formal education.

2.1 RADIO'S ROLE AMONG ALTERNATIVES FOR FORMAL EDUCATION

This section delineates the broad alternatives possible for organizing a formal education system and identifies the potential roles radio can play within those alternatives. Before turning to that discussion, though, we should indicate what types of activity we denote by the phrase "formal education."

DEFINITION OF "FORMAL EDUCATION"

By formal education we refer to education that has two characteristics. First, its subjects are predominantly in the cognitive skills area. At the elementary and secondary levels these skills include effective use of the national language, mathematics, social and natural science, and second languages. At the higher level specialized skills such as agronomy, engineering, and medicine would be included. Second, formal education typically will lead to certification of a sort that is readily understood internationally: one can label the product of a formal education system as "having a university degree," "having completed primary," and so forth. Though research is under way to find more meaningful descriptors of educational attainment than the time-based ones now associated with formal systems, it is reasonable to expect that present methods of describing educational attainment will remain important for quite some time. When accepted alternatives to present methods exist, it will become reasonable to define formal education simply as education in cognitive skill areas. There is nothing in the above definition of formal education implying that formal education need employ traditional pedagogical techniques. Such distance-learning systems as the Open University of the United Kingdom provide formal education by nontraditional techniques.

Nonformal education is education in subject areas specific to the development needs of individual regions of a country. Some nonformal education may deal with cognitive skills, e.g., adult literacy training, but most of it will utilize whatever cognitive skills the individuals already have to assist in the transfer of development-relevant knowledge. This knowledge might concern local agronomic practice, public health, personal hygiene and nutrition, community organization, and so forth. Coombs and Ahmed (1974: 8-9) further distinguish nonformal education from informal education, which is typically acquired from acquaintances or mass media; nonformal education differs from informal in that it generally involves structured presentation of a body of information the usefulness of which extends over many years. Provision of nonformal education is one important task of development communications, as indicated in Table 1.2, and one to which we shall return in Chapter 3.

ALTERNATIVES FOR FORMAL EDUCATION

In this subsection we describe in broad terms the alternatives for formal education. First we categorize these alternatives along a number of dimensions; we then discuss both the conventional and technological options available.

Categorization of alternatives.[1] The categories of alternatives to be considered are:

(1) the degree of physical centralization of students for instruction;

(2) the mix of instructional methods (including the extent of use of radio);

(3) the amount and distribution of time students spend in school;

(4) the curriculum mix; and

(5) certification, promotion, and retention procedures.

We discuss each of these briefly below, then focus in more detail on those most critical for examining radio's role.

Advances in communication and information-storage technology have made possible a considerable decentralization of schools. A first level of decentralization would be to very small neighborhood schools; this possibility is important in allowing the establishment of schools in low population-density rural areas. A more marked level of decentralization is represented by the distance-learning concept, in which the students receive their lessons at home by printed materials and audio (stored or off-the-air) and interact with the school system by mail and/or periodic personal contact. Distance learning need not preclude gatherings of students for athletics, social occasions, or seminars and discussions. As already indicated, its use shows substantial promise for reducint the cost and improving access for secondary and higher education in developing countries.

The second category of alternatives concerns the mix of instructional methods. We use the term *mix* to emphasize that in most departures from present methods of instruction the student will be learning from several instructional techniques during the day. In one mix there might be, for example, two hours of radio in a class of 60 students with one paraprofessional and one older student monitoring, two hours of conventional class activity (size 30), and 1/2 hour with a teacher in a discussion group with 5 or 6 other students. Subsequent subsections discuss alternative instructional methods, both conventional and technological, in more detail.

The third category of alternatives concerns the amount of time students spend in school—the number of hours per day and the number of days per year. In most countries elementary students spend 4 to 6 hours per day for about 180 days. Using present techniques of instruction, the length of the school year impacts very strongly indeed on costs and it is probably of considerable importance in student learning (Wiley, 1977). There is one further aspect of the "time" question that is much discussed by economists; for students in the higher grade levels, there is an opportunity cost to the economy of having the students in school. In estimating the true cost of education one should, then, add in the earnings foregone by students due to their being in school. In an overview of results in this area Schultz (1971) estimated that approximately half the cost of schooling at the upper levels in developing countries may be in earnings foregone. In rural areas even the time of children of elementary-school age can have value. Increasing problems of unemployment, however, reduce these opportunity costs.

The fourth category of alternatives is that of curriculum mix. We will provide no discussion of this obviously important area of choice except to note that the importance attached to various components of the curriculum can have a bearing on the choice of radio versus conventional instruction for two reasons. First, in some subject areas (e.g., mathematics or second language) teachers are apt to be relatively weaker than they are in others. Radio is a more attractive option if substantial importance is attached to such subject areas. Second, if there are to be *changes* in curriculum or pedagogical technique (e.g., a decrease in rote memorization), radio is potentially capable of implementing these changes more rapidly. Thus curriculum objectives can impact on the choice of instructional medium.

The final category of alternatives concerns promotion, retention and certification procedures. The range of options here depends to some extent on the state of testing technology. Though testing and certification procedures have only a small direct impact on cost, they have an important indirect impact through their influence on the number of students in the system.

We now turn to a more detailed discussion of the second category of alternatives, that dealing with the mix of instructional methods. We begin with discussion of conventional alternatives, then turn to technological ones.

Conventional alternatives. The conventional alternatives to present systems fall into several relatively simple categories. These are:

(1) changes in teacher quality (i.e., level of ability, education, or experience);

(2) changes in the average number of students per class;

(3) changes in the average number of hours per week and weeks per year the students spend in school;

(4) changes in the quantity of books and other support material available per student; and

(5) changes in the utilization rate of classrooms.

The set of economically feasible, conventional alternatives can be characterized for any given annual budget, B, and number of students to be enrolled, N.[2] The simple equation in the footnote summarizes all conventional alternatives in broadbrush terms. It fails to capture nuances but it specifies, nonetheless, all combinations of teacher quality, class size, hours of class per week, instructional-materials usage, classroom usage, and students enrolled, that are economically feasible at the prevailing budget, price, and wages.

Technological alternatives. It is somewhat more difficult to categorize the technological alternatives than to categorize the conventional ones. There are two broad dimensions along which the alternatives can be arrayed. The first is alternative technologies and the second is alternative uses for technology. Alternative technologies include:

(1) motion video (i.e., television, film);

(2) still video (slides, charts, still-frame television);

(3) audio (cassettes, records, radio); and

(4) computer-assisted and computer-managed instruction.

Alternative uses for technology include at least the following four possibilities:[3]

(1) *Enrichment of learning,* i.e., provision of occasional lessons or experiences that the classroom teacher would find difficult to provide.

(2) *Direct instruction,* i.e., carrying the major portion of the instructional burden in one or a few subjects.

(3) *Extending in-school education,* i.e., providing direct instruction in enough subjects so that a qualified teacher can be replaced by a monitor with little or no more education than the students.

(4) *Distance learning,* in which, as previously discussed, a technology combined with textbooks and occasional personal interactions completely replaces the teacher and school.

The first three of these uses of technology take place in school; they thus occur in combination with some mix of conventional alternatives. The final use, distance learning, is potentially capable of dramatic cost reductions through elimination of the basic schooling infrastructure; the extent to which this potential is realized will depend on local conditions, on the efficiency of the distance-learning system, and on the extent to which economies of scale are realized through large enrollments. The next subsection further discusses experience with radio's use and the role of radio among these alternatives.

THE ROLE OF RADIO

The preceding subsection outlined the alternative technologies that might be used for education, and alternative uses for them. How does radio stand among the alternative technologies? What evaluation information do we have on its effectiveness? Which uses might it best serve? We discuss those issues briefly here, then turn in the next major section to a more detailed discussion of a number of specific cases.

The effectiveness of instructional radio. Three surveys review information relevant to the effectiveness of instructional radio. One is Section VI of Chu and Schramm's (1967) comprehensive review of learning by television. The second is a paper by Forsythe (1970) that, in an earlier form, was prepared for the President's Commission on Instructional Technology. The third is a survey of all media, including traditional instruction, which was undertaken by Jamison, Suppes, and Wells (1974). Sources of further information on instructional radio may be found in a 432-entry, indexed bibliography compiled by R. Madden (1968), and in the annotated bibliography in this volume; an early review of research undertaken primarily in the late 1930s and early 1940s may be found in Woelfel and Tyler (1945).

Chu and Schramm (1967) numbered the principal conclusions of their extensive survey. The ones most relevant to instructional radio follow:

> 53. Given favorable conditions, pupils can learn from any instructional media that are now available. [p. 151]

> 54. The use of visual images will improve learning of manual tasks as well as other learning where visual images can facilitate the association process. Otherwise, visual images may cause distraction and interfere with learning. [p. 162]

> 60. Student response is effectively controlled by programmed methods, regardless of the instructional medium. [p. 172]

Their general conclusion is that radio, particularly when appropriately supplemented by visual material, can teach effectively and, for many purposes, as well as other media.

Forsythe (1970) reached a similar conclusion. In summarizing studies of radio's effectiveness he concluded:

Research clearly indicates that radio is effective in instruction. Experimental studies comparing radio teaching with other means or media have found radio as effective as so-called "conventional methods". Even through radio has been critized for being only an audio medium, studies have shown that visual elements in learning are not uniformly important. In many educational situations visuals may be more harmful than helpful. Also, the efficiency of combined audio and visual media has been challenged by studies which show that multi-channel communications may not be inherently more effective than single-channel presentations.

Jamison, Suppes, and Wells (1974: 33-34) conclude in a similar vein:

> Radio has been used extensively for formal classroom instruction in the United States (more in the past than at present) and elsewhere. There exist, however, only a limited number of good evaluations of the effectiveness of instructional radio. These evaluations indicate that instructional radio (supplemented with appropriate printed material) can be used to teach most subjects as effectively as a live classroom instructor or ITV. Due to the limited number and scope of good evaluations now available, and to the potential economic significance of instructional radio for developing countries, much more research—both survey and experimental—is highly desirable.

In order to give a more concrete sense of what the effectiveness studies report, we are including, virtually unchanged, information from two tables in Schramm (1977: 50-52). This information appears in Table 2.1, which also includes information on learning from audio distributed in other ways than by open-circuit radio.

The examples in the table indicate that radio, properly used, can teach as well as (or, in some cases) better than traditional instruction. There are two directions that subsequent studies should take to extend these findings. The first of these is exemplified by the Radio Mathematics Project in Nicaragua; there they are investing substantial resources to extract the maximum they can from the radio medium. Results from that project differ qualitatively from the results re-

TABLE 2.1
Examples of Learning from Instructional Radio

Author	Study	Results
Constantine (1964)	Science taught by radio in elementary school.	Students gained on the average 14 months, in one school year, on standardized test of scientific information, and 15 months on standardized test of work study skills.
Heron and Ziebarth (1946)	Learning from radio lectures compared with that from classroom lectures by the same teacher in college-level psychology. Groups changed places half-way through the course.	No significant differences.
NHK (1956a, b)	Japan Broadcasting Corporation used radio to teach English and music in 3rd, 5th, and 7th grades.	Reported learning gains in every case at or above level of conventionally taught classes.
Wisconsin Research Project in School Broadcasting (1942)	12 elementary school classes that received 25 minutes weekly of radio teaching of music, plus 40 minutes of classroom practice, compared with 8 classes taught same material for 75 minutes weekly in classroom.	Radio classes significantly better in tests of ability to recognize note values, read at sight, and recognize rhythms; no significant difference in ability to take musical dictation.
Xoomsai and Ratanamangala (1960)	Very large sample study of teaching of social studies and music in 2nd and 3rd grades, English language in 6th and 7th grades of rural Thai schools. Compared with control groups.	Experimental controls doubtful, but gains of radio groups reported as comparing very well with usual gains in those classes by conventionally taught students.

TABLE 2.1 (Continued)

Author	Study	Results
Lumley (1933)	High school students taught foreign languages with the aid of radio.	Pronunciation of students who heard radio lessons better than that of students who did not.
Popham (1961)	Two sections of a grad course in Education matched on aptitude and subject matter pretests; one section taught by lecture, the other by tape recordings of same lectures.	No significant differences.
Menne, Klingenschmidt, and Nord (1969)	Recorded lectures from introductory university psychology course, and provided students who wished to work at their own pace with their own tape recorders and printed chalkboard notes. 209 students chose to study from tapes, 408 from live lectures.	Overall, no significant differences. Lowest quartile showed clear advantage for tape. Only 5 out of 209 tape students dropped out of course, while 58 out of 408 dropped out of lecture sections.
Elliott (1948)	Compared use of taped with live geography lessons in private secondary school.	Lower IQ students gained relatively more from tape.
Bureau of Public Schools (1969)	Compared English language performance of first-grade students in the Philippines who received two 15-minute radio lessons per week with those who received only classroom instruction.	Significant difference in favor of radio group on end-of-year tests.

SOURCE: Items in Table 2.2 are combined from Tables 2.6 and 2.7 of Schramm (1977), with the exception of the item on the Philippines.

ported in Table 2.1. Searle, Matthews, Suppes, and Friend (1977) report dramatic student achievement gains when primary students receive their mathematics instruction by carefully programmed radio. The next section further discusses the Nicaragua case, which illustrates a remarkable (but usually unrealized) potential for radio to improve instructional quality.

A second direction in which research should be moving is into an examination of the effects of introducing radio (and other changes in pedagogical technique) on student dropout and repetition rates. These rates are critical in modeling the cost-effectiveness of possible change in pedagogical technique in either in-school or distance-learning systems. Very little is known about the effects of alternative school policies on either of these outcomes, but particularly on repetition rates.[4]

Radio among alternative technologies. A widely held view is that the choice of a medium of instruction will in most cases be a complicated one. It will involve careful analysis of the learners' needs and situation, of the instructional task, and of the locally available media and their costs. Two lines of evidence suggest, however, that the task of media choice may be less complicated than it might at first seem.

The first line of evidence, which was just reviewed, suggests that students learn effectively from any medium, if it is used properly. Variations in learning outcomes depend much more on how the material is structured and presented than on which medium carries the information. An exception to this finding of equal effectiveness may be for extending schooling; as we shall see, there seems to have been little success with radio for this purpose.

The second line of evidence arises from cost studies. These we review in Chapter 4. In contrast to the findings of no sigfinficant differences across media in terms of learning effectiveness, there are, as one would expect, striking differences in cost among media. Computer-assisted instruction costs 10 to 50 times as much as instructional television, which itself costs 3 to 10 times as much as instructional radio. Both computer-managed instruction and still-frame television are more expensive than ordinary television, the latter because of the cost of receivers capable of holding a video frame on the screen.

We conclude from the above lines of argument that radio should generally be the medium of choice in low-income countries if an electronic medium is to be used at all.[5] The difficult choice will usually (but not always) be between radio and conventional instruction and not between radio and some other medium. (Whether to use open broadcast radio or recordings will depend on local conditions, including the size and geographical distribution of the population.)

Alternative uses for radio. The list of uses for technology presented earlier in this chapter included enrichment, direct instruction, extending in-school education, and distance learning. By far the most widespread use of radio in formal education is for enrichment. This use is easy to organize and inexpensive. It will typically involve one or two 15-minute supplemental lessons per week, in different areas of the curriculum, which are used at the discretion of the teacher. Though little or no systematic evidence exists on the effectiveness of enrichment lessons, their impact is probably quite limited (but, perhaps, worthwhile since costs are frequently so low). This volume discusses no case studies of radio used for enrichment.

Radio's second use, for direct instruction, has been tried in many countries and a number of evaluations now exist. The term "direct instruction" covers a range of intensities of use. At one extreme is relatively light use of radio to provide several short lessons per week in the same subject. This use is more systematic than radio for enrichment though requiring only somewhat intensive use of radio. Nicaragua's

Radio Mathematics Project makes substantially heavier use of radio. In that project primary-school students receive 30 minutes of radio instruction in mathematics daily. Most of the studies reported in Table 2.1 use radio for direct instruction at some level of intensity.

Radio's third potential use is for extending in-school instruction to regions otherwise unreached. This volume summarizes two case studies from Mexico—describing projects in San Luis Potosi and in the Tarahumara region—that use radio in this way. These cases illustrate both the potential and the major difficulties associated with this use of radio; by and large the experiences are disappointing.

A final use for radio is as a component of a distance-learning system. Australia, Germany, Great Britain, France, and Japan make extensive use of radio for distance learning at the secondary and higher levels, usually in conjunction with correspondence and sometimes in conjunction with television, and an increasing number of low-income countries are also experimenting with this use of radio (Schramm, 1977; MacKenzie, Postgate, and Scupham, 1975; Lefranc, 1974). Kenya has many years of experience with a radio-correspondence approach to teacher learning, and the next section summarizes a case study on their experience (Kinyanjui, 1977). The Dominican Republic has used radio plus correspondence to provide elementary and beginning-secondary equivalency instruction to adults (White, 1977a). Their work draws on Spanish efforts in the Canary Islands (Cepeda, 1976; Gallego, 1974). The South Koreans are providing secondary-school instruction through radio and correspondence (KEDI, 1976). The instances could be multiplied. Because of its potential for improving access and reducing cost, distance learning is perhaps the most attractive potential use of radio for formal education.[6]

2.2 SUMMARIES OF CASE STUDIES

This section summarizes the five case studies dealing with radio's use for formal education that appear in the volume edited by Spain, Jamison, and McAnany (1977). The material here draws heavily on the case studies though, where appropriate, additional material has been included. The first case we summarize is Searle, Suppes, and Friend's (1977) description of Nicaragua's Radio Mathematics Project, which uses radio for direct instruction in mathematics at the primary level. The next two cases that we summarize—by Schmelkes (1977) and Spain (1977)—deal with attempts in Mexico to extend the reach of in-school elementary education to rural areas. Finally, we summarize two case studies of distance-learning projects, Kinyanjui's (1977) description of Kenya's radio-correspondence system for teacher training, and White's (1977a) description of *Radio Escuela Santa María* in the Dominican Republic, which provides elementary and secondary-school equivalency for rural adults. While there is much additional information about instructional radio, some of it summarized in the preceding section, these five cases are among the best studies now available. Our summaries of them here should help provide an indication of the potential and the problems of expanded use of radio in formal education.

THE NICARAGUA RADIO MATHEMATICS PROJECT

In early 1975 a group of AID-sponsored researchers and mathematics-curriculum specialists began working with Nicaraguan counterparts in Masaya, Nicaragua on radio programs to teach elementary-school mathematics. The Radio Mathematics Project (RMP) has now initiated its third operational year and is reaching several thousand first- and second-grade students. During 1977, programming is being extended through the third grade, and a carefully controlled evaluation of a large-scale implementation of the first-grade curriculum has just been completed. Present plans call for continued expansion of curriculum coverage to higher grade levels and for implementation of the radio curriculum throughout Nicaragua. The case study by Searle, Suppes, and Friend (1977) describes the present status of the project in detail, and, of particular importance to other project developers, it emphasizes the psychological principles underlying the project's use of extremely frequent student response as a pedagogical technique. Two other salient features of the RMP that Searle, Suppes, and Friend describe are its heavy use of formative evaluation in curriculum preparation, and its concern from the outset with problems of cost and operational implementation of the project results.

The project. The Radio Mathematics Project provides all of the mathematics instruction children receive. A daily lesson consists of a 30-minute radio presentation, followed by approximately 30 minutes of teacher-directed activities, for which instructions are contained in a project-developed teacher's guide. No textbooks are used and printed materials are limited to a one-page worksheet for each child each day. (For reasons of cost, the RMP subsequently eliminated the use of printed worksheets.)

Before the broadcast portion of the lesson, the teacher gives each child a worksheet on which the child writes his name and student number, a task that most first-graders can learn to do adequately. Then the broadcast lesson is turned on. During each lesson two main characters join with one or two subordinate characters to sing, play, and talk mathematics, usually inviting the children to join in. The children are asked to respond orally, physically, and in writing, and they do so up to 100 times during each 30-minute lesson. Initially the RMP used stories to engage the children, and embedded mathematical work in a story context to maintain interest. Early tests of lessons with stories, using kindergarten and first-grade children in California and first-grade children in Nicaragua, convinced the curriculum developers *"that the mathematical activities are intrinsically interesting to the children and do not need story support, as long as the children are asked to respond frequently"* (Searle, Suppes, and Friend, 1977: 12).

Sometimes children handle concrete materials during the broadcast, for example, counting or grouping small objects. Dialogue between radio characters introduces new mathematical material and children are asked to respond orally. In later lessons, the same exercises are repeated and the children respond individually on their worksheets.

After the radio transmission, the teacher continues the lesson, following the directions given in the teacher's guide. Usually children continue working on the worksheet during this portion of the lesson. During the experimental phase of the project, worksheets are collected and returned to the project office for analysis.

Research objectives. The research aims of the project can be broadly characterized as falling into three realms: (1) radio and educational achievement, (2) the economics of radio as a technology of instruction, and (3) the generalizability of the results to other settings. Among the educational questions of concern are: Can mathematics be taught effectively using radio as the primary source of instruction? How are achievement gains related to student characteristics? How does achievement of students' learning by radio compare with learning in the conventional classroom? How does the instructional program affect student and teacher attitudes towards mathematics, towards school, towards learning by radio? Do attendance and dropout patterns change when radio instruction is introduced in the classroom? Does the failure rate attributable to mathematics change? Does performance in other school subjects change? The bulk of the project's substantial research budget is devoted to seeking at least partial answers to these questions.

The economic aspects of the instructional system are the second major research concern. What are the development costs of the program? What are the operational costs? Can the cost of implementing the system in a different setting be estimated? What are the economic consequences of using radio in the classroom? Is the rate of flow of students through the school system, and hence the per-pupil cost of education, affected? What is the cost of each of the components of the system and how is that cost related to its effectiveness? How much teacher training is necessary to maintain an effective level of instruction? How much supplementary material must be prepared for students? How much supervision will teachers need in order to use the radio in the classroom?

The third research area, that of generalizability, is less well defined than the preceding two, but perhaps more critical to the ultimate success of the RMP. Even if it turns out that the RMP is a major pedagogical success, and that its costs are low, if disseminating results proves difficult the project will have been of limited value. Project developers are thus experimenting with alternative approaches to diffusing the project within Nicaragua, and other countries are considering experimentation with the RMP's broad approach.

Evaluation results. The RMP evaluated students' performance at the first-grade level in both the 1975 and the 1976 school years. The 1975 evaluation was preliminary: there were no random assignments of classrooms to radio versus control; the radio curriculum was still being developed; the sample size was relatively small; and, for some of the schools, the occasional presence of project personnel for formative evaluation may have affected the results. Nonetheless, reasonably good data were collected, and Searle, Friend, and Suppes (1976: Ch. 9) analyzed the effect of exposure to radio on mathematics achievement. They found that students who had radio scored about 67% correct on the end-of-year test, while students who had no radio scored only about 58%; this difference is highly statistically significant and reflects a difference of about half a standard deviation.

Jamison (1977a) also examined the 1975 data to ascertain whether the RMP affected the likelihood a student would be forced to repeat first grade. He used a multivariate logit model to examine two mechanisms through which radio could plausibly affect repetition propensity. One hypothesized mechanism was direct, that is, exposure to radio was entered directly into the regression equation predicting repetition propensity. The result was that the direct effect was to *increase* the student's likelihood of repeating, but only by a small and statistically insignificant amount. The second hypothesized mechanism was that radio would *indirectly* affect repetition by improving the student's mathematics performance which would, in turn, reduce repetition. Jamison found the RMP to induce a highly statistically significant reduction in repetition propensity through this mechanism. He calculated that the probability that the typical student repeat would drop from .36 to .22 if the student were exposed to the RMP.[7] The study also examined the effect of RMP on the likelihood that a student would drop out of school, and found very little effect.

The evaluation of the RMP based on the 1976 data provides much more conclusive results than do evaluations based on the 1975 data. The sample size was larger; the students were randomly assigned to treatment and control groups; and, perhaps most important, a tested and revised version of the curriculum was in use. Searle, Matthews, Suppes, and Friend (1977) report on this evaluation; Table 2.2 contains some of their more important results. Perhaps because the curriculum had been improved, the results show an even more dramatic difference in favor of the radio students than was found in the 1975 data. The radio students performed a full 1.26 standard deviations better on the posttest than did the controls; they answered half again as many questions correctly. The impact of radio on repetition rates for the 1976 data remains to be ascertained.

TABLE 2.2

Descriptive Statistics for 1976 First-Grade Posttest

	Radio Group	Control Group
Number of classes	30	23
Number of students	571	438
Number of test items	84	84
Mean item score (% correct)	65.6	40.6
Standard deviation	19.9	18.9
95% confidence interval about mean	61.3 − 70.0	36.5 − 44.7

SOURCE: Searle, Matthews, Suppes, and Friend (1977: Table 4).

We have discussed the RMP and the results of its evaluation at some length. We are aware of no other educational
intervention in a low-income country that has resulted in
achievement gains of this magnitude, including interventions
making extensive use of television. It is to be hoped that a
vigorous research and development program will continue
with the RMP, both to assess the extent to which success
can be continued at higher-grade levels, and to evaluate
alternative implementation strategies.

RADIO SCHOOLS OF THE TARAHUMARA

The Sierra Tarahumara is a mountainous, 15,000 square-
mile region in the state of Chihuahua in Northwest Mexico.
In 1960 the total population of this area was 125,000, of
which 50,000 were Tarahumara Indians. The Tarahumara
remain relatively isolated from Mexican society, forming a
distinct indigenous subculture, with their own language and
customs. The Catholic Church has had a Jesuit mission in the
region since 1900, and the Jesuits have run boarding schools
for the Tarahumara since the early 1900s. The radio schools
were begun in 1955, with the intent of extending the educational work of the Jesuits to a larger proportion of the native
population. Although initially much of the education had a

religious focus, since about 1960 the Jesuits have cooperated with the Mexican Secretariat of Public Education, which has few public schools in the region, to provide a secular education through radio schools. These schools follow the official government curriculum and utilize the official textbooks, but provide most of their basic instruction by radio for the first four grades of primary school. The aim has been to provide an education sufficient to allow graduates of the radio schools to continue their studies in the public schools if they so desire. The case study upon which this summary is based reports on an evaluation of the system conducted in 1971 and updated in 1975 by Sylvia Schmelkes de Sotelo of the Center for Educational Studies in Mexico City (Schmelkes, 1977). The interested reader is referred to her case for many more details.

Instructional radio lessons are broadcast from the Jesuit mission headquarters in Sisoguichi; all lessons are prepared by two teachers from a nearby primary-teacher training school. In 1971 there were 46 radio schools, serving 1,081 students spread throughout the region. Each school had one or two auxiliary teachers, individuals who had no more than a primary education themselves, to organize and supervise the classes and to guide and correct the students' work. The teachers' education is supplemented by summer training at the Jesuit mission. In about 75% of the schools, students from all grades are combined into a single classroom, while the remaining schools divide the students into two classrooms, the average class size being about 19 students. The 15-minute instructional radio lessons are grade specific, and are broadcast continuously throughout the school day. During the 45 minutes of each hour when they are not receiving broadcasts directed to their grade level, students engage in individual exercises.

Most of Schmelkes' study is devoted to an evaluation of the radio schools' outcomes. In terms of imparting cognitive knowledge, her sample of fourth-grade, radio-school students scored slightly better than their traditional-student counter-parts in arithmetic, geometry, and Spanish. However, these results plausibly stem from factors other than utilization of the radio lessons; out of the 24 radio schools visited during the study, only 7 schools had a radio operating. Further, high dropout rates and nonattendance were significant problems; of those students who continue to the fourth grade, few, if any are Tarahumara (non-Tarahumara Mexcians make up the majority of enrolled students, despite the initial mission to educate the Tarahumara). Schmelkes was unable to find any relevance of the school curriculum, which was transferred intact from the traditional, urban-oriented, primary-school curriculum, for local employment opportunities. She finds that, at best, the schools encourage the student to leave the community (and "thus the community loses its better human resources"), and in general they contribute to "an education that serves the white population of the Sierra and keeps the Tarahumara in a marginal position."

Similar criticisms of the relevance of curriculum carried by instructional technology appear elsewhere (e.g., see Spain, 1977; or Mayo, McAnany, and Klees, 1975). It is inappro-priate to conclude from such observations that instructional technology is incapable of meeting rural development's edu-cational needs, but rather that more concern must be given to examining those needs as educational systems evolve. Since, however, a thorough understanding of the relation between education and rural development is far in the future, it is probably both economically and politically unwise to postpone the provision of any education at all until educa-tional "needs" are fully understood.

The Radio Schools of the Tarahumara are currently en-gaged in a complete reevaluation of their efforts (the radio lessons have been temporarily discontinued since the 1973-1974 school year, pending this reevaluation), perhaps in large part due to the evaluation and recommendations made by Schmelkes. Those responsible for the schools are now focussing their attention on how to reorient the schools more directly toward the needs of the Tarahumara community.

MEXICO'S RADIOPRIMARIA

The *Radioprimaria* system, which began in 1969, was designed to extend access to the upper levels of elementary schooling to rural areas of Mexico that are presently unreached. During the 1969-1970 school year, 29 schools in the Valley of Mexico and the Federal District utilized *Radioprimaria*, but discontinued it after the first year, except for one classroom in the Experimental Education Center in Mexico City. At the beginning of the 1970-1971 school year, the system was tried out on a small scale in the state of San Luis Potosi and remains in use there.

Spain's (1977) case study presents an analysis of *Radioprimaria* as instituted in San Luis Potosi, and what we report below is based directly on his study.

Radioprimaria was mainly intended to allow a school with four teachers to offer all six grades of primary schooling. Three teachers handle the first three grades in the traditional manner; the fourth teacher has the fourth, fifth and sixth grades in one classroom and instructs them with the assistance of radio lessons. Some instructional radio programs are grade specific while others are directed to all three grades in common. When grade-specific lessons are broadcast, the students in the other two grades are supposed to engage in work on their own. It should also be noted that the above structure implies that students may be directed to listen to the same common broadcasts each year for three years.

A team of eight radio teachers prepares the instructional radio lessons at studios located in Mexico City. They are shipped by bus to San Luis Potosi, where they are broadcast by the University of San Luis Potosi radio station (at no charge) within a 30-mile radius. The station broadcasts every school day, Monday to Friday, from 9:00 a.m. until 12:45

p.m. In Mexico City, the programs are broadcast one hour earlier over Station XEEP, in order to be utilized by the experimental classroom, as well as by some traditional primary schools that use the lessons informally.

Each lesson last 14 minutes and about five programs are broadcast each school day. The subjects of the broadcast are taken from the official primary-school curriculum and are keyed directly to the required textbooks. Emphasis is placed on Spanish, arithmetic, history, and geography, although the system also broadcasts lessons dealing with physical education, nature study, and practical activities. Every fortnight, classroom teachers receive a mimeographed document that contains the radio lesson schedule and suggested activities to complement the broadcasts.

Utilization. In 1972 there were 43 schools serving about 2,800 fourth- fifth- and sixth-grade students. Contrary to the original plan, only 7 of these schools, out of a possible 70 in the state, were originally incomplete schools offering fewer than 6 grades of primary school. Nonetheless, about 60% of the schools that did have all six grades had fewer than six teachers, so often two or three of the higher grades had already been combined into one classroom with one teacher. In addition to serving these schools in San Luis Potosi, it is known that the Mexico City broadcasts are picked up and utilized by regular schools, but no data are available on the extent of such use. Also, since the broadcasts are open circuit, over normal radio-band frequencies, in both San Luis Potosi and Mexico City, it is thought that there are many adults who tune in to the lessons. Indeed, one of the original goals of *Radioprimaria* was to allow participation by adults who had failed to complete primary school.

During the school year about 1,200 14-minute programs are broadcast, or approximately 280 hours. About 80% of the programs are directed at the combined fourth-, fifth- and sixth-grade audiences, with the remaining 20% distributed among three grades.

Effectiveness. Spain gave pretests and posttests over a semester period to a random sample of radio and nonradio students in the sixth grade. He concludes from the test results that *Radioprimaria* "has produced (test) scores that are comparable to those of the children in direct-teaching schools" (Spain, 1977). However, there are some doubts as to the reliability of the results generated, which Spain himself explicitly recognizes. For example, although the rural radio classes had higher gain scores than the nonradio classes, only a few of the radio classes are the type of class for which the *Radioprimaria* system was originally intended. In spite of the modesty of Spain's claims for the cognitive effectiveness of the radio system, and of the difficulty of drawing firm conclusions from the data he had available, his data suggest that students in the radio schools performed better than those in nonradio schools in both Spanish and mathematics, and the difference in Spanish was statistically highly significant.

In some respects, Spain's evaluation of other aspects of the *Radioprimaria* system is more enlightening than the analysis of cognitive outcomes described above. Through visiting all the radio schools and several of the nonradio schools, and by talking with system participants, a number of problems were uncovered. Spain estimates that 15% to 20% of the classes miss the first half hour of broadcast due to teacher and/or student late arrival. Furthermore, of the 44 radio schools visited, one was inexplicably closed, and 18 others made no use of radio that particular day—either because the receiver needed repair, or the power had failed, or the teacher had decided the lessons were useless.

No federal funds are allocated for receiver purchase and, consequently, receivers must be bought and maintained by the teacher or the community; in one case no receiver had been purchased because the teacher and the community were unable to agree on who would pay for it. Of the remaining 25 schools found using radios, seven had inaudible receivers.

Spain reports widespread reception problems, which is not surprising given funding arrangements nonconducive to the purchase of adequate receivers and their maintenance.

Spain attributes many of the above problems to a lack of resources allocated for school supervision. Perhaps for the same reason, schools have been dropping out of the *Radioprimaria* system; in the first year of operation there were 49 radio schools; in 1971-1972 there were 44; and in the following year there were only 37. Spain describes how the initial acceptance of *Radioprimaria* was fostered by the Director of the local Audiovisual Center, through frequent visits to the classrooms, using his own automobile. This individual's automobile broke down at the end of that first year and no resources were forthcoming from the federal government to support such efforts in subsequent years. Consequently, Spain feels that enthusiasm for the system has been waning.

Finally, Spain also examines the potential benefits of the *Radioprimaria* system's expansion of primary-school education in rural areas. Contrary to the avowed government intention to have the system aid in rural development, Spain found that parents and students see primary-school graduation as a means to leave the rural areas and compete in the urban labor market. Spain's assessment of the employment market in the chief urban area of the state, San Luis Potosi, indicated even more unfortunately, the existence of widespread unemployment and an excess supply of primary-school graduates.

Discussion. The *Radioprimaria* system is an innovative attempt to overcome the lack of sufficient educational opportunities in rural areas that exists in Mexico and most other developing nations. Although its costs may appear somewhat higher than other instructional radio projects, this is entirely due to its present experimental, low student-utilization format; if the number of students included in the system were expanded, costs per student would fall substantially.[8] The unique configuration of the system, which combines several grades with one teacher, results in considerable cost savings over the traditional direct-teaching system. Of course, despite a favorable cost comparison, the merits of the system must be judged by cost data combined with information on relative pedagogical effects and long-run benefits.

In terms of pedagogical effects, Spain's analysis appears inconclusive, even though radio schools scored better on the tests, since there was no clear comparison made of joint fourth-, fifth- and sixth-grade classrooms with radio, versus direct teaching with one teacher assigned to each grade. Spain indicated that there may be some problem with the grade-specific, instructional radio-lesson format utilized in *Radioprimaria,* in that the students not receiving the broadcasts showed little concentration when they were supposed to be working on their own. This is not unsurprising since it is likely that the ongoing radio lesson would be difficult to ignore. In addition, Spain questions whether common fourth-, fifth- and sixth-grade broadcasts, which are likely to be repeated to a student each year for three years, are a beneficial pedagogical tool. Thus there would be risks in adopting some variant of the *Radioprimaria* approach in another country, or in expanding it in Mexico, before more rigorous effectiveness comparisons have been undertaken. On the other hand, the cost advantage of *Radioprimaria,* and its capacity to extend schooling to places where it would otherwise be unavailable, might well make those risks worth taking.

TEACHER TRAINING BY RADIO
AND CORRESPONDENCE IN KENYA

A case study by Kinyanjui (1977) describes the history, operations, and existing evaluation information concerning the radio-correspondence approach to teacher upgrading being used in Kenya. The Kenya Education Commission first suggested the use of radio-correspondence instruction in

1964; two years later the government of Kenya approached AID for technical assistance in establishing a Correspondence Course Unit (CCU) in the Institute of Adult Studies, University College, Nairobi (now the University of Nairobi). The principal efforts of the CCU have been directed toward teacher training, and in what follows we draw heavily on Kinyanjui's account of that effort. In an earlier paper Kinyanjui (1974) described the Kenyan project in the context of other, somewhat similar, teacher-training projects, and we refer readers interested in other projects to that paper.

Purpose and operation of program. At the time of creation of the CCU, the Kenyan government perceived there to be a major shortage of adequately qualified primary teachers in Kenya. According to the Annual Report of the Ministry of Education, there were 37,923 teachers employed in Kenya's primary schools in 1968. Of these, 10,438 were professionally unqualified. Of the 27,285 qualified teachers, 16,992 were "P3" teachers who were the mainstay of the primary schools, comprising about 60% of the qualified teaching staff and almost 45% of the total teaching staff. The two major teacher-training efforts of the CCU involved creating a program to upgrade an unqualified teacher to the "P3" level and another to upgrade "P3" teachers to "P2." The second of these began first, in 1968, and the in-service training course for unqualified teachers began in 1969.[9]

The course for upgrading "P3" teachers prepares students to pass the Kenya Junior Secondary Examination; after passing the examination, the teacher is eligible for promotion to "P2." The program for unqualified teachers is conducted in two phases. The first is professional training in methods of teaching organized by the Kenya Institute of Education and consisting of a year's study divided into three, short, residential courses during school holidays. Between the residential sessions, the courses are supplemented by radio lectures. Candidates who successfully complete the first phase of the program are then admitted to the second year's academic course conducted by the CCU. The unqualified teachers, however, study only three subjects (English, mathematics, and either history or geography) at the first-year secondary level. Those who successfully complete the correspondence course and pass the final examination are upgraded to "P3" status.

The instructional program provided by the CCU comprises a synthesis of the following:

(1) correspondence study guides, textbooks, and other teaching materials such as maps, mathematical instrument sets, science experiment kits, and so forth;

(2) supplementary radio broadcasts covering the material in one or more lessons of the study guide;

(3) marking of students' lessons by qualified secondary and university teachers; and

(4) face-to-face teaching during occasional residential sessions.

The correspondence-course material in one or more lessons is supplemented by a 15-minute radio program that is broadcast twice a week over the Voice of Kenya. The CCU radio programs are allotted a fixed air time from 5 p.m. to 6 p.m. every weekday throughout the year.

The radio lessons are optional, and there are many students who work ahead of the radio programs; some of these do listen to the programs at later stages. The radio lessons are particularly aimed at the slower students and are used to pace and encourage them. The radio teacher tries to highlight the important points in a lesson and to provide a summary at the end of each teaching unit. Occasionally the radio teacher will arrange for a question-and-answer type of program in which problems common to many students are discussed and common mistakes are corrected.

Evaluation results. Though Kinyanjui reports no completion figures for the upgrading of "P3" teachers, he does point out that, in the four-year period from 1969 to 1972, over 10,000 unqualified teachers successfully completed their radio-correspondence upgrading to the "P3" level. This completion rate is one important index of success; another is that the supervisors of upgraded teachers, according to a survey, reported that about 95% of them improved their performance after taking the upgrading course.

There is a somewhat sharper measure of performance for teachers being upgraded from "P3" to "P2" in that they must pass the Kenya Junior Secondary Examination. Even here there are difficulties in comparing CCU-trained students with graduates of traditional schooling: no control data are available to allow matching students' backgrounds and abilities, and, as a source of definite bias in favor of the CCU students, traditional students must take all five examination subjects at one sitting whereas CCU students need not. This discrepancy notwithstanding, the difference in pass rates in favor of CCU students is still impressive: the average pass rate for CCU candidates was close to 50%; for others for most years, it was less than half that.

Conclusion: Kenya's radio-correspondence courses provide an effective mechanism for upgrading teacher quality. The CCU students are learning the prescribed material. The system's cost is substantially less than for traditional instruction,[10] and, probably more important, it allows teacher upgrading to occur without demanding either an expansion of the teacher-training force or a withdrawal of teachers from their ongoing teaching responsibilities in the primary schools.

It is worth noting, however, particularly in a volume dealing with radio, that the CCU radio-correspondence courses are principally *correspondence* and only supplementarily radio. This is probably true for almost all distance-learning systems that utilize a broadcast medium.

RADIO ESCUELA SANTA MARIA IN
THE DOMINICAN REPUBLIC

In 1964 a radiophonic adult-literacy program modeled on the Colombian Radio Sutatenza was begun in the Cibao region of North Central Dominican Republic, and, during the next six years, more than 25,000 adults received literacy certificates. However, many participants perceived these radiophonic schools to be remedial and inferior to traditional schools. In 1971, therefore, *Radio Santa María* initiated a much more comprehensive adult-education program, partially modeled on the radiophonic adult-education program of the Canary Islands (Cepeda, 1976). *Radio Santa María* now provides elementary- and secondary-school equivalency programs through a daily one-hour broadcast, accompanied by lesson sheets and weekly sector meetings with a field teacher. Five radio stations in other parts of the Dominican Republic also began to broadcast the daily radio lessons, so that by 1975 a primary- and intermediate-level education was available in virtually all rural communities in the country. Examinations at the end of grades six and eight are held in accordance with the regulations of the Secretariat of Education, so graduates of the radiophonic schools receive official diplomas. White (1977a) provides a detailed description on which most of this summary is based.

Adult education has been a well integrated part of the conventional educational systems of the Dominican Republic since 1953. The *Direccion General de Educación de Adultos* used day-school facilities in towns and cities, and offers a primary education through grade eight to the very large number of youths and adults in the Dominican Republic who missed this opportunity earlier in their lives. The adult-education program has provided educational opportunity for over 30,000 students from 1968 to 1975 but primarily in urban areas. The difficulties of recruiting teachers and finding well-lit classrooms for nighttime use in rural areas has almost completely prevented the spread of the government adult-education program to rural areas.

Radio Santa María's adult educational program encourages students to listen to general education and cultural broadcasts, as well as to instructional programs, and assumes that they will participate in community organizations as part of their education. The academic material presented in instructional broadcasts and weekly worksheets is offered at an accelerated pace so the adult student can complete eight years of schooling in four calendar years.

Radiophonic students meet with a field teacher once a week at which time there is discussion of the previous week's lessons, and the worksheets for the next week are distributed. The median age of the field teachers is 24, about 85% have some secondary education, and all have another job or are secondary school students. As was found in the Nicaragua Radio Mathematics Project in teaching young children, White found the active participation of the adult student during the instructional broadcast to be an important pedagogical technique: "To insure that the learning process is an active search and not just a passive listening to the broadcast, a series of small completion exercises are built into the presentation: a word to be underlined or written into the text; a small mistake which the broadcast dialogue helps the student to detect and correct, etc." (White, 1977a: 179).

In the 1974-1975 school year, the fourth year of the program and when it had been expanded to a nationwide program, there were about 20,000 students attending classes; about 2,000 students took the eighth-grade exam with a 96% pass rate. "One of the most notable achievements in the program is the high retention rate of students who enroll, given the great flexibility of the system. Even if one allows for the fact that enrollment is closed at the midsemester point, that retention is approximately 70-75 percent in some of the advanced grades is remarkable compared with most radiophonic adult education programs" (White, 1976a: 87).

Retention in the first four grades is considerably lower, in part because the students are mostly dropouts from the regular primary school.[11]

Two studies have compared the academic achievement of radiophonic students and those in conventional adult-education programs. In 1973, a small study compared 15 students from the radiophonic schools of Santa María with 15 from the official adult-education program in the city of La Vega. Students tested were from the second, fourth, and sixth grades. At the second-grade level, there was no significant difference in scores, but at the fourth-grade level the radiophonic students had a mean score of 66, while the conventional students had a mean score of 40; and at the sixth-grade level, radiophonic students had a mean score of 69, while conventional students had a mean score of 47 (Decena-Dilone, 1973).

In 1975, White conducted a more comprehensive comparison in two different education districts. Students at the end of the sixth and eighth grades were compared, and both groups were given the examination prepared by the District Office of the National Office of Adult Education; this examination was similar to the one usually given to the radiophonic students, but it was in a different format and covered some unfamiliar curriculum material. Therefore, a few questions not pertaining to curriculum covered in the radiophonic program were omitted in scoring the exams for research purposes. An example of comprehensive scores for sixth-grade students in District II can be seen in Table 2.3. The scores of radiophonic students in District I were relatively more favorable. Our conclusion from these data is that radiophonic students can perform as well as the students from the conventional system. Only 8 of the total of 21 comparisons show a difference in score of 5 points or more, and of these, 4 favor the radiophonic students and 4 favor the conventional students. Evidence of academic performance of radiophonic students equal to that of conventional

TABLE 2.3
Comparison of Median Examination Scores of Sixth Grade Students in Schools With Radiophonic and Conventional Classroom Methods: District II

	Radiophonic Students					Conventional Classroom Students				
	No.	% Less Than 60	% 60–79	% Higher Than 80	Median Score	No.	% Less Than 60	% 60–79	% Higher Than 80	Median Score
Spanish Language	198	11.1	64.2	24.7	73.0	87	17.2	70.1	12.6	70.7
Spanish Grammar	198	40.9	39.4	19.7	63.9	83	44.6	42.2	13.2	63.5
Mathematics	199	82.9	13.6	3.5	Less than 50.0	33	72.7	24.3	3.0	50.6
Natural Sciences	199	36.2	50.8	13.0	64.9	52	59.6	38.5	1.9	57.4
Dominican Economy	200	74.5	24.5	1.0	Less than 50.0	52	71.2	28.8	—	54.2
Social Studies	201	62.1	33.4	4.5	54.4	60	66.7	31.7	1.7	55.8

SOURCE: White (1976a: Table 7.2).

system students seems particularly significant, however, given that all the conventional students were from urban communities, while 78% of the radiophonic students were from rural backgrounds. As might be expected, within the radiophonic group, urban students scored somewhat higher than rural students.

The equal performance between students of the two systems is also significant in light of the lower per-student cost of the instructional radio program over the conventional system. Cost information on both systems of adult education is insufficient to allow a complete cost analysis, but a broad-brush comparison suggests substantially lower per-student costs for radiophonic students; Chapter 4 provides further information on the cost of *Radio Escuela Santa María.*

NOTES

1. A category that will not be discussed here is that of organizational alternatives. In the United States there is discussion of a number of organizational structures differing from those now in common use; these include performance contracting, community control, and voucher finance.

2. It is possible to express the range of alternatives quantitatively. Let q be a measure of teacher quality (for operational simplicity, q may have to be a simple measure such as percentage of teachers fully qualified or average educational attainment of teachers) and let $W(q)$ be the average annual wage (for full-time work) of teachers when their quality average is q. Let C be the average class size, i.e., the average number of students in a classroom with a teacher and let h be the average number of hours per week a student is in class. Assuming, and this assumption can easily be relaxed, that a full-time teacher is in class 36 hours per week, the student-to-teacher ratio, S, is given by $S = 36\ C/h$. Increasing class size thus increases S, as does decreasing h. To continue, let U be the average usage rate of classrooms, i.e., the average number of times they are used per day, and let P be an imputed annual price for a classroom. Since the available budget was B and the number of students was N, an average of B/N per student per year is the basic cost constraint. Each student consumes $1/S$ or $H/36C$ teachers and $1/UC$ classrooms during the year. Assume, further, that the annual value of books and other instructional materials used per student is V. Then the following equation holds as an approximation that includes only the major costs: $B = [(h/36C)W(q) + P/UC + V]\ N$.

3. This categorization is based on Schramm (1977), but differs from his in placing greater emphasis on distance learning. Schramm has an additional category: use of technology to catalyze major educational reform. We have deleted it here since such catalytic efforts (in Samoa, El Salvador, and the Ivory Coast) have heretofore used television. It is at least possible, however, that massive use of radio could be used to catalyze reform.

4. The economic evaluation of the Nicaragua Radio Mathematics Project will attempt to assess radio's imapct on dropout and repetition; Jamison (1977a) reports early results indicating radio to reduce repetition rates. Macken, van den Heuvel, Suppes, and Suppes (1976: 33-34), in a survey of home-based education in the United States, report on several studies in which different approaches to correspondence instruction affected students' propensity to remain involved with the course.

5. The cost argument leading to this conclusion may be less important in high-income countries. There the entertainment value of TV can be more easily afforded and the value of student time saved by computer-assisted instruction in certain special areas may be high enough to offset its cost.

6. Holmberg (1977) provides an up-to-date practical discussion of problems in the design and implementation of distance-learning systems, and the World Bank has initiated a research program to acquire improved information on distance learning's costs.

7. Jamison further concluded that even though introducing radio would increase the cost per student per year from $54 to $57, it would reduce the cost per first-grade graduate (by reducing repetition) from about $88.50 to $79.20. Such a cost reduction would allow an increase of about 12% in the number of first grade graduates without increasing expenditures.

8. Chapter 4 contains more information on the cost of *Radioprimaria.*

9. At the time of this writing (October, 1977) the CCU has, at least temporarily, discontinued its teacher training courses.

10. An analysis of the cost of the CCUs teacher upgrading programs is just being completed for the World Bank; its conclusions suggest these programs to have been substantially more expensive than previously thought.

11. When considering the number of students who benefit from a radio or television distance-learning project, it is important to keep in mind the spill-over effect. It is likely that there will be many people who are not officially enrolled, and who may not be regular listeners, but who nonetheless derive educational benefit from some of the broadcasts.

chapter 3

Radio for Development Communication

As we have stated earlier, the two premises on which this book builds are that radio is, and will remain for the next decade or two, the single most pervasive means for communication with the majority of the world's population, and, second, that many countries will use this important national resource to promote development goals. The range of goals for which radio has been used is indeed as broad as the range of goals set for the development process.

As governments face the task of communicating to their people the goals and methods of their development programs, they will inevitably consider seriously the nature of the role radio can play, and how they may best incorporate previous experience into planning radio use. This chapter provides a framework for thinking about how to use radio for development communication and summarizes available evidence concerning its effectiveness. Section 1 reviews the *goals* development-communication projects attempt to achieve; Section 2 reviews the effectiveness of different *strategies* for using radio to achieve these goals.

3.1 THE VARIETY OF GOALS

This section categorizes a number of the ways in which radio has been used to promote social, political, or economic goals. The distinction is often made, at least in Western countries, between the informative or persuasive uses of communication, on the one hand, and those that are cultural or for entertainment, on the other. Examination of programming schedules reveals the extent to which it is difficult to make such distinctions consistently. While music seems most obviously to fall into the entertainment category, even there the distinction is often hazy; music with lyrics that express a view about life or even politics can be an important persuasive experience, especially for cultural subgroups like the young. The issue is a difficult one, but for the purpose of economy in the present volume we will limit our examination of radio projects to those that have some stated purpose other than entertainment. We do *not* wish to indicate that we believe the entertainment potential of radio to be unimportant, only that it cannot be treated here.

We have, in Table 1.2, delineated four goals for development communication: motivation, general information, nonformal education, and directed behavior. Let us look at each of these briefly so that when we examine the evidence concerning the effectiveness of different strategies for radio use, we will be aware that in the projects reviewed there are frequently several different goals being pursued. Often a single radio project attempts, either explicitly or implicitly, to attain multiple goals. As a consequence, the evaluation of projects with these intermingled objectives is more because such projects may be relatively successful at achieving one goal but less so for another. Nevertheless, as our list of goals includes the ones that are most often established for projects, study of these will provide the best summary of the success of radio for development.

TO MOTIVATE

A communication system in a society is most often used to reinforce existing values and behavior patterns (such as popular cultural messages in radio soap operas), or to persuade to a new behavior (such as the advertising spots on radio and television). Although there are cognitive elements in such messages, the primary thrust of the content is in the affective or motivational area. Development communication is certainly often devoted to this general goal, whether it is to motivate a country politically toward national unity, or to arouse the public against a common external enemy, or to motivate a group toward a self-development activity.

There are numerous specific examples of how radio has been used to motivate people. Many of the Latin American church-related radio stations, called radio schools (see the strategy of listening groups for more detail), have adopted as one of their primary goals the task of consciousness-raising among poor, rural audiences. White (1977b) speaks of this in Honduras, Cabezas (1975) in the Dominican Republic, and de Kadt (1970) in Brazil. What seems to have happened over the past five years in most development work is that poor, rural people are being called upon to help themselves to change their situation. Whereas before many radio programs stuck to literacy teaching as though learning to read and write were enough stimulus for adults to enroll, now people are being motivated much more specifically to help change their situation through common activity. Working together takes motivation, and radio is helping to provide this.

There are a number of other uses of radio that primarily motivate. Kenya (UNICEF, 1975) uses a humorous 15-minute drama each week to attract rural listeners to think about their families' health problems. The use of dramatizations, soap operas, and stories are all common forms of motivating people to become literate, to participate in a family planning program, or to adopt an agricultural practice. Sometimes programming is created by community members themselves on the premise that such programming will more likely stimulate the audience to listen and participate in the community activities (Hudson, 1977; El Hadj Badge and Robert, 1972; and Gunter and Theroux, 1977).

Finally, national campaigns have been enlisted along with other resources to mobilize large numbers of people (see the campaign strategy). Tanzania (Hall and Dodds, 1977) in its health and food growing campaigns and Cuba in its literacy campaign (Fagen, 1969) used radio as an important part of the motivation or build-up period. These, then, are some of the ways that radio has been used to motivate its audience.

TO INFORM

Information in this context refers to a wide variety of things: local, national, and international news; messages about the availability of social services; and announcements concerning an event of importance to the audience. One of radio's important functions is to inform its audience about what is going on; it serves this role in both high-income and low-income countries.

Radio has played the role of information provider and has even created in rural people the need for more information. In the literature on adoption of innovation, the stage of awareness or first learning about a new idea or method is often best initiated by some form of mass media (Rogers and Shoemaker, 1971).

Some countries have no other feasible way of reaching their rural people with government plans or policies. Botswana, for example, decided to use radio primarily as a means of informing its largely illiterate population of the contents of the first National Development Plan (Colclough and Crowley, 1974).

TO TEACH

Radio can be used to teach—i.e., for nonformal education— in both the basic cognitive-skill area and in the work-skill area. In the present context we wish to distinguish radio's use for nonformal education from the other goals of development communication. Education is a process that uses organized learning experiences to teach abstract, cognitive skills—usually ability to read and write, but also ability in numeracy and a more generalized abstract skill often called learning-to-learn, or ability to transfer cognitive skills to a new learning situation. Simple transfer of information does not imply learning a skill or process but acquiring a product, some concrete bit of knowledge. The work skills referred to in our categories are the more concrete cognitive or psychomotor processes by which someone can better earn a living, be it through skills of bookkeeping or bricklaying. The acquisition of the latter is often said to be the result of training, whereas education is a broader and more encompassing term that speaks of the general cognitive skills as well as the socialization in the values and norms of society. While some of radio's use for nonformal education is directed toward impartation of basic cognitive skills, outside the formal education system its use is more often directed to the teaching of work skills, and we will discuss this goal further.

As we stated, work skills refer to concrete cognitive or psychomotor processes, or habitual ways of thinking and acting that are used in day-to-day life. Several examples are the skills demanded in carpentry, or in the construction of a latrine, or in cooking. Other examples include the skill required to use a certain kind of new seed variety to best advantage, to use a diaphragm in family-planning practice, to keep simple books, to learn a new surgical procedure, or to repair an internal combustion engine. All of these skills have obvious applicability to real problems of everyday life, and one could develop a list of many more. How has radio been able to deal with teaching skills?

The history of skills' development through formal education in low-income countries has generally been discouraging. Technical education is expensive and reaches relatively few people in comparison to needs. Nonformal education's record appears no better (cf. Ahmed and Coombs, 1975; Foster and Sheffield, 1974; Sheffield and Diejomaoh, 1972). Radio has played a limited role in this field for several reasons. The first is motivational. Skills promoted by some radio projects have had insufficient perceived benefits for the amount of sustained effort required, and dropout rates have been high in these radio projects. Second, radio is not the ideal means for instruction in a work skill. Typically, skills of this kind are best acquired through observation and guided imitation in a face-to-face setting, on-the-job or in a school workshop. Moreover, even when skills are needed by isolated rural people and there are few instructors, radio has usually been considered inappropriate for this work. As a consequence, in isolated rural areas, needed work skills are seldom taught by radio or even by any other means.

There have been, however, several examples of attempts to teach work skills by radio, and, where proper supporting elements were included, some success has been achieved. A large-scale experiment in Ecuador using radio alone or radio with audiovisual aids (Spector and Torres, 1963) showed that skills such as latrine making or fruit canning could be taught to a rural audience. Tanzania (Hall and Dobbs, 1977; Dobbs, 1972) has used radio and the simple printed materials to teach latrine building as well as to present some courses in village bookkeeping in a distance-learning approach. Health aides (Kreimer, 1977) in Alaska and primary school teachers (Kinyaajui, 1977) in Kenya have been given in-service training.

Thus, although the record of radio has been somewhat spotty in supporting acquisition of work skills, a careful review of an appropriate strategy may indicate greater scope for radio than the overall record would suggest.

TO CHANGE BEHAVIOR

Changing behavior is the most difficult goal to achieve of the ones outlined in this series, yet it has a great importance for the typically isolated rural dweller. Radio provides the only reliable communication system that reaches large portions of rural populations in many countries. A strong station whose signal reaches most of a country's territory will often substitute for a nonexistent, rural telephone system. Once or twice a day such a station will typically devote 10 to 40 minutes to official announcements for isolated people. The message might be from the Ministry of Education asking certain teachers to attend a meeting the next day in the capital, or from the Provincial Government to the mayor or chief of a village about an administrative matter, or from the health agency announcing a vaccination schedule in rural clinics. Such announcements are not simply the provision of general information, but usually guide behavior in some way.

Other examples reinforce the notion that radio can substitute for the telephone, the newspaper, and the mail system of many rural and even urban areas. Hudson (1977) relates how a two-way radio system among widely dispersed, Sioux Indian villages in Canada was used for giving instruction, calling meetings, or settling business. Tanzania (Hall and Dodds, 1977) used radio as the only feasible means of instructing rural dwellers on how to vote for the first time. Kreimer (1977) provides the most precise case, where a doctor gives health-care instructions to a rural health aide in Alaska by two-way radio. A radio spot in Ecuador (Manoff, 1975) announced to rural people why they should use iodized salt in their diet. Radio can more effectively provide exact instructions or directions for behavior change when few people are involved and they have a two-way capacity, but even where instructions are for large masses of people and the message is one-way only, radio often functions for instructing people in certain behaviors.

We have discussed four goals for development communication: to motivate, to inform, to teach, and to change behavior. The section that follows describes several strategies for using radio to reach these goals, and reviews the success of experience with the various strategies.

3.2 RADIO STRATEGIES FOR
DEVELOPMENT COMMUNICATION

As we have noted, this chapter is devoted to reviewing the evidence on audience coverage and on a number of different strategies or organizing modes for using radio.[1] For each strategy, we will use one case study as the primary example to illustrate the potential of radio and we will try to summarize other evidence about the strategy from the existing literature. Our purpose here is to present cases to illustrate the variety of experiences with different ways in which radio has been used, to examine the evidence critically about the actual level of success attained, and to assess the potential of different approaches where changes and improvements can be made.

OPEN BROADCASTING

This strategy encompasses a broad variety of experience. What distinguishes it from other strategies is the primary emphasis it puts on the message. Although the audience may be well defined in an open-broadcast project, there is no attempt to organize listeners or to put much supporting materials in their hands. The amount of interface with other organizations that will carry on more direct contact with listeners will vary according to the nature of the project. To summarize the characteristics of many open-broadcast projects we could say that they are message-centered; typically reach people in their homes; do not attempt to teach complicated concepts or behaviors, but rather to motivate and get across modest amounts of information; and are often geared to some simple behavior change. *Sesame Street* for television might be the clearest example of an open broadcast program for the reader to keep in mind as s/he continues this section.

Gunter and Theroux (1977) have summarized many of the advantages of this approach in their paper on the subject. Let us summarize their suggestions and then present two more cases that illustrate the open-broadcast approach. The authors' basic assumption is that the mass entertainment media of most countries attract and educate much larger audiences than do most typical, educational broadcast programs. They suggest that development-communications strategists adopt a more creative approach to their work, and devote more time and money to improving program quality and attracting larger audiences for educational radio. They argue that many development objectives can be achieved without the expenses of organizing an audience. They cite three examples of how radio might achieve valuable learning results.

First, the authors review advertising and its possible application to education, which they call "edvertising." Second, they talk of audience participation in program production, and finally, of a specific example of an educational quiz show.

The authors review advertising principles and argue that these can be adapted to the achievement of educational goals. Commercial radio advertising takes as a basic principle that it must motivate the audience to listen. Educational radio tends to assume that this motivation already exists and, therefore, does not use persuasive techniques. Perhaps this is because it has had a captive audience in schools for so many years. Gunter and Theroux believe that this motivation cannot be assumed. They suggest short radio spots using advertising techniques for educational purposes, but do not cite any cases in which this approach has been used.

Gunter and Theroux cite a second approach of open broadcasting that creates programs that are community controlled and participative. In a small Andean town in Ecuador, a local radio station experimented with using cassette recorders to create audience-made programs. The idea was to have the rural people record their own programs. Local helpers were given recorders and asked to meet with people in their areas and record meetings, entertainments, discussions, and complaints, and then give the tape to the local radio station to edit and play in one or two half-hour community programs.

This method for creation of open broadcast material is both relatively cheap and appealing to its audience. People speak about what concerns them and communicate ideas, information, and entertainment to a large number of their fellow citizens. This approach they call participative programming.

As a final example of educational programming for a non-organized audience, the authors refer to an educational quiz show developed and tested at the University of Massachusetts. In a laboratory setting, the quiz-show format showed a superior learning gain for participants over those who learned by a lecture method. They argue that this format can stimulate audience attention and continued interest for learning.

If one were to summarize the main arguments of Gunter and Theroux favoring this strategy, they might be: better, more creative programming will motivate people to attend to and learn from radio messages; investing in better programming will capture a larger portion of the potential listening audience and, therefore, will be a better investment of funds than concentrating on a much smaller, organized audience; and creative programming can break traditional, passive ways of learning and get more people to participate in their own learning. It is important to keep in mind that most radio projects outside the formal schooling sphere depends on the good will of a volunteer listener. The participant can always drop out or turn his radio to another station. This is especially true of open-broadcast programs. This makes audience interest of such vital importance for this strategy.

Two arguments advanced have backing from other evidence sources. First, the analogy with advertising calls upon the considerable evidence that advertising can use mass media to change the amount of knowledge, the attitude, and most importantly, the behavior of an audience. No evidence is cited for the educational effectiveness of "edvertising" but the argument that if soap or beer commercials work, then literacy or health commercials might also work, seems reasonable.

The second analogy in the Gunter and Theroux argument is the power of good entertainment to motivate and to teach.

The best example is the soap operas or *novelas,* as they are called in Latin America. There is no doubt about the large audiences that these programs attract all over the world. There are some studies on their effects on audience attitudes and values (e.g., Colomina de Rivera, 1968). Many educational broadcasters have argued that the *novela* format would be an excellent educational medium. Two examples can be cited. One, a television soap opera from Brazil (D'Arinos, 1975) teaches basic education to adults, apparently with some success. More recently a Mexican educational soap opera has appeared on television. During the early months of its airing it got one of the highest ratings for viewership of all programs, commercial or educational. The commercial producers of the programs make their money selling advertising, while the Secretary of Public Education organizes part of the listening audience. Although no hard evidence exists, it is reported that 260,000 adults have signed up for classes organized around the program.

A radio program on health in Kenya is reported to be one of the most popular programs on the air in 1975. Whether or how much it teaches has yet to be determined, but a survey conducted after its first year of existence indicates a large audience even in rural areas (UNICEF, 1975). Another rural radio program in Guatemala (AED, 1976) seems to have made a clear contribution to knowledge, attitude, and behavior change. The experimental project distinguished between organized and unorganized listening groups, and preliminary results indicate that open broadcasting had clearly superior results in comparison with controls, and showed even some relative advantages over the organized approach.[2] What seems evident from examples like these or from *Sesame Street* is that educational programs can have mass appeal, and that there is reason to believe that radio can attract a large listening audience in rural areas of developing countries if programming makes an appeal to audience interest.

A second example of this strategy comes closer to the Gunter-Theroux example of "edvertising." The Manoff advertising agency has been experimenting with short, radio-spot announcements to help improve nutrition in low-income countries. The attempt is to create messages centered on one or a few specific behaviors and, with the use of reported and varied messages over a period of a year, to change listeners' knowledge, attitudes, and especially behavior. The first project in Ecuador (Manoff, 1976) had a variety of problems, but showed a significant impact on the awareness, knowledge, and attitudes of a large rural audience. Behavior was more difficult to change, but in one practice, the use of iodized salt, behavior did shift significantly over 15 months. Similar projects in the Philippines and Nicaragua are underway. Preliminary results in the Philippines indicate improvement in behavior concerning nutritional practices.[3] What seems important in this example is that brief radio spots can apparently change eating behavior without an organized-audience context for persuasion. The messages are carefully made, the objective is specific and instruction simple, but the audience is voluntary and listens at home. No materials are supplied and no backup from health agencies is called for directly in the home.

A final argument of Gunter and Theroux is that the open-broadcast approach reaches far greater audiences than do the organized-audience approaches. Good programming, it is maintained, will reach a much larger audience and have a relatively greater impact than the same amount of investment divided between programming and field supervision for an organized audience. There are two requisites to confirming this argument. First, in an open-broadcast approach it is necessary to assess the level of listenership and, with more difficulty, the amount of impact the programming is having. The examples we have provided appear to speak to the first criterion of audience coverage, at least. In the cases cited for Mexico, Kenya, Ecuador, and the Philippines, there have been audience surveys that indicate a wide listening audience, certainly much wider than the usual numbers participating in organized-audience efforts. The second question of impact has only been measured thus far in the case of the nutrition campaigns. The evidence indicates a positive impact on audience awareness, knowledge, and attitude. There is less evidence for behavior change, but indications are that given the right objectives and conditions, simple behavior can be changed.

What conclusions can we make about the strategy of open broadcasting? The examples given were mostly positive, but there is much more experience of failure than of success in using radio to reach and to educate an unorganized audience (McAnany, 1973; Arana, 1971; Spain, 1971). The criticism of Gunter and Theroux, however, seems to be well taken: emphasis on the quality of the message and concern about its broad appeal is a likely way of improving the reach of the message. The development goals to be achieved are a critical element in the choice of strategies. If the objectives involve informing people, making them aware of an issue or motivating them to change a relatively simple behavior, then the open-broadcast strategy is a potential use of radio that is attractive for development communication.

Two questions remain unanswered regarding this strategy and will be treated further. First is the question of the cost of this strategy, and of the comparison of cost with the reach and impact it has, especially in comparison with other strategies. Second is the question of feasibility, or of how difficult it is to make such a strategy succeed. The first question is addressed in Chapter 4, the second in Chapter 5.

RADIO CAMPAIGNS

The second strategy, radio campaigns, is between the open-broadcast and the organized-listening-group approaches. It has a number of historical predecessors, including the organized discusion group in Sweden and the mass-mobilization campaigns common to socialist countries such as the People's Republic of China and Cuba. There are few examples of campaigns in which radio has played a predominant role. The Tanzanian case to be outlined has made a unique contribution in combining radio and discussion in campaign format. Some of the distinguishing features of a radio campaign are the following: its concentration of effort into a relatively short period of time; its focus on the achievement of one or a few well-defined goals that have broad appeal; its efforts to motivate and involve a large portion of the population in its activities; the organization of a listening audience during the campaign period; the long preparation for the campaign and the need of coordination of many insitutions for its success; and the role of public support for the campaign goals. Other features make the campaign similar to other organized groups' strategies: radio's use for publicity of the activity, organized listening groups with trained leaders, printed supporting materials, and regular programs once or twice a week.

The radio campaign on which most of this section is based originated in Tanzania about a decade ago and much of the evidence comes from the half dozen radio campaigns created during the intervening years. Since Hall and Dodds (1977) have summarized much of the experience in the 1973 health campaign, a reporting of their findings seems appropriate. Before turning to more detailed consideration of the Tanzanian experience, we should note the results of a recent survey by Leslie (1977) of evaluations of the use of mass media in nutrition education. She reports on seven projects that use radio, five of which are campaigns (including one in Tanzania); Table 3.1 summarizes her findings on those seven projects.

The Tanzania Radio Campaign. Hall and Dodds trace the beginnings of the method to the combination of a radio effort by the Institute of Adult Education, and a correspondence course developed for members of local cooperatives by the Co-operative Education Centre. Reaching the scattered, rural-adult population was a shared goal of both groups. They began with an experimental, radio-study-group campaign in 1969 with about 20 groups and less than 1,000 participants,

TABLE 3.1

Evaluations of Radio's Usage for Nutrition Education Campaigns

Project	Description			Available Evaluation Measures					Findings
	Media	Objective	Duration	Outreach	Knowledge Changes	Behavior Changes	Health Status Changes	Cost	
The Stanford Three Community Study (U.S.A.)	Radio and television	To reduce dietary risk factors in cardiovascular disease	A two-year campaign, 1972-1974	No	Yes	Yes	Yes	No	Fat consumption decreased by about 25% for all experimental groups but did not change for the control groups. The increase in knowledge of dietary risk factors was greatest for media plus face-to-face instruction.
The North Karella Project (Finland)	Radio and newspapers	To reduce dietary risk factors in cardiovascular disease.	Ongoing, begun in 1972	No	Yes	Yes	Yes	No	The fraction of males consuming low-fat milk increased from 24% to 62%. Distribution of leaflets by mail or newspapers was more successful than by schoolchildren.
The Trinidad and Tobago Breast-feeding Campaign	Radio and newspapers	To reverse the decline in breastfeeding	A six-week campaign June-July 1974	Yes	Yes	Yes	No	No	85% of recently delivered mothers were aware of the campaign. Mothers who were most aware of the campaign delayed introduction of supplementary bottle feeding.
Advertising Technique Nutrition Education Campaign (Ecuador)	Radio and posters	To increase breastfeeding and to increase use of iodized salt	A 15-month campaign, 1974-1975	Yes	Yes	Yes	No	Yes	Knowledge of legumes as a protein source increased 45%. Reported use of iodized salt increased from 5% to 98%.
The SUNAB Project (Brazil)	Radio and newspapers	To encourage consumption of nutrition foods in accordance with changing agricultural flows	Ongoing, evaluated for the year 1974-1975	Yes	No	No	No	No	Of the sample surveyed, 26% were aware of radio messages and 22% were aware of newspaper advertisements.
The Tanzanian "Food Is Life" Campaign	Radio and booklet	To improve nutrition through improved techniques of agriculture and food preservation	A 16-week campaign, June-Sept. 1975	Yes	No	No	No	No	The broadcasts reached three million adults, although only half that number was projected. Some progress was made in eliminating food taboos.
CARE Mass Media Nutrition Education (South Korea)	Radio and comic book	To improve nutrition through knowledge of five food groups	A one-year campaign in 1970	Yes	Yes	No	No	No	The broadcasts reached almost 90% of the sample interviewed and the comic book reached 80%. 20% of those interviewed had learned the five food groups.

SOURCE: Leslie (1977, Tables 1 and 4).

studying a popular version of the new five-year plan. In the following year, a larger effort was made, and about 200 groups were formed throughout a wider portion of rural areas. This campaign was stimulated by the national elections. It was decided to provide a 2 to 3 month study period for citizens to teach them about the electoral system, and to make them politically aware of their rights and duties before they were to vote for the first time in their history. Two more campaigns are described, one in 1971 concerning the history and achievements of Tanzania on the tenth anniversary of its independence. This was the first truly nationwide campaign, with about 1,500 to 2,000 groups and over 20,000 participants. The campaign in 1973, called Man is Health, shifted to a mass level with 75,000 groups and about 2,000,000 adult participants, and emphasized not only study but action. A closer look at the health campaign will provide evidence for the effectiveness of the approach.

Hall and Dodds in their summary provide an important historical perspective in showing how the campaigns grew from a small experiment to a national mobilization, and in discussing the elements that were important to this successful growth. They point out three features that were common to all four campaigns: the series of radio programs (usually one each week for 2 to 3 months), the printed materials (a text for literate participants, plus a manual for group leaders), and the organized study group with a discussion leader (the latter usually a primary schoolteacher, but in the health campaign often a local farmer). There have since been refinements over the five years covered in the report. Later campaigns rebroadcast programs. A fifteen-minute introduction was added to the radio program to provide music, poetry, and announcements relevant to the campaign and to allow a "gathering time" before the main program began. Group-leader training grew in importance and complexity. To train the 75,000 leaders for the Man is Health campaign required a carefully coordinated, three-stage training of three days each, where each group would help train others. Greater participation in terms of total numbers has been achieved, but it is recognized that sometimes large discussion groups limit the active participation of members.

Two other important features of campaigns are noted. First, there is in addition to the actual campaign of about 12 weeks, a planning period where the relevant ministries define campaign objectives, prepare appropriate written and radio material, and launch an important publicity campaign (including radio and poster announcements). Second, the Institute of Adult Education must get the collaboration of various ministries and agencies for planning as well as for recruiting and training group leaders.

The campaigns since 1970 have always attempted to provide some evaluation of results. These evaluations have grown in size and sophistication with the campaigns, but still they remain rough estimates of results. The single most impressive fact is that for the health campaign in 1973, about 2,000,000 rural adults participated. In the same campaign, the authors report a 47% gain on a knowledge test from pre- to post-test; also, participants gained significantly more than controls. In terms of action, Hall and Dodds estimate that about 750,000 latrines were constructed, and many less easily discernible public-health measures such as boiling drinking water or clearing away mosquito breeding areas were adopted. In a sample of participant villages, there was a 60% improvement in health-related practices.

The reported costs are very crude estimates, but in the health campaign the total cost estimate was $610,000 or about $0.47 per participant. Swedish aid contributed $210,000 of these costs.

The authors point to the following positive features that have emerged in the campaigns: multi-institutional coordination has been achieved, but this could not have happened without the strong political backing from the central government the campaigns have enjoyed and the increasingly long periods of careful preplanning (18 months lead time for the health campaign); the short period of the campaign seems to have achieved a high audience-retention rate; the impact of the campaigns has gone beyond the direct participants and has involved others in the actions advocated by the government. There are several problems to be faced in these campaigns: for example, the failure of the distribution of printed materials at times, the lack of feedback and follow-up mechanisms, and the lack of highly trained leaders who might, as subject matter experts, immediately answer participants' questions. There is very little doubt that the Tanzanian campaigns have demonstrated how radio can be integrated into wide-scale learning experiences that have a significant impact on rural areas.

The experience of Tanzania with campaigns is impressive. On both criteria of reach and impact, the radio-campaign strategy seems to have succeeded quite well. Examining only the health campaign, the 2,000,000 adults involved in the discussion groups is an unprecedented figure for such development projects using mass media. The relatively careful documentation of impact is also impressive. There is evidence for a low dropout rate, a high participation rate in discussions, and an acceptable amount of learning and follow-on action. Hall and Dodds point to several particular advantages of the radio-campaign strategy: first, its power to mobilize such a large number of people; second, the discussion-learning method that does not have the teacher as information-giver of the group, but a local person simply trained to lead the discussion; third, the peculiar fit between the strategy and Tanzanian-defined development goals stressing mobilization, popular participation, and a self-help approach to achieving them.

Implications outside Tanzania. Several critical questions need to be raised lest one success story create the impression of a universal panacea.

First, do most low-income countries have development goals that are related to the strengths of the campaign approach? The amount of mobilization and the level of participation achieved in Tanzania may rest on circumstances peculiar to Tanzania, or at least to its political goals as a socialist country. Many governments do not share the same political model with Tanzania. The mass-mobilization-campaign approach has been common to many socialist countries, but there are few cases where such an approach has been used in nonsocialist countries outside wartime mobilizations in many countries. Botswana (Colclough and Crowley, 1974) is a nonsocialist country that is trying to recreate the same radio strategy for purposes of development. They are in the midst of their second campaign, but no clear evidence is yet available on the outcome.[4]

Second, it is not clear how many governments are interested in mobilization of rural masses through such a campaign approach. Can there be such a high level of participation without mobilizing people?

Third, can most governments agree on national campaign goals and get the collaboration of a number of agencies in the planning and execution stages? It seems that the more usual case is for a large campaign to be the work of a single government agency. Moreover, when interagency coordination is called for, failure often stems from the central government's inability to overcome the bureaucratic isolation of its own institutions.

Having said all this, we return to the evidence from Tanzania and the descriptions of efforts in Botswana, and we suggest that the strategy is a promising approach for using radio to achieve change. There is reason to believe that radio campaigns can achieve limited but concrete goals, perhaps short of the broad social mobilization achieved in Tanzania (Schnitman, 1976). We are not yet sure of the outcomes of this strategy in the nonsocialist development context, but the time is ripe for a good test of its viability.[5]

REGULAR LISTENING GROUPS

The regular-listening-group stategy consists of a combination of radio messages, broadcast on a consistent schedule, usually with some printed support material, and a group organized to listen to the broadcasts together and, subsequently, discuss them or share some common learning experience. The meeting may result in group decision and/or common action as a consequence of the discussion. There is a rich variety of experiences of this kind, and the following sections will analyze three of the more prominent organizing methods.

The Radio Schools. The radio school is a form of organized listening that originated in Colombia thirty years ago, and that has spread, as the map showing the regions served by Latin American radio schools indicates, to many nations in Latin America. The radio schools began when the originator, a Catholic priest, began to broadcast religious and educational messages to his scattered parishioners. Gradually he began to send out written material and finally to pick and train a group leader or monitor to hand out support materials, answer a few questions, and be a feedback person from the group to the production center. As the system spread, the organization became more complex (see Brumberg, 1975), but the essential group learning mechanism remained unchanged. The important element that distinguishes the radio schools from the other listening group strategies is its continual commitment to teaching literacy and nonformal education skills. Although radio schools also later included farm practice and agricultural innovation in their goals, like the farm forums to be discussed, they remain primarily dedicated to their original educational goals. Again, we may distinguish most regular listening groups from the radio-campaign strategy because the former create and maintain their groups on a permanent basis, while most campaigns only create ad hoc groups for the brief duration of the campaign.

The case we will use to illustrate radio schools is not the original and most commonly known example of ACPO (Popular Cultural Action) of Colombia, but an offshoot,

ACPH (Popular Cultural Action of Honduras). White (1976b and 1977b) undertook a long-term evaluation of ACPH, and our summary comes from his findings.

White provides an analysis of ten years of experience of both ACPH and its companion *campesino* organization, the Popular Promotion Movement (PPM). Founded in 1961, the radio schools of Honduras were an almost direct copy of the Colombian ACPO model. However, as White notes, there has been a gradual evolution in both goals and structure of the organization over the last 12 to 15 years, so that from the original emphasis on literacy, there followed stages of Freirian consciousness-raising, community organizing, and finally a more action-oriented, pressure-group phase of pushing for greater social and economic power for the *campesino*.

The author asks three research questions in his study: (1) whether the ACPH/PPM has been *effective* in achieving immediate objectives in promoting skills in literacy, health, and agriculture, and in raising the consciousness and organizational capacity of its audiences; (2) whether these goals, if accomplished, are *relevant* to the *campesino*; and (3) what in the ACPH/PPM strategy contributes most to rural development in rural Honduras?

White begins with an historical analysis of the traditional power base in rural Honduras. He traces the large landholder as the key power holder and link with the urban elite. He also points out that with the coming of "modernization" to Honduras after World War II, and the greater concentration of land and technology in the hands of large landholders, the *campesino's* level of subsistence worsened. During the 1960s the ACPH and the PPM began working in literacy, health, and agricultural areas as well as to raise the *campesino's* consciousness and to help him organize to work for improving his lot. White's evaluation attempts to discover whether these organizations succeeded in their goals and whether such success in turn made a difference in the quality of the *campesino's* life.

White evaluated the effectiveness of the literacy work of the radio schools for the 10-year period (1961-1970) by

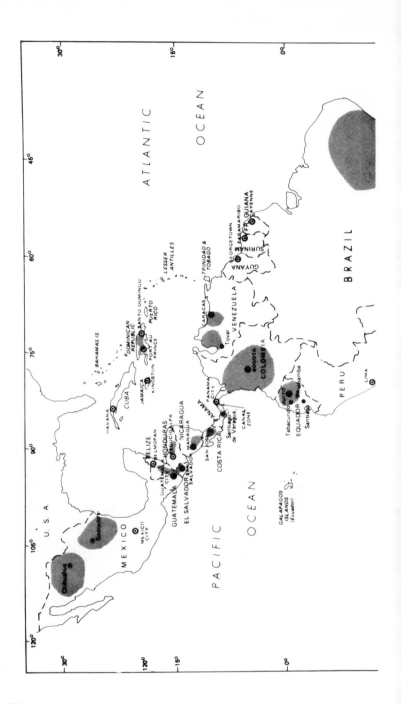

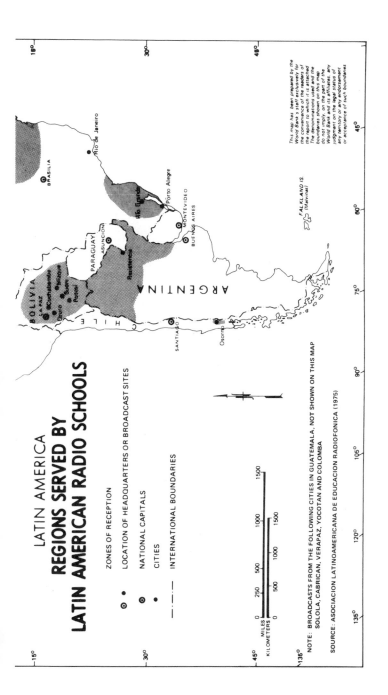

LATIN AMERICA
REGIONS SERVED BY
LATIN AMERICAN RADIO SCHOOLS

⊙ ZONES OF RECEPTION

⊙ LOCATION OF HEADQUARTERS OR BROADCAST SITES

⊙ NATIONAL CAPITALS

• CITIES

–·–·– INTERNATIONAL BOUNDARIES

MILES
KILOMETERS

NOTE: BROADCASTS FROM THE FOLLOWING CITIES IN GUATEMALA, NOT SHOWN ON THIS MAP
SOLOLA, CABRICAN, VERAPAZ, YOCOTAN AND COLOMBA

SOURCE: ASOCIACION LATINOAMERICANA DE EDUCACION RADIOFONICA (1975)

This map has been prepared by the
World Bank's staff exclusively for
the convenience of the readers of
the report to which it is attached.
The denominations used and the
boundaries shown on this map
do not imply, on the part of the
World Bank and its affiliates, any
judgment on the legal status of
any territory or any endorsement
or acceptance of such boundaries

drawing a sample of 595 students or ex-students of ACPH and testing them in literacy and numeracy skills. He found that many students in radio schools had had one or more years of regular school and that this seemed to make more difference in literacy attainment than time spent in radio classes. ACPH had a 45% dropout rate, reached 107,715 students in 10 years, but seemed to have benefited only about 10% of the population in a significant way in attaining permanent literacy. White argues that the PPM policy after 1972 to organize *campesinos* and pressure government for land and other resources should make literacy more relevant to the Honduran *campesino*. He concludes that increased power for the *campesino* is likely to increase his interest in literacy, rather than the attainment of literacy is likely to increase his power.

In health and agricultural knowledge and practice, White found the radio-school villages were higher on knowledge in both, but that only in health were they higher in practice as well, when compared with nonradio-school villages. Again, he believes the lack of success of ACHP/PPM in making a difference in farm practice was because knowledge without resource inputs does not help the farmer improve his life. He points out that the women's household clubs in villages, begun by PPM in 1967, may have helped women to implement health practices better than similar organizations were able to help men in agricultural practices.

The author tried to do a comparative study of the consciousness-raising process, examining the village's knowledge of organization principles and its ability for collective action. He found a higher level of consciousness in radio villages than in nonradio villages. He did not find greater organizational skills in radio villages, but he did find that radio villages had carried out more community projects than nonradio ones. Still, he observes, when, because of increasing land scarcity, *campesinos* began more pressure tactics to obtain land, the radio schools did not seem to prepare them for this kind of directly political work.

He concludes that the ACPH/PPM, using radio and the communication network of village leaders, has helped to create the basis of a new *campesino* culture; it has helped develop a participatory decision-making structure and helped develop a base for interest-group action.

The author asks how the accomplishments of the radio schools helped overall rural development in Honduras. He concludes with some generalizations growing out of the study: (1) structural change is more important for promoting adult education than is adult education for promoting structural change; (2) to be relevant and successful, adult education must be closely integrated with resource delivery and other, rural-development efforts; and (3) consciousness-raising (awareness of problems and consequent value changes) is only effective with solid bases of power in increased economic productivity and *campesino* organization.

A review of the radio schools (McAnany, 1975) more generally concluded: "The positive features of the radio school approach in Latin America for nonformal education are several. First, radio schools have historically always focused on the *campesino* audience in rural areas where learning needs are greatest. Second, several features of their approach fit in with important learning principles: the group-learning approach; multi-media instructional methods (radio, printed booklets, newspapers, and audio-visual aids) coordinated around learning objectives; supervision by a local person who can relate to and motivate the learning group. Third, the radio schools have been built up on an already existing and important structure in rural areas, the parish church. The priest is an important legitimizing factor that has helped radio schools survive in the rural areas where the power structure is generally oppressive to *campesinos.* Fourth, the radio schools, by being mostly private and church sponsored, have been free of identification with the government and its policies.

"There are, however, some negative features that also must be faced regarding radio schools; several have already been mentioned. First, the heavy emphasis on literacy seems to be a misdirection of effort. There is a much wider range of information/education concerning rural areas that may well need to precede literacy and may best be conveyed by radio and through the monitor of listening groups who presumably would be literate. Second, radio schools often do not involve themselves in community development, claiming to be strictly educational. The Freire critique of such a 'banking' kind of education would suggest that the education learned in radio schools be applied to real problems of *campesinos*. There is a tension here, of course, between attacking real social problems and remaining in business. The experience of MEB in Brazil suggests that careful consideration of consequences of social action is necessary. Third, until now the radio schools have remained relatively small and their impact on rural life limited. These results may be partly due to lack of proper financing, but may also come from poor planning and management of the existing projects. Fourth, radio schools may have lost their appeal for real change in rural life and may be seen only as another half-hearted attempt by the power structure—this time the church and not the government—to give *campesinos* the minimum of social services so that they are satisfied with their position in society. There is some evidence, moreover, that even in rural areas the relatively better off are the most likely to benefit from such services. Finally, the major efforts of radio schools seem to be focused on the mass media messages without giving sufficient attention to feedback from rural groups in order to reflect their needs and interests in the messages."

The number of people radio schools are now reaching varies according to the particular project. ACPO in Colombia reports more than 150,000, by far the largest. In comparison with what other projects are doing for the rural adult in Latin America, the radio schools are reaching a significant number and their potential for greater reach is primarily limited by financial constraint. The effectiveness of this method of organizing the audience varies according to the goals being prepared and the particular project in question. The White evaluation is critical but not negative toward the strategy. Other evaluations of radio schools (McAnany, 1975) suggest that if the strategy can be properly supported and the administration is well organized, the radio-school approach can achieve a great deal for nonformal education and other development goals for rural adults.

The Radio Farm Forums. According to Rogers and his colleagues (1977) "a radio forum is a small listening group that meets regularly in order to receive special radio programs, which members then discuss. On the basis of the program and discussion, they decide what types of relevant action to take." The last part of the description distinguishes the radio farm forums from the radio-school approach just reviewed. The radio forums are usually decision groups geared to a group action; the radio schools are usually learning groups, but sometimes they make common decisions for action as well. The other way in which these two types of radio listening groups have been distinguished is by their origin. Historically, radio forums began in Canada among farmers and were spread to India and then to a number of other Asian and African countries through the sponsorship of UNESCO. As we saw, the radio schools were begun and have spread primarily in Latin America and have been usually sponsored by the Catholic church.

Although Rogers and colleagues (1977) do not concentrate on a single case, they present the relevant experience from the best-studied cases. The constituent elements of radio forums are the organizers who establish and help serve the forum, written discussion guides, regularly scheduled radio programs, and regular feedback reports of both discussions and group actions, as well as questions, to broadcast programmers. The basic advantage of the forum idea is its multimedia approach of combining the mass medium of radio with the interpersonal communication of group discussion and feedback through the monitor. The authors argue that neither radio nor group discussion alone can have all of these advantages.

A number of different radio-forum experiences are briefly presented with main results. India's use of forums began with a highly successful experiment in Poona where forum members learned significantly more in ten weeks than individual listeners or those who did not listen at all. When the forums were spread nationwide shortly afterward, the experience was not as positive, probably because the new forums did not experience the same national attention, the forums went on for years instead of ten weeks, and the financial and personnel support were a great deal less than in the experiment. A similar experiment was tried in Ghana where similar positive results were found during the initial period. No follow-up report was made on forums outside the experimental period.

The authors conclude with a number of generalizations about radio forums. Among others are: radio is the single mass-media channel reaching the widest rural audience; radio needs to be supplemented by other media such as printed and audiovisual materials; radio has the advantage (over television) of being able to reach specialized rural groups in their own language; greater effectiveness seems to lie in a small number of themes that are featured over a relatively brief period in an integrated manner; forums seem to be effective with illiterates as well as literates; radio forums are more effective when group leaders have a basic training in leading discussions; forums are compatible with village experiences and cultural preferences; and feedback from forums can help to change government perceptions about what rural people need.

It is possible to draw certain basic conclusions from the long history of radio farm forums. What seems common across these experiences is both the structure (radio, small organized group, group leader and secretary, discussion and group decisions) and the general results (usually an advantage in learning and action of group over individual listeners to radio programs). The authors admit that there is not sufficient evidence to prove that forums are an effective strategy in every case, but that potentially the combination of interpersonal and mass communication can be effective, especially in increasing knowledge. What seems evident from the experiences in India, Benin, and Indonesia, where large field tests of forums were made, is that the problems associated with capitalizing on this potential are formidable. Essentially, it is much easier to organize the radio message than the audience. In all three cases the eager recruitment of new groups was not sufficiently followed up with supervision and distribution of printed materials. Moreover, feedback often failed, and groups whose sole contact was the radio message itself often disappeared quickly after formation.

The settings in which some of the large-scale tests of farm forums were created suggest, perhaps, that the strategy was not sufficiently integrated into other rural-development processes. India expected the radio forums, without other supporting activities, to create change. Although still prevalent, this belief in the sufficiency of radio forums by themselves has been undermined by lack of significant change in most rural areas. A great deal of skepticism has since overtaken development planners as well as mass-media experts.

To date, the evidence is not overwhelming but perhaps encouraging. The potential reach is quite large as both the Indian and Indonesian projects (Rundfunk und Fernseh, 1974) show. In their expansive phases each had several thousand groups organized. Their relative failure at this point does not invalidate their potential for reaching large segments of rural people. The clearest evidence of impact is in learning. It seems clear that farmers exposed in groups to agricultural information can and do learn more than farmers who listen to radio by themselves, or those who do not listen at all. The Guatemalan Basic Village Education Experiment, however, showed some advantages for radio alone over the organized audience (AED, 1976). This is not an insignificant finding for rural areas that are overwhelmingly agricultural. Technical information about farming is still a crucial input to improved agricultural practice and increased productivity.

Obviously, changed behavior must follow, but information (knowledge) is a prerequisite to action. One may argue quite accurately that change in rural areas must go much beyond improved agricultural techniques, to land reform and change in basic social structures. But no radio strategy outlined in this essay will be sufficient to accomplish this by itself. The farm forum experience has demonstrated that the radio, combined with the interpersonal communication of the group, can help to improve knowledge and practice. If other structural changes have been accomplished, then radio has the potential of helping improve agricultural productivity. If such changes are not made, as White points out about Honduras, then increases in agricultural knowledge and even in practice may not make much difference in the lives of poor farmers.

The Radio Animation Groups. This strategy again is a form of organized listening groups. We wish to distinguish it from the other two organizations of groups discussed above. The technique of animation grew out of a French tradition of group dynamics that was applied to development projects in the early 1960s, especially in Africa (Colin, 1965). The classic animation approach had clearly distinct historical assumptions from both radio schools and farm forums. At least in theory, the animation approach stressed the participation of the community in defining its own problems, the nondirective nature of the social animator's role, the degree of awareness necessary for the community to recognize its problems, and the self-help nature of its development action. In practice, many of these elements are not emphasized in radio projects in Francophone countries, and many of the original goals of animation have been partly adopted by other listening-group strategies, thereby blurring the distinction.

It may be worthwhile, nevertheless, to review one case of the animation approach. Cassirer (1977) has prepared a rather lengthy description of Senegal's rural radio project. In 1968, Senegal, through UNESCO sponsorship, began radio broadcasts for rural groundnut farmers in the regions of

Thies, Diourbel, and Sine Saloum. Fifty-seven radio clubs were established for the pilot area, but many more were informally created during the following years. Cassirer's paper traces the history of Radio Educative Rurale (RER) from 1969 through June 1971, with an added postscript in March 1975.

The very severe conditions of the peasants in the groundnut area during 1968-1970 provided an important historical backdrop for the form in which RER evolved. A creation of joint efforts by various ministries (Information, Education, Health, Rural Development, Agricultural), the radio was conceived as a two-way system. Two-thirds of the programming in this period (1969-1972) contained material recorded in the field, and thus allowed input from the peasant audience itself. In addition, President Senghor backed the creation of a written feedback system called *Disso* (or "dialogue" in the national language), which solicited letters from rural people concerning their problems. These letters were translated into French, printed, and distributed to relevant government officials every three months. In the first two and a half years of the project 2,300 letters from 500 villages were received.

The strong, critical response of the farmers in the groundnut areas in the first years made some government officials wish to stop the radio programs and the feedback. One minister made a tour of rural areas where radio had prepared rural audiences for what to expect in his set speech. They demanded action and got it in the form of cancellation of credit debts.

The schedule of two radio broadcasts a week to rural listening groups has continued for a number of years. The broadcasts provide technical information concerning agriculture, health, credit, and other aspects of rural life. The input of local audiences, as well as the written feedback, makes the project unique. The fact that the project is now fully funded with national resources and has expanded into other areas with locally adapted programming is an indication of its success in Senegal.

A preliminary cost study by Trabelsi (1972) was incorporated into the Cassirer historical account. Since the study provided little detail and made no comparisons with other radio systems, the figures are less meaningful than they might have been. Cassirer argues that radio is a relatively cheap substitute for some work that extension agents often do. He does not argue for complete substitution of radio for these personnel, only that once capital costs are amortized, more intensive use of radio to reinforce activities of rural workers would be quite attractive economically.

The author draws three lessons from the experience: a rural broadcasting system like the RER takes a great deal of effort as well as political help to create (given in this case by the president of the country); a project of this kind is not excessively costly and can be economical if it functions to its capacity; and the programming that allows audience input and encourages dialogue is more important than the content of broadcasts.

If one of the principal objectives of the animation strategy is to promote participation, the Senegal case seems to have achieved that at least at the beginning of its work. There is evidence of strong peasant response to the government invitation to send letters concerning problems peculiar to the countryside. The government translated and published these letters for circulation to government officials. Although it is not clear whether this dialogue measurably helped the peasants' lives after the first crisis of debt repayment was resolved by the government, still the creation of such a mechanism between peasants and government through radio is promising.

The evidence from the Senegal case and that of Niger (El Hadj Badge and Robert, 1972) indicates that the animation method can have a significant reach. One limit to this is the amount of local participation that the project allows. In both Niger and Senegal there is an attempt to localize programming and direct input of participants into program production. This principle followed to its logical conclusion would mean a local radio station for each community. Lack of resources has limited the number of local stations and thus the amount of local participation in both Senegal and Niger.

What impact can such a strategy have? The evidence from Cassirer is inconclusive. There is evidence that a number of farmers did participate and the program is reported to be still very popular among rural groups. There is evidence from other sources that programming in their first language has special appeal to illiterate peasants. Both Senegal and Niger have provided such programming. The dialogue that the Senegal project promoted between government and peasants did have some impact on government decision making, at least during the early period. One questions whether the same attention is given peasant input once the crisis is past. The danger is not only indifference of government officials, but the manipulative possibility of giving peasants the impression that by having their letters printed and circulated among officials something is being done about their problems.

More generally, the strategy faces four problems. First, the nondirective nature of the animation approach can mean endless dialogue and little action. Second, local participation must be defined for each radio project and examined for its feasibility and its eventual impact on rural life. Too vague and ideal a notion of participation may be counterproductive to achieving concrete gains by the participants, as White points out in the Honduran radio-school case. Third, participating with the government may contain serious dangers of co-optation by the power holders who are inclined to short-term solutions. Collaboration or confrontation is often a serious strategy question for development-project leaders who solicit and gain popular participation of large masses of rural people. Finally, the desire of localization manifested in the two cases we have mentioned means that radio often loses some of its advantage as a mass medium and becomes more like a local telephone system or a community radio station.

The promise of the strategy, however, makes it worthwhile to promote for those development goals that involve participation.

THE TELECOMMUNICATION/
TWO-WAY STRATEGY

Radio in its broadcast mode is ordinarily a one-way medium. To achieve a number of development goals that call for more direct participation of rural people or depend on immediate feedback, a two-way communication system would have significant advantages. Radio in this strategy would operate more like a telephone system, but with multiple interconnections. Given the right kind of technical and social planning, a radio system can be designed to serve both telecommunications and broadcast purposes (Parker and Lusignan, 1977).

How has the telecommunications use of radio worked in a development context? We will review two cases to illustrate its potential. There have been relatively few development projects that have used this strategy, and further cost and effectiveness data need to be gathered.

The first case is Kreimer's report (1977) on the use of the ATS-6 satellite to provide a reliable signal in a radio-based health project in Alaska. The main endeavor involved about 25 remote villages in one health district in rural Alaska. Ten villages were provided with small, satellite ground stations to help improve the technical quality of two-way radio contact between native health aides in villages and physicians at the regional hospital. Aides in other villages were contacted by a terrestrial HF radio system. Bad climate conditions had impeded use of the regular system to less than 15% of the possible contact days. Locally selected, paid, and supervised aides are given only 16 weeks training and can benefit from consultation with trained personnel in handling cases in their remote villages. The evaluators assessed the impact of improved radio contact in the ten participating villages over a two-year period from 1971 to 1973. Evaluation questions included whether better reliability would increase aide-physician consultation, whether aides would change their care of patients, whether aides would find increased contacts helpful and reassuring, whether increased contact and consultation would change health care (and improve health), and whether hospitalization rates would change.

The purpose of the Alaska health-care delivery service was straightforward: to improve the reliability of the two-way radio signal and thereby increase the likelihood of use of the consultation service between health aides in distant villages and doctors in the central hospital. Certain results were clear. In the first 2 years of the improved reliability of radio contact, consultation in the experimental villages increased almost 500%. There were, in addition, increases in cases treated and confirmation by doctors that, in their opinion, health care had improved.

The second case, reported by Hudson (1977), was set in Northeast Ontario, Canada. There was a long-standing need expressed by native peoples in the area for better communication, and the Canadian government provided a two-way radio system to interconnect all 25 villages of a Sioux tribal group. Hudson found that when two-way radio equipment was installed in the villages, the uses to which the system was put included administrative affairs of the tribal council, weather, news, and personal contact between families and friends. There were immediate benefits to the participants in the system. Chiefs of the area used the radio to carry out the work of their regional council and thereby saved time previously spent in travel from one village to the other (usually by plane). Increased information flow and contact with other native communities was made easier. This increased exchange among people speaking the same language and sharing the same culture, and helped to defend the minority culture from being eroded by the dominant white culture. The formation of a local group to help manage the radio may be the first sign of how the introduction of a technology may help to stimulate community cohesion. This, in turn, may point to the role of two-way radio in promoting greater political unity among minority groups. Finally, Hudson emphasizes that unless communication technology is under the control of the users of the system, genuine access may not be available.

There is no question that use of two-way radio will grow along with the increasing sophistication of technology, especially with satellites. What conclusions are suggested from these two experimental cases? One point seems clear: people have a range of information and learning needs that communication technology can serve. These needs are most often for exchange of information that may be necessary for various aspects of development. Use of radio, and especially use for development, will depend on the level of awareness of the community. If it has already developed a series of well-defined goals, both political and informational, that better communications can serve, then the level of use and the efficiency and the effectiveness of the system is probably assured. These conclusions obviously depend on further testing, and on better observation and measurement of results over longer periods and in different settings.

Two more examples might be briefly mentioned. Hudson, in the previously mentioned study (1977), also reports on the use of a low-watt radio station as a stimulus to community development among an Eskimo group in Northern Canada. Her argument is that in this kind of very isolated community, a local radio station in local hands provides more control over messages coming into the community and a stimulus to the community for common action to solve problems and organize people.

The final example is one dealing with the use of two-way radio in nonformal learning groups. Clark (1972) reports on a study group in a land-development project in Malawi. The idea was to have different adult listening groups (in this case learning English) in the region be able to ask the radio teacher questions. Unfortunately the experiment was not carried out very carefully and no conclusive results were available. It seemed clear, however, that students liked the opportunity to ask questions directly of the radio teacher. It is not clear that learning was enhanced. The limit on numbers of groups participating in such direct interaction poses some question about cost in this case.

Let us examine these cases of the two-way radio strategy in the light of the two criteria of reach and effectiveness. First, there is an inherent limitation of reach in the case of two-way radio. The advantage of the telephone is that it substitutes for face-to-face communication and can often serve the same purpose. But a mass medium like radio can reach many people simultaneously. The cases under review here have failed to resolve the trade-off dilemma of either reaching more people, or having a more functional two-way communication opportunity. In Hudson's two-way case, 25 Sioux villages were served; in Alaska, Kreimer's case involved 14 village health aides who conferred regularly by radio with doctors at a distant regional hospital. Nevertheless, indirectly through health aides and village chiefs, these systems served moderate populations. Parker and Lusignan (1977) argue that with better technical planning a flexible radio system can be created that could serve both broadcast and two-way purposes.

The effectiveness of two-way radio depends on the particular development goals to be served. Kreimer's and Hudson's cases indicate a clear demand for two-way systems in their respective areas. Health aides in Alaska want a chance to consult with doctors about their patients and take the opportunity when it is offered. The two-way system among the 25 Sioux villages was heavily used for a number of purposes. These are only pilot projects, however, and further evidence will be necessary to examine two separate aspects of two-way radio communication. The first is one of cost. How expensive will an operational system be for remote rural areas? What kinds of demands will the creation of such a service put on the regional or national system in terms of more sophisticated and centralizing hardware such as satellites? Second, more evidence is needed on the social relevance of two-way radio. Will the availability of telecommunications for rural areas increase genuine social participation and to what extent will it bring economic advantage to traditional marginal areas? The answer to these questions should grow out of improved evaluation of the demand for telecommunication that communities feel and the continued experimentation with different ways of providing telecommunications services to meet development goals.

NOTES

1. McAnany (1973) and Evans (1976) have previously discussed these matters, organizing them in a somewhat different way.

2. A final report on the Eastern zone of the project (AED, 1977) contains evidence of a more conclusive nature. Radio certainly contributed significantly to knowledge and adoption of new practices. The relation between these changes and increased production remains less clear.

3. Cooke and Romweber (1977), in a final report on the projects in Nicaragua and the Philippines, claim that the radio messages changed awareness, knowledge, and even behavior in the areas intended. The claimed behavior changes, though substantial, are self-reported and would probably be difficult to document statistically. Cooke and Romweber also provide a valuable discussion of the methods used in their radio advertising approach to nutrition education.

4. Cf. a recent paper by Crowley and Kidd, "Radio learning group campaigns in Botswana." This paper was prepared for International Extension College's Workshop in Distance Teaching and Rural Development, Dartington Hall, U.K., 1977.

5. Cuca and Pierce (1977) describe the use of mass media campaigns involving radio to promote family planning and contraceptive use in Iran (pp. 154-156), South Korea (pp. 182-183), and Taiwan (pp. 214-216). Open radio broadcasting was tested in Colombia (pp. 103-104). These efforts seem to have been successful.

chapter 4

The Cost of Radio

Our purpose in this brief chapter is to discuss the cost of providing radio for education and development communication. More information is available on the cost of radio for in-school education than for distance learning, and more is known for distance learning than for development communication. This should be kept in mind in reading what we write about the costs of each.

This chapter contains three sections: in the first we discuss the elements of cost of a radio system; in the second we discuss the methods of cost analysis; and in the third we apply those methods to a study of the costs of a number of the case studies summarized in the preceding two chapters.[1]

4.1 THE ELEMENTS OF RADIO SYSTEM COSTS

The costs of providing radio for education or development communication divide naturally into five major elements: (1) costs of administration, planning, and evaluation; (2) costs of program conceptualization and production; (3) costs of transmission; (4) costs of reception; and (5) costs of complementary inputs such as printed materials or training of teachers to use the system. The absolute and relative importance of each of these cost elements varies tremendously from project to project.

Administrative, planning, and start-up costs can be substantial, particularly for distance-learning projects, which are, in effect, creating new routes for completion of entire cycles of a formal school system. Radio campaigns, too, can have relatively high planning and administration costs; other uses of radio for development communication might have quite low administrative costs. These are costs that are occasionally ignored in planning, but they are often of sufficient magnitude that they require explicit budgeting.

The costs of program production are perhaps the mostly highly variable of any element of costs. The Nicaraguan Radio Mathematics Project (RMP), discussed in Chapter 2, spends about $2,000 in producing an hour's worth of radio programming; the Mexican *Radioprimaria* spends about $115. Part of the pedagogic success reported for the RMP is undoubtedly due to the extreme care with which its programs are initially prepared and the careful (but costly) formative evaluation that goes into this process. While reasonable levels of effectiveness can be attained with far lower programming costs than those of the RMP, even its programming costs can be quite low on a *per-student* basis if the using audience is substantial.

The third cost element listed was that of transmission. The capital costs of transmission include purchase of a transmitter, construction of a building in which to house it, and construction of a tower for the transmitting antenna.[2] In addition, there are recurrent costs of operating personnel, maintenance, and electric power. Table 4.1 shows the costs of radio transmitters of varying power levels; the higher the power, the greater the signal coverage area. To the costs in the table must be added $5,000 to $10,000 worth of control

TABLE 4.1
Radio Transmitter Costs

Power	Cost
AM Transmitters	
250 w — 500 w	$ 4,400 — 6,500
1 kw	6,500 — 6,800
5 kw	18,500 — 22,900
10 kw	20,500 — 24,900
20 kw	50,200 — 59,900
50 kw	97,500 — 104,000
100 kw	120,000 — 135,000
FM Transmitters — MONO	
250 w	$ 5,000 — 9,900
1 kw	6,700 — 7,600
3 kw	10,000 — 13,500
5 kw	13,500 — 15,600
10 kw	18,000 — 21,900
20 kw	25,000 — 29,300
40 kw	60,000 — 66,500
FM Transmitters — Stereo Applications — Add	
1 kw	$ 1,500
40 kw	3,500

SOURCE: Warren (1973: Table 10).

equipment, tower costs of $10,000 to $50,000, and building costs (Rathjens, 1973; Warren, 1973). It should be noted that these cost figures are now several years old and that advances in solid-state electronics are reducing acquisition, operations, and maintenance costs of new transmitting facilities.

Many educational applications will require only limited amounts of transmission time, and the purchase of dedicated transmission equipment is therefore necessary. For example, the RMP leases transmission time from a private broadcasting station at a rate varying from $11.50 to $14.50 per 26-minute time slot, depending on the time of day.

The fourth cost element is that of reception. The cost of reception has two major components—that of the radio

TABLE 4.2

AM/FM Radios: Price, Quality, and Battery Life

Model	Price[a]	FM		AM		Tone Quality	Battery Life[b]
		Sensitivity	Selectivity	Sensitivity	Selectivity		
Panasonic RF900	$60	VG	G	VG	F	G	17
Sony TFM7 250W	45	G	VG	VG	F–G	F	6
Penney 1860	50	G	F	VG	F	G	10
Hitachi KH1047H	50	F	VG	VG	F–G	P	20
Sears 22696	25	P–F	G	VG	F	P	19
Magnavox RD 3035	45	F	P–F	VG	G	F	18
Juliette FPRI286	40	P–F	F	VG	G	P	18
Lloyds NN8296	30	P–F	F	G	F	P	21
Lafayette 1702349L	28	P–F	P–F	VG	F	F	10
Soundesign 2298	29	F	P–F	VG	F	P	24

SOURCE: **Consumer Reports,** July 1975: 438-439.

Key: P — Poor, F — Fair, G — Good, VG — Very Good.

a. This is the retail list price in 1975 U.S. Dollars.

b. This is the life in days of four C-type batteries if the set is operated for four hours per day at high volume.

receiver and that of the power required to operate it. If mainline power is available, the cost of power is negligible for radio; in nonelectrified areas, however, the cost of batteries can be important.

Table 4.2 provides a comparison of AM/FM receivers in the range of $25 to $60 (list price in the U.S. in 1975). The comparison gives some indication of the relationship among initial price, battery life, and three important design characteristics: tone quality, sensitivity (ability to pick up a weak signal), and selectivity (ability to receive a station without interference from another station). Sensitivity is important in order to provide reception of adequate quality in rural areas that may be substantial distances from the transmitter. Selectivity is important in areas with multiple-channel broadcasting on closely spread frequencies. All models of radio in the table use four C-size batteries. The battery life was tested by playing the radio for four hours per day at high volume (conditions that would be similar to classroom use). The batteries, which have a replacement cost of approximately $1.00 for a set of 4, lasted from 6 to 24 days.

The receiver prices listed are retail and substantial reductions would, of course, result from wholesale purchase. Prices for radios without the FM option would also be lower, although Krishnayya (1976) has advanced a number of reasons for favoring FM. However, though it is occasionally argued that one might also reduce costs by acquiring radios capable of receiving at only one frequency, Warren (1973) cautions that this approach might well increase costs; and, in some places where it has been tried, it has resulted in increased maintenance costs due to students tampering with the receivers to try to change frequencies. It should also be noted that, while much less expensive receivers are available than those listed in Table 4.2, less expensive ones are probably unsuitable for group or classroom listening.

The final cost element to be considered in planning radio's use is that of complementary inputs. Training teachers for the radio's use or providing printed material can be expensive; indeed, until cutbacks were made, these items dominated the replication costs of the Nicaraguan RMP. Little can be said about the general pattern of these costs, but they are often of sufficient importance that their allocation needs to be carefully planned.

4.2 COST FUNCTIONS FOR INSTRUCTIONAL RADIO PROJECTS[3]

In the preceding section we discussed the various elements of an instructional radio system whose costs need to be considered. Our purpose in this section is to describe the basic concepts of economic analysis that are required to pull these elements together into an understanding of the overall cost behavior of an educational radio system.

This section begins by discussing the concept of a cost function, and the related concepts of total, average, and marginal cost. To a first approximation cost functions for educational technology fit into a convenient form that separates "fixed" and "variable" costs, and we next discuss that case. Capital costs for educational technology are high, and for that reason it is important that planners deal with them properly; we touch lightly on these matters in this section.

TOTAL, AVERAGE, AND MARGINAL COST

It is useful to think of costs as functions rather than as numbers: a total-cost function gives the total cost required to finance instructional radio as a function of the number of students to be reached. To take an example let

$$\text{Total Cost} = TC = TC(N),$$

where $TC(N)$ is the total cost required to provide instructional radio to N students. Total cost will, of course, increase as N increases.

The average-cost function (or, equivalently, *unit-cost function)* is defined to equal the total cost divided by the number of students served:

$$\text{Average Cost} = AC(N) = TC(N)/N.$$

Just as the total cost depends on N, so may the average cost; typically average costs will decrease as N increases.

The marginal-cost function gives the additional cost of providing one more unit of input (i.e., in this example, of providing instructional radio to more than one student) as a function of the number of units already provided. Stated slightly more precisely, the marginal cost function is given by:

$$\text{Marginal Cost} = MC(N) = TC(N+1) - TC(N).$$

That is, the marginal cost at any given level of student utilization, N, is equal to the total cost for N+1 students minus the total cost for N students. It is often feasible to assume the marginal cost of adding one more student to a system is constant, that is, it is independent of the number of students already served.

To illustrate the concepts above, let us construct a simple example. In Table 4.3 the first column indicates the number of students served by a particular educational program, while the second column indicates the total costs of serving that

TABLE 4.3
Total, Average, and Marginal Cost Example

Unit (students) N	Total Cost TC (N)	Average Cost AC (N)	Marginal Cost MC (N)
0	$ 0	$ 0	—
1	30	30	30
2	70	35	40
3	105	35	35
4	120	30	15
5	130	26	10

number of students. We see that the example has been constructed to indicate that total cost is some function of the number of students; that is, total cost increases as the number of students increases. From the information presented in the first and second columns we can derive the average- and marginal-cost information presented in the third and fourth columns. The average cost is simply the total cost divided by the number of students, while the marginal cost is the addition of total costs caused by the addition of one more student to the system. The average cost is most useful as an historical summary of the system's efficiency in doing its task, while the marginal-cost measure is more useful in examining the cost consequences of expanding or contracting the system, in terms of the number of students served.

FIXED AND VARIABLE COSTS

When the total-cost function can be approximated by the simple and convenient linear form,

$$TC(N) = F + VN,$$

it becomes possible to separate costs into fixed costs and variable costs. In this example, F would be the *fixed cost* because the value of cost contributed by the first term on the right-hand side is independent of N; V is the *variable cost* per unit of input because the value of total cost contributed by the second term on the right-hand side varies directly with N. When the total-cost function is linear, the average cost is simply equal to the fixed cost divided by N plus the variable cost $[AC(N) = F/N + V]$; the marginal cost is equal to V. Thus the average cost declines as N increases (by spreading the fixed cost over more units) until, when N is very large, the average cost is close to the marginal cost.

The above equation is a reasonable approximation to the cost behavior of instructional-technology systems.[4] Program preparation and transmission tend to be fixed independently of the number of students using the system. Reception costs, on the other hand, tend to vary directly with the number of students.

CAPITAL AND RECURRENT COSTS

A *capital cost* is one that is incurred to acquire goods or services that will have a useful lifetime that extends beyond the time of purchase. *Recurrent costs,* on the other hand, are incurred for goods or services that are used up as they are bought. The principal cost of schools is the recurrent cost of teachers' time; since teachers are paid while they provide their service, the useful lifetime of what is actually purchased simply coincides with the pay period. (In this example we neglect the human-capital-forming aspect of teacher-training colleges.) The cost of a pencil would seem to be a capital cost since, depending on one's penchant for writing, it could last for several months. In fact, pencils are treated as recurrent costs for the reason that their expected lifetime is less than the accounting period (usually one year) of school systems. The line between capital and recurrent costs is, then, conventionally drawn at one year; if the lifetime of a piece of equipment exceeds a year, its cost is usually treated as a capital cost. Coombs and Hallak (1972: Chapter 9) point out that school systems often adhere only loosely to this one-year convention, and they provide a valuable practical discussion of how to examine school building and facilities costs.

An occasional source of confusion, even among economists, is between fixed costs and capital costs. There can be fixed costs that are recurrent; an example is the electric power required to operate a television transmitter. Likewise, there can be capital costs that are variable; an example is the receiver component of reception costs. Thus the concepts of fixed costs and capital costs are distinct, though it is often true that major capital expenditures are associated with substantial fixed costs.

How does one construct the cost functions discussed in the preceding subsection if capital costs are present? Let us say that a school system buys a radio transmitter and 6,000 receivers in year one for a total cost of $220,000. It would clearly be inappropriate to include the entire $220,000 as a year one cost in attempting to determine the unit cost of the radio in year one; likewise it would be inappropriate, in computing year three costs, to consider the use of transmitter and receivers as free. In order to construct a useful cost function it is necessary to *annualize* the expenditure on capital equipment.

In annualizing a capital cost one must take account both of how long the capital equipment will last and the interest rate one could receive on the capital if it were invested in, say, bonds instead of in the transmitter and receivers. The resulting annualization can reasonably be thought of as the annual *rent* one would have to pay if the equipment were leased rather than purchased. To continue with the example of the preceding paragraph, if the $220,000 worth of equipment had an expected lifetime of ten years, and if the interest rate were 7.5% per year, the annualized cost (rental value) of the equipment would be $32,051 per year. Cost calculations for instructional-technology projects can be rather sensitive to the interest rate chosen, as Jamison, Klees, and Wells (1978) have shown; we use 7.5% in this book as a reasonable intermediate value.

4.3 THE COSTS OF SEVERAL PROJECTS

In this section we use the concepts of the preceding section to assist in the analysis of the costs of several projects.

COSTS OF IN-SCHOOL RADIO

We begin this subsection with a discussion of the Nicaragua Radio Mathematics Project (RMP), then compare its costs with those of several other in-school uses of radio. We use the cost estimates for the RMP presented in Jamison, Klees, and Wells (1978: Chapter 5) as modified by Searle, Friend, Suppes, and Tilson (1976: 27-32). In order to obtain a cost function for the RMP, we need to ascertain the parameters of the cost function for it: $TC(N) = F + VN$; that is, we need to ascertain the values of F and V.

Table 4.4 summarizes the various components of the cost of the RMP, under the assumption that the project provides instruction to students in three grade levels. We see from the table that the annualized variable costs, V, are $1.64 per student per year. The total cost function for the RMP is, then:

$$TC(N) = 169,200 + 1.64 \, N.$$

If, after the project were partially operational in Nicaragua, it reached 40,000 students at each of 3 grade levels, then N would equal 120,000. For N = 120,000, $TC(N) = 169,000 + (1.64) \times (120,000) = \$366,000/\text{year}$. If the total project cost is $366,000 per year, then average cost (i.e., total cost divided by the number of students) will equal $3.05 per student per year. Notice that this remains substantially above the value of marginal cost, V, of $1.64 per student per year, which is the cost of adding another student to the system. This average cost is higher than marginal cost because it includes the per-student allocation of fixed costs; naturally as the number of students increases, the fixed cost *per student* will decrease and average costs will fall closer in value to marginal costs.

To facilitate comparisons across projects it is sometimes useful to compute the cost per student per hour of radio (or television) instruction. This can be done by dividing the average cost per student per year by the number of hours per year of instruction. Since the RMP broadcasts 165 30-minute lessons per year, with an average cost of $3.05 per student per year (assuming 40,000 students per grade), we arrive at a cost per student-hour of $.037.

TABLE 4.4

Costs of the Nicaragua Radio Mathematics Project (in 1975 U.S. dollars)

Item	1 Capital Cost Component	2 Annualized Capital Cost	3 Recurrent Cost	Annualized Cost (= 2 + 3)
A. Elementa of the Fixed Cost, F				
Start-up cost[a]	$335,000	$33,000/yr.	0	$ 33,000/yr.
Project administration			$59,000/yr.	59,000
Radio lesson preparation for 3 grade levels[b]	480,000	70,000		70,000
Transmission for 3 grade levels			7,200	7,200
TOTAL				$169,200

	Annualized Cost Per Student
B. Elements of the Variable Cost, V	
School supervision	$ .11/yr.
Receiver[c]	.10
Batteries	.09
Teacher's guide and teacher training	.42
Blank paper and miscellaneous supplies	.92
TOTAL	$1.64

a. Start-up costs are annualized over 20 years at a 7.5% interest rate.
b. Radio lessons are annualized over 10 years at a 7.5% interest rate.
c. Receiver costs are annualized over 5 years at a 7.5% interest rate; 2 classrooms are assumed to share one receiver.

The RMP's costs are high for a radio project—in part because of the heavy investment in high-quality programs, and in part because of the higher level of supplementary resources provided to the student. While we make no effort at detailed cost-effectiveness analyses in this chapter, it is perhaps worth noting that, even though the cost per student is relatively high, adoption of the RMP would almost surely reduce costs per graduate because of the effect it has on reducing repetition rates.

We have discussed the costs of the RMP at some length in order to exemplify the methodology and results of cost analysis of projects; in the remainder of this chapter we treat other project costs more briefly.

Another project for which reasonably good cost estimates are available is the Mexican *Radioprimaria* (Spain, 1977); Table 4.5 reports on its costs. The average cost per student per year assumes *Radioprimaria* utilization levels of the year 1972: 2,800 students and 280 hours broadcast. The cost-per-student-hour figure reflects the common broadcast feature of the *Radioprimaria* system; that is, students receive about 242 hours of instructional radio each year even though only 280 hours are produced in total for all three grades. The reason for this is that 80% of the broadcasts are aimed at the combined three grades' audience. The ratio of average cost per student to variable cost per student indicates that production costs dominate system costs, which is unsurprising given the tentative, experimental nature of the system at this date. Average costs per student could be lowered substantially by expanding to include more students in the system.

Jamison, Klees, and Wells (1978: Chapter 6) undertook a tentative comparison of the cost of providing students in a rural area with fourth-, fifth-, and sixth-grade education in three classrooms with three teachers, versus putting them in one classroom with one teacher and one radio for three years. Even if enough teachers could be found who were

TABLE 4.5
Cost Summary of Four Instructional Radio Projects[a]

Project	Year of Information Source	N	h	F	V	AC (N)	Cost Per Student-Hour
Nicaragua[b]	1976	120,000	250	169,000	1.64	3.05	.037
Mexico Radioprimaria	1972	2,800	280	45,600	.19	16.44	.068
Mexico Tarahumara[c]	1972	1,081	640	56,300	.50	52.86	.331
Thailand[d]	1967	800,000	165	125,800	.28	.44	.018

SOURCE: Jamison, Klees, and Wells (1978: Chapter 12).

a. Values in this table were computed with an interest rate of 7.5%; all values are in 1975 U.S. dollars. The symbols are defined as follows: N = number of students using project (in the given year, unless otherwise noted); h = the number of **hours** of programming broadcast per year; F = annualized fixed costs; V = annualized variable cost per student; AC (N) = average annual cost per student for the given value of N; and the student-hour cost is the annual cost per student-hour of viewing for the given values of N and h.

b. The values of N and h chosen for the RMP in Nicaragua reflect hypothetical utilization of the system.

c. Though the cost per student-hour of the Tarahumara project is extremely high (because of the low enrollments), the radio schools in which they operate are, overall, less expensive than traditional primary education because of their use of auxiliary teachers receiving about half the pay of a qualified primary teacher.

d. See Schramm, Coombs, Kahnert, and Lyle (1967) for a description of the Thai instructional radio project and for the cost data upon which this cost function is based.

willing to work in rural communities (which is a problem in Mexico), their results indicated that the *Radioprimaria* alternative is much less expensive than the traditional system ($101 per student per year rather than $164); this advantage would be increased if student utilization were hypothesized to be greater than 2,800. The additional costs of the instructional radio components of the *Radioprimaria* system are more than offset by the reduced teacher and facility costs resulting from the combination of three grades into one classroom with one teacher. Whether these cost savings are cost-effective is a matter of judgment.

Table 4.5 also contains cost information on two other in-school radio projects, as well as a summary of the RMP and *Radioprimaria* examples. The other Mexican project also uses radio to extend schooling and is described in the accompanying volume of case studies (Schmelkes, 1977). The Thai project uses radio principally for enrichment; its production techniques are relatively simple, but its audience is large indeed, resulting in low per student costs.

In order to provide a comparison of in-school radio costs with those of television, Table 4.6 provides cost information on a number of in-school television projects. The Mexican TV project, like the radio ones, was used to extend schooling—at the beginning secondary level in this case—to areas otherwise unreached (Mayo, McAnany, and Klees, 1975); the other projects were principally for quality improvement in existing schools.

COSTS OF RADIO
FOR DISTANCE LEARNING

Table 4.7 presents cost functions for three distance-learning systems in developing countries that use radio; this table shows a quite reasonable range of average costs. Schramm (1977) provides cost information on two other distance-learning projects that use radio, both from developed coun-

TABLE 4.6

Cost Summary of Four Instructional Television Projects[a]

Project	Year of Information Source	N	h	F	V	AC (N)	Cost Per Student-Hour
El Salvador	1972						
Total Costs		48,000	540	1,395,000	1.38	30.44	.179
GOES Costs[b]		48,000	540	999,000	1.38	22.19	.130
Hagerstown, USA	1973	22,000	1,440	1,467,000	.81	67.79	.575
Korea[c]	1976	1,000,000	560	1,757,000	2.26	4.03	.056
Mexico	1972	29,000	1,080	726,300	5.31	30.34	.084

SOURCE: Jamison, Klees, and Wells (1978: Chapter 12).

a. Values in this table were computed with an interest rate of 7.5%; all values are in 1975 U.S. dollars. The symbols are defined as follows: N = number of students using project (in the given year, unless otherwise noted); h = the number of hours of programming broadcast per year; F = annualized fixed costs; V = annualized variable cost per student; AC (N) = average annual cost per student for the given value of N; and the student-hour cost is the annual cost per student-hour of viewing for the given values of N and H.

b. The GOES costs refer to the costs incurred by the Government of El Salvador; the difference between total costs and GOES costs results from external financial assistance.

c. The N and h for Korea reflect planned utilization of the system as discussed in Jamison and Kim (1977). Though studio facilities are now complete, and pilot testing of programs is underway, the Korean ETV System remains to become operational.

TABLE 4.7

Cost Functions for Three Distance-Learning Projects[a]

Country	Source(s)	Nature of Project	Cost Function (dollars per year)	N	AC (N)
Kenya[b]	Krival (1970)	In-service certification and upgrading of primary-school teachers	TC (N) = $250,000 + 9.77N	10,100	$34.50
Korea[c]	Jamison and Kim (1977)	Radio-correspondence high school covering three grade levels	TC (N) = $168,000 + 25N	30,000	30.60
Dominican Republic[d]	White (1976a)	Primary-school equivalency for adults using radio, workbooks and weekly meetings	TC (N) = $152,000 + 8.7N	20,000	16.30

SOURCE: Jamison (1977b).

a. These cost functions are expressed in terms of 1975 U.S. dollars, with capital costs annualized at a 7.5% interest rate; N is the approximate annual enrollment in the system; and AC (N) is the average cost per student per year, using the enrollment level given.

b. This cost function was constructed as an approximation to the cost data given in Krival (1970); the data date from 1969. While the evidence on this from Krival is unclear, this cost function probably fails to include costs that students incur for their texts and workbooks, which might be substantial. See also footnote 10, Chapter 2, p. 58.

c. The high marginal cost for the Korea system results from its heavy reliance on textbooks; of the marginal cost of $25.00, $21.00 is for texts.

d. This cost function was constructed as an approximation to the cost data given in White (1976a: Section 9).

113

tries. One is the Australian Radio-Correspondence Schools, which began operation in 1933. These schools serve students in remote regions of Australia who are unable to attend regular classes. In New South Wales the Radio-Correspondence Schools reached about 7,000 students in 1967 and cost about $310 per student; this is about 17% higher than traditional instruction. The high costs probably result from the very low student enrollment *per grade level.* The second project for which Schramm reports cost data is the NHK radio-television-correspondence high school in Japan; their costs of $308 per student per year compare with traditional costs of about $540.[5]

While there is difficulty in comparing the cost per enrollee of a distance-learning system to the comparable cost of traditional instruction, rough comparisons are possible. For the projects listed in Table 4.6 we can tentatively conclude that the costs of the radio-correspondence systems are 35% to 50% that of traditional instruction. However, until much better comparative cost studies are available, these estimated ratios must be considered highly speculative. The extent to which these systems will in fact realize potential savings depends on the size of the audience to be reached and its dispersal. A further economic advantage of distance learning is that it need not withdraw the learner from productive work; he can continue with his job. Much more needs to be learned, though, about the cost of distance learning and about how its costs can be reduced.

COSTS OF RADIO FOR
DEVELOPMENTAL COMMUNICATION

Relatively little is known about these costs. They are often rather small, frequently buried in the budgets of larger organizations, and usually available only for the portion of costs financed by the government. A relatively inexpensive research effort could substantially improve our knowledge of

TABLE 4.8

Costs of Several Development-Communication Projects Using Radio[a,b]

Source (s)	Description of Project	Program Production	Transmission	Remarks
KENYA — —	Weekly serial of 15-minute radio programs on "Giving Birth and Caring for your Children."	$225 per 15-minute program	$85 per 15-minute program	This project has been popularly received in Kenya and similar projects are under development in Tanzania and Zambia.
NEPAL Mayo, Herm, Jamison, Sahdev, and Smee (1975)	Family planning, maternity, and child health program, producing two 15-minute programs per week plus one-minute spots.	$20 per 15-minute program; $60 per one-minute spot	$10 per 15-minute broadcast	Transmission costs are based on cost estimates rather than use charges.
TANZANIA Hall and Dodds (1977)	'Man is Health' mass campaign reaching several million villagers with information on creating a healthy environment and using community medical services.	— —	— —	Cost estimated to be about $.50 per villager reached, including cost of $.10 for two 48-page booklets.
SENEGAL Cassirer (1977) Trabelsi (1972)	Rural educational radio to establish two-way dialogue between government and peasants; approximately one hour per week of programming.	$615 per hour	$15 per hour	

a. All cost estimates in this table should be regarded as highly tentative.
b. These projects rely on the listeners to provide their own receivers.

the costs and financing of radio's use in development communication; in the absence of such a research effort, Table 4.8 tentatively presents aspects of the costs of a few projects.[6]

NOTES

1. This chapter provides information only on cost analysis and omits the somewhat more technical discussion of combining cost and effectiveness information into a cost-effectiveness analysis; Jamison and Leslie (1977), in the companion volume of case studies, describe a cost-effectiveness analysis of radio's use for in-school education in Indonesia. Also in the companion volume is a discussion of the technological alternatives for distributing radio with their cost implications (Parker and Lusignan, 1977). Audio cassettes provide a close substitute for radio and it will in many cases be desirable to consider their use as an alternative distribution system; Colle (1976) provides an imaginative discussion of the range of uses to which cassette systems might be put.

2. The tower itself serves as the transmitting antenna for AM applications; for FM an antenna can cost from $2,000 to $20,000.

3. This section draws heavily on Jamison, Klees, and Wells (1978: Chapter 1), which treats these matters in substantially more detail. While the cost functions we present carry an air of precision, we wish to emphasize their approximate character. Carnoy and Levin (1975) argue that there is a natural tendency to underestimate costs of educational technology, and Klees and Jamison (1976) found that this had indeed happened in the Ivory Coast. Fisher (1971) provides an excellent practical guide to handling these and other problems of cost analysis.

4. It should be emphasized that this linear formulation of the total-cost function is in many cases only a rough approximation. For example, as the system expands to cover students from more heterogeneous cultures, more geographically distant locations, or less densely populated areas, the marginal cost per student may well vary.

5. Cost information is also available for the British Open University (Laidlaw and Layard, 1974; Lumsden and Ritchie, 1975). Because this is more heavily *television* and correspondence than radio, we do not report these cost figures here. Kanocz (1975) presents sketchy cost estimates for the German radio-correspondence *Funkkolleg*, which indicate it to be far cheaper than conventional instruction, and, even less specifically, Krawcewicz (1976: 10-11) claims that "we may state that (the Polish Radio-Television University for Teachers) is almost certainly less expensive than the traditional forms of education."

6. After preparing this chapter we received a copy of an interesting cost study, by Etherington (1977), of a radio campaign in Botswana.

chapter 5

Constraints on Implementing the Radio Strategies

I t is clear in the assessment of the effectiveness, reach, and cost of the different radio strategies for education and development communication that numerous constraints can hinder the realization of radio's potential. There are few good case studies of either successful or unsuccessful projects that have thoroughly documented the process of implementation and identified the ways in which these projects met and overcame certain implementation problems. (An exception to the dearth of evidence is an administrative history of the ETV project in El Salvador by Mayo and Mayo, 1971).[1] The conclusions about the effectiveness of different radio strategies must take into account not only the strategy's potential, setting, software, and particular development goals, but also a series of other factors both in the environment and within the radio system itself that affect outcomes.

These factors are often crucial to whether the application of a particular strategy succeeds or fails. We have divided our discussion of constraints into parts dealing with those that are external to the radio project and those that are internal to it. The first constraints, those of the environment, deal with problems outside the project over which there is less control; the second deal with more down-to-earth problems that face managers within the project.

5.1 EXTERNAL CONSTRAINTS

STRUCTURAL

Perhaps it is too obvious to speak of the constraints imposed by social and economic structures, but education and development communications radio strategies have often failed or partially failed because these constraints were insufficiently considered. To take an example from a formal education project, Schmelkes (1977) shows that in a project in Mexico, the Indian students for whom the radio strategy was intended benefited a great deal less than non-Indian students because of the social and cultural constraints placed on the mobility of Indian students. White (1977b) shows that in Honduras those who benefited from the radio schools were those among the *campesinos* who already were better off. Cook et al (1975) have shown that there is a widening of the effects' gap between lower- and middle-class watchers of *Sesame Street*. A number of people have begun to examine the structural constraints on communication for development purposes (Grunig, 1971; Felstehausen, 1973; Golding, 1974; Beltran, 1975; Roling, 1975). The radio strategies outlined above are constrained by the setting in which they are applied. If equity is an important goal of development, then the success of the different strategies must be examined in the light of distribution of education or information benefits, rather than solely in terms of their absolute impact.

IDEOLOGICAL

The value question is an important one that touches the uses of radio. All radio communication has a content and that content reflects basic values and beliefs. Whether we are talking about a formal school curriculum in Mexico or a program of consciousness-raising in rural Honduras, the issue of ideology is important. This issue is particularly sensitive where there is strong public consensus on a need for change, as is the case in many low-income countries. What is debated is the way of changing, and opposing value systems often come much more into evidence in such public debates. The value question may be less of a problem in some formal school subjects, but history, social studies, and even language are often brought under serious ideological question.

For the development communication strategies, the ideological question is even more critical. The Latin America radio schools, for example, have repeatedly felt called upon to clarify their ideological position (de Kadt, 1970; Musto et al, 1971; OSAL, 1972; Cabezas, 1975). When a radio project is attempting to motivate rural people to self-help or to bring information or education to these people, the cause of the rural "problem" is an important element to clarify for one's audience. In examining the causes of poverty, malnutrition, and lack of schooling, the question of ideology is necessarily touched upon.

POLITICAL

The distinction between the ideological and the political constraints is that the former concerns the value system underlying the content of radio and educational messages, and the latter the question of power to allocate resources to achieve one's goals. Although the two types of constraints are related, it is useful to make a distinction in the discussion. The most obvious reason that radio projects are political is that radio is a mass medium and can reach large numbers of people with its messages. Many countries tightly control their radio and television stations; evidence of their political importance is that these media are often the first targets of

coups d'etat. Second, there is the politics of money. Sometimes radio projects may command a good deal of money and
there is a political struggle over their control. Third, radio
projects may have a certain amount of prestige connected
with them in some countries, and political parties that are
competing for power often seek control and hope to gain
political favor if the project proves successful. Fourth, the
radio strategies summarized here most often address themselves to poor rural people. It is difficult to treat rural problems seriously in most developing countries without the
projects becoming political. The political-power holders
are often very suspicious of any attempt to organize, mobilize, or even communicate with a large mass of the rural
poor. The danger of politicization is that the government
will intervene or close down the project radio station, as has
happened in northeastern Brazil.

A second and important constraint is the political will of
the government to carry out a radio development project.
No matter how attractive a radio strategy might be for
achieving certain goals, if the political leadership fails to
support the goals and their achievement, then a project will
have difficulty succeeding. Some of the goals take a strong
national determination to carry out because they are complicated and costly of solution. The success of the radio campaigns in Tanzania, for example, is at least partly explained
by the national commitment that the government has to the
mobilization of people for their own development, and the
concomitant investment of resources in rural services. Other
projects fail or only manage to survive at a low level because
there is no more than a verbal commitment to the proposed
goals.

LEADERSHIP

This is a crucial though often uncontrollable constraint, yet
one that can make a major difference in success or failure of

projects. What we mean here is not an administrator (the lack of which is an internal constraint), but a leader who is fully committed to the goals and project strategy, and who has both vision and the political skill to win backing and get others to cooperate with him. Colombia's radio school project, ACPO, mentioned in Chapter 3, owes a great deal of its success to its founder and leader for thirty years, Father Salcedo. Radio Santa María in the Dominican Republic (White, 1977a) also can partly attribute its success to a dynamic leader. A common problem for radio projects is that although government officials agree that the idea is a good one, it has often come from an external technical-assistance agency and there is no leader to make it work locally. An added problem is that trained leadership talent in low-income countries is often in short supply and there is quick turnover of these people in their jobs as they move up the career ladder.

INSTITUTIONAL PERMANENCY

Radio strategies for development and education often suffer from a lack of permanency. They begin as "experiments" or "pilot projects" and often, despite success, cease to exist when the experiment ends or the government that sponsored them changes. Radio strategies are often an amalgam of several bureaucracies, a ministry of information, for example, and a ministry of education or agriculture. Their success depends to a large extent on the cooperation of these institutions. But a project based on this interagency cooperation has an impermanent base and will become permanent only if it can put down some institutional roots elsewhere. There are examples of successes, of course, but there are probably many more failures; innovative and experimental projects often fade away because they fail to find an institutional home. Honduras's ACPH that White (1977b) speaks of grew outside of government. Cassirer (1977) refers to a successful project in Senegal that got presidential backing and later became a permanent part of the ministry of information, but serves education and rural development. There are, especially in the files of bilateral and international aid agencies, countless histories of pilot projects and experiments that did not remain. A careful study and reflection on these cases would perhaps improve the chance of useful radio-based projects to succeed and grow into more permanent institutions.

5.2 INTERNAL CONSTRAINTS

There are internally many constraints to a radio project. They may be thought of as relating to the main functions of most radio strategies: finance, training, planning/management, content development, production, distribution, and reception. There are perhaps a few commonly experienced constraints that do not fit into this framework, but it serves the purpose of reviewing the common problems radio strategies face in implementing a project.

FINANCE

If we begin with the most obvious constraint of money, it is not that success is guaranteed by its presence. The problem of self-financing is an important one facing the large number of privately operated projects. Among radio schools in Latin America, this problem is a serious constraint on almost all elements of the systems, including the director's time, which is often devoted largely to fund raising. On the other hand, large government projects often achieve little more than poorer, private ones. Colombia's ACPO (Brumberg, 1975), the Dominican Republic's Radio Santa María (White, 1977a), and the Canary Islands' Radio ECCA (Cepeda, 1976) are three major projects that are largely self-financing. Though publicly financed projects do not have to raise funds, they often must wait for budgets to be approved by other agencies. If private projects need to develop self-financing strategies, government-sponsored ones need to develop political strategies to ward off the pressures to reduce their budget by others who are competing for the same resources. If, as we have said, a radio project does not have a permanent base by the time it passes the pilot stage (and external financing ceases), then it is in trouble for its continued existence.

A second problem is a budget allocation strategy that fits with the knowledge of which parts of the radio system are most effective in attaining project objectives. We have no sound evidence to give us absolute guidance on this point. In the cases reviewed in this volume, there have been a variety of budget allocations. The Radio Mathematics Project in Nicaragua spent a large amount on development of curriculum materials, programming, and feedback. The Tarahumara (Schmelkes, 1977) and Tanzania (Hall and Dodds, 1977) projects spent very little money on programming. Cassirer (1977) indicated that the Senegal project spent a great deal of its budget on programming and little on field supervision, and yet he says that the project worked successfully. The Rogers et al (1977) review of India's radio-forum project reports that a serious problem was its lack of funding for field personnel. There are at this time no generalizations available to make a decision on allocation easier. Each project needs to be analyzed with regard to the most effective way of allocating its resources to those components that best achieve project goals. In one case it may be to develop information for agricultural programs, in another to provide more field support, and in a third to produce more interesting programs by using more creative talent.

TRAINING

The constraint involving lack of trained people for radio projects is one that cuts across several operational areas. Low-income countries often lack trained people for radio in a variety of fields including engineering, creative writing, and management. The problem of finding enough trained people is often solved by outside technical assistance, which helps in the short term to begin the project but often introduces a series of other problems. When time and financing are found, allowing people to be trained, the result is often that the people are so much in demand that they quickly leave the position for which they originally were trained. But more often, what happens is that training gets ignored. Because projects often must begin quickly while political momentum lasts, training is postponed and the project may struggle on with untrained people and consequently have poor results. The best solution that radio projects have found to many of these training and personnel problems is to recruit local people dedicated to the project and to train them locally. This often lowers costs and lowers the likelihood of the training being used by participants to move out of the project.

PLANNING AND MANAGEMENT

The need for careful planning and organization of radio strategies seems to be one of the great constraints on their success. There is not only a problem of finding well-trained planners and managers, but also of determining the administrative structures within which such projects must function (Chambers, 1974). The location of decision-making authority will often dictate how radio will be organized. If a radio project is under the ministry of information, as is often the case in low-income countries, then other ministries like education, health, agriculture, labor, or rural development must struggle to coordinate their programs that use radio with this other bureaucracy.

The planning function may often be performed once at the beginning of a project and be neglected thereafter. Objectives are often vague or undefined and no allowance is made for their growth or change. A major additional problem is that planning may often be performed by foreign technical assistants who do not properly understand the social and cultural setting. In this case, or even when local people are involved in planning, there is little involvement of others, especially recipients, in the planning process. Hudson's cases (1977) of the local radio projects in Canada are an exception to this rule.

Part of the solution to the problem is training people to be better managers and planners. But another part in applying simple management techniques (Chambers, 1974) and in involving recipients in the planning so that goals do reflect needs.

CONTENT DEVELOPMENT

There are two main problem areas, one related to the more formal educational radio projects and another related to the development communication projects. The first constraint on content development in formal and even nonformal education programs is that not enough careful planning is given to curriculum development and instructional design. Radio is often used simply as a way of reaching more people and not as a part of a learning system. Account is often not taken of the difference between direct and mediated teaching, and the radio message is created as if the student were being addressed face to face. Searle et al.'s (1977) account of the Nicaragua project demonstrated the care with which a radio mathematics course was developed. The development of radio teaching of adults in various primary subjects in the Dominican Republic is another is another example of careful planning being given to the development and delivery of content.

For the more open kinds of messages such as agricultural and nutrition information, the problem is often a question of appropriateness and timing. Agriculture follows a cycle and may have a variety of regional differences. The problem of adapting the agricultural information to a particular region is both costly and time consuming. Food preparation often depends on what is available in certain geographical areas and to certain social classes. Radio content of a kind that might be applicable to everyone is often already known or too general to be useful.

Solution to these constraints may consist in some people being trained in curriculum development and instructional design for the more explicitly educational radio strategies. For those that deliver information for immediate application, the allocation of resources to make sure the information is correct and timely is essential.

PRODUCTION

Gunter and Theroux (1977) argue that the single greatest production constraint is the quality of radio programming. They say that educational programs are poorly made, dull and uninteresting, and therefore fail to attract a large or faithful audience. Most school teaching is routinized and dull, and radio reflects this "school" mentality. They have no simple answer, but they point to alternative ways of teaching by radio that are interesting and effective. We have reviewed several of these ways and some costs have also been reviewed. It is not clear that more money necessarily buys quality in production. Kenya (UNICEF, 1975) produces a popular, weekly health program on a low budget. A Guatemalan agriculture program (AED, 1976) is expensive to produce but has developed a large regular audience. Both programs are interesting and of good quality, yet cost different amounts for production. We might think of examples of unsuccessful, poor quality programs that varied a great deal on production cost as well. The ideal, of course, would be to produce high quality programs of low cost, but whether this is possible depends on the specific objectives that each project is seeking. In Kenya, the project wishes to entertain and provide motivation to rural people to be concerned about their family's health. The amount of explicit health information present in each program is low. In Guatemala, the daily half-hour program on agriculture is meant to provide a great deal of explicit information for application.

DISTRIBUTION

There are three areas of distribution constraints on radio projects: the distribution of the message, that of accompanying printed materials, and that of other resources often called upon in some follow-up action. Difficulties of signal strength often hinder good reception, and this most frequently occurs in the more isolated cases. Radio ownership is another problem. Sets are unevenly distributed in the population, and in many countries the most geographically isolated and lower social classes have no access to radio. Set maintenance or replacement of batteries is another related problem that many radio projects cannot control. Again, problems of this kind are often more acute for isolated populations. An almost universal problem facing radio projects is making sure that printed materials arrive on time to be properly coordinated with the radio message. Hall and Dodds (1977), for example, refer to this as one of the problems in the otherwise successful Tanzanian health campaigns. The final problem is material-resources distribution. Both White (1977b), in his Honduras case, and Hall and Dodds refer to the problem of having material resources to carry out suggested actions in health and agriculture. Often, like printed-material distribution, there is a management or coordination problem, but also there may be a failure to invest in the necessary resources or infrastructure. If the radio advocates certain agricultural practices, for example, but no agency can provide listeners with the material to carry out the advocated practice, then no effect except frustration can be expected. These three distribution problems are major constraints on the achievement of radio project goals. Better planning and management can help solve some; others are up to other government agencies who must provide material resources.

RECEPTION

Reception of the message primarily concerns the audience, which in most radio strategies is an organized one. The reception constraints on the effectiveness of radio strategies may be divided into four areas: organizational structure, motivation, feedback, and participation. There are a number of ways of organizing the listening audience, from formal groups meeting in classrooms to individuals listening at home. The structuring of the audience is a critical element, and trained field staff are needed to make it work. A form of supervision or coordination of field staff is another level of organization, interacting with both the program center and the individual reception groups. This field staff may be voluntary or paid, but whoever bears the cost, it must function well if people are to receive and apply the radio message. A common cause of failure among radio projects outside formal schools is the inability to reach and organize the audience. Tanzania (Hall and Dobbs, 1977) was able to organize almost 2,000,000 people in its health campaign, but a large part of its success was due to a long, prior-planning period and a helping hand from the cell system of the ruling TANU party. Distance learning in the Dominican Republic builds part of its organizational structure on the primary schools where it recruits part-time teachers.

There is a great deal of discouraging evidence concerning the failure to motivate people properly in educational radio. High dropout rates from volunteer adult-learning programs make the cost of each student produced less attractive than the mass medium of radio might suggest. In literacy programs the motivation of the audience has been a key factor in their effectiveness (Oxenham, 1975). Those radio projects able to tap a strong motivation in their audiences have been successful. Kinyanjui's case (1977) of Kenyan teachers studying by radio illustrates this. If teachers passed certain exams at the end of their studies, they would be promoted and get a raise in salary. Radio provided them a means of studying for their exams at home. Kreimer's (1977) case also shows that Alaskan health aides wanted more consultation from doctors and made great use of an increased opportunity through satellite radio to do so.

Feedback is a mechanism by which information from the audience concerning the reception of the message is provided to the originator so that improvements or other adjustments may be made. In a previous review of radio projects in a development context (McAnany, 1973), we concluded that most projects did not have a functioning feedback system, and therefore were message-creation centers that had no knowledge of what was happening in the field, much less whether the message was having an effect. There are two kinds of feedback involved here: the first kind is a formative feedback or pretesting of materials to assure the quality of the radio message or the printed material. The Nicaragua project (Searle et al., 1977) is the best example of this effort currently available. The second is how the message is actually received among the listening groups or classrooms. There are two purposes to the second—an educational goal to see whether the message is being understood and actually fulfilling its learning objectives, and a management goal to see how the system is functioning, whether radio sets are working, materials arriving, and group leaders or teachers showing up on time. Although nearly all the projects see the need for such feedback, there is little evidence to convince us that systems are gathering relevant and continuing information from the field. The added problem for projects that do succeed in getting feedback is to know how to use the information to improve materials or change management decisions.

Two constraints suggest themselves in addition to that of how to create feedback systems. First, creating good feedback is expensive, as the Nicaragua case shows. Second, production units and management may be slow to change, even in the face of evidence that there are problems in the system. No case as yet has indicated exactly how these constraints can be overcome to increase the effective running of radio projects.

A mass medium like radio presents problems for the active participation of its audience. Yet participation is one of the commonly invoked goals of many rural development projects. There are degrees of audience participation in a radio project, from a minimal amount of feedback from the audience to participation in production, management, and ownership of the radio station by the community. The two projects in Canada that Hudson's (1977) case study discusses place a great deal of emphasis on local participation, even though the initiative came originally from outside. Cassirer (1977) speaks about the participation of Senegalese farmers in the shaping of radio program production, as well as government policies for rural areas through feedforward and feedback. White (1977b) seems to indicate that the ideal of the Honduras radio school was a greater participation by the *campesino* in his own development, but he gives no indication of how this took place within the radio project. On the other hand, the campaign approach in Tanzania by Hall and Dobbs (1977) seems to leave little room for feedback and participation in shaping the radio message. It is clear that, although there is a need for participation in most strategies, the word has distinct meanings for the audience in each case.

5.3 CONCLUSION

This chapter has catalogued a number of common problems that radio projects have encountered that limit the potential of technology in accomplishing information and education goals in development. Chapters 2, 3, and 4 have reviewed and presented the evidence for radio's effectiveness, reach, and cost. It is clear from a number of the cases cited that radio used in a variety of ways can be an attractive tool. The present chapter outlines the common areas of constraint for the different radio strategies. When these problems are confronted in the planning or early implementation stage of a project, they can be partially or even totally avoided. It is the hope of the authors that an increasing number of planners and decision makers recognize the necessity for overcoming constraints and make radio's potential for contribution to development even greater.

NOTE

1. A second administrative history of the kind we refer to was completed by S. Grant in late 1977. This covered a four year history of an out-of-school television program for rural adults in the Ivory Coast, West Africa, and contains valuable insights into the constraints on media used for rural development.

chapter 6

Conclusions

This volume has reviewed the recent history of radio's use for formal education and for development communication. Within both of these categories we examined the experience of a number of projects in terms both of *strategies* they employed for using radio and of the *goals* they used it to attain. In this final chapter we sum up what we feel can be learned from these experiences.

6.1 RADIO FOR FORMAL EDUCATION

In Chapter 1 we spoke of three objectives for radio in helping formal education systems to meet their goals. The objectives were: improving educational quality and relevance; lowering educational costs; and improving access to education, particularly in rural areas. These objectives consist, principally, of using radio to assist a formal education system to provide its existing services more cost-effectively to a broader audience, rather than to meet new goals. Nonetheless, if new goals are set for the education system—in terms, say, of increasing the development-relevance of the curriculum or of fostering a sense of national unity—radio may in some cases provide a quick and effective mechanism for reaching these new goals; instruction in agricultural science or in the national language (in a linguistically heterogeneous county) are two examples.

Chapter 2 discussed four alternative *strategies* for using radio to meet these objectives. These strategies were:

(1) *Enrichment of learning,* i.e., provision of occasional lessons or experiences that the classroom teacher would find difficult to provide.

(2) *Direct instruction,* i.e., carrying the major portion of the instructional burden in one or a few subjects.

(3) *Extending in-school education,* i.e., providing direct instruction in enough subjects that a qualified teacher can be replaced by a monitor with little or no more education than the students.

(4) *Distance learning,* in which a technology combined with textbooks and occasional personal interactions completely replaces the teacher and school.

In Table 6.1 we summarize our assessment of the potential of each of these strategies for radio's use to meet the three objectives we listed.

TABLE 6.1
Uses of Radio in Formal Education

	Objectives		
Strategies	**Improve Access**	**Improve Quality**	**Reduce Cost**
In-school, enrichment	No	Maybe	No
In-school, direct instruction	No	Yes	Usually No
Extended schooling	Maybe	Maybe	Maybe
Distance learning	Yes	Usually No	Yes

NOTE: The entries in the table indicate our best estimate of the **possibility** of reaching a stated objective if radio is used in the indicated mode. For example, the evidence indicates it is definitely possible to improve quality by in-school use of radio for direct instruction; such use of radio will not, of course, **necessarily** improve quality.

This volume has provided little discussion of radio's use for enrichment of in-school education; the reason is that such use of radio provides little prospect for substantial change in education. On the other hand, the cost of this use of radio is usually low indeed and there may well be some benefits; our point is simply that this strategy holds no promise for major improvements.

In contrast, use of radio for direct instruction in one or more subjects shows substantial promise for major improvements in the quality of education. The Nicaraguan Radio Mathematics Project provided a striking example of how much impact on student achievement a carefully designed radio curriculum can have. While this project is reasonably costly by the standards of instructional radio, it appears that its costs are more than offset by the project's reduction of student repetition rates and hence of the (substantial) burden of providing places for repeaters in the Nicaraguan educational system. Use of radio for direct instruction has, however, little promise for improving access to schooling; nor is there yet sufficient experience of its success to allow complete confidence that the results from Nicaragua could be repeated elsewhere.

The principal purpose of using radio for extending schooling is to improve access in rural areas. We earlier summarized two case studies of projects in Mexico that used radio to extend schooling—one near San Luís Potosi (*Radioprimaria*) and one in the remote Tarahumara region. Experience with both these projects was mixed, but principally disappointing. While both projects showed evidence of being able to use radio to teach at about the level one could expect in traditional elementary schools, neither project expanded beyond the pilot stage and the Tarahumara one has recently ceased broadcasting. Whether better financing and a firmer government commitment would contribute to greater success for subsequent projects using radio to extend schooling remains to be seen. We feel that further exploration of the potential is well worthwhile, but that such exploration must be assumed to have an element of risk.[1]

The final strategy for using radio in formal education is as a component of a distance-learning system. The experiences we reviewed from Kenya and the Dominican Republic were both highly favorable. In Kenya, radio was combined with correspondence to upgrade the quality of the teachers. In the Dominican Republic similar methods were used to provide elementary and secondary school equivalency for adults. Both projects appear to have maintained pedagogical quality and provided access to education to groups otherwise unable to receive it. (In Kenya, teachers would have been unable to be upgraded without leaving their jobs. In the Dominican Republic, traditional adult education simply failed to reach the rural areas.) There is by now a substantial history of use of radio for distance learning in both high- and low-income countries; an educational planner can be reasonably sure that this use of radio can be effectively implemented. However, though their costs appear low, much remains to be learned about the economics of distance-learning systems and for what types of educational problems they provide the most cost-effective solution.

6.2 RADIO FOR DEVELOPMENT COMMUNICATION

Our discussion of radio's use for development communication focused on the experiences of a number of projects that used differing radio strategies for four basic purposes: to motivate audiences, to inform them, to teach them cognitive or work skills, and to change specific items of behavior. The principal strategies for attaining these goals are open broadcasting, radio campaigns, and radio programs tailored to organized listening groups. Two-way radio has also, to a lesser extent, been used to reach these goals. Table 6.2 summarizes our assessment of how well the different radio strategies can

TABLE 6.2
Goals and Strategies of Radio for Development: Effectiveness and Reach

| | | | Effectiveness in Reaching Stated Goal | | | |
| | | | | To Teach (nonformal education) | | |
Radio Strategies	Reach	To Motivate	To Inform	Cognitive Skills	Work Skills	To Change Behavior
Open Broadcasting	High	4	5	1	1	2
Radio Campaigns	High	5	2	2	1	3
Listening Groups	Medium	4	3	3	2	4
Telecommunications (two-way radio)	Low	5	4	2	3	2

NOTE: A value of 1 in the table indicates low effectiveness; a value of 5 indicates high effectiveness.

be expected to perform for each of the four purposes; the table rates performance both in terms of how wide a reach the strategy has and in terms of its effectiveness.

Table 6.2 indicates that, as radio strategies for development communication become more closely committed to organizing their listening audience, the more limited their reach becomes. Thus, open broadcast needs only to concentrate on getting out an interesting message, but the listening-group strategies (radio schools, farm forums, radio animation) must expend resources and time in organizing and providing materials for their audiences. However, the more heavily organized strategies clearly have advantages in promoting more complex and long-term changes among their clientele. The conclusion is not to force a choice of any one strategy on communication planners, but rather to make them aware that radio can be used in a variety of ways, for a variety of goals, and that the objectives of the development project should best dictate the choice of strategy.

But let us go one step beyond this general conclusion to review briefly some cases where radio has achieved its goals with special success. Four examples come to mind: The Kenya health broadcasts (UNICEF, 1975), the nutrition radio campaigns (Manoff, 1975), the Guatemalan agricultural-information programs (AED, 1976), and the Tanzania radio campaigns (Hall and Dodds, 1977). Let us consider the strategy in which radio was used, the development goals, the project achievements, the special characteristics that make the approach most promising, and conclusions about its usefulness for the future.

The Kenya health program, already described in Chapter 3, has achieved a large audience among both urban and rural audiences. Its health messages are carried in humorous format to many households that otherwise would have had no exposure to the educational purpose it espouses. It has achieved three of the goals that Gunter and Theroux (1977) have advocated for the open-broadcast strategy. It reaches a large audience, at a low weekly cost, with entertaining and educational health messages. There are no impact data, but an audience survey indicates that audiences are listening. Radio can be enlisted in a positive and inexpensive way to reinforce the important work of health or nutrition.

The Manoff nutrition radio campaigns are another illustration of the open-broadcast approach. The evidence is inconclusive, but the repetition of the experience in several countries is beginning to illustrate the viability of the idea that advertising techniques and research can be used to change behavior in socially important areas like nutrition, and not just for selling consumer products.

The Guatemalan Basic Village Education Project has shown that careful programming, closely geared to the audience's interests, can win the attention of a large rural audience and create change as well. The programs provide agricultural information that is precisely geared to the timing of the crop cycle. Thus the information, in addition to being accurate, is also highly relevant and is therefore more likely to be applied. The audiences are organized in part of the project, but there is evidence for high learning gains and innovation adoption even among nonorganized audiences.

The first three cases illustrate several points: that radio can play a role in such important development areas as health, nutrition, and agricultural productivity; that it can attract a wide audience and get its messages across without necessarily organizing its audience; that in two of the cases it effects behavior changes as well; and further, that this has been done at reasonable cost. This evidence would seem to indicate that most countries could make better use of a national resource like radio to pursue important development goals.

The last example is one of a radio campaign; review of the Tanzania experience brings out some of its potential. The large number of people that the Tanzanian campaigns have been able to mobilize (2,000,000 adults in 1973) dramatically indicates that the strategy has potential for reaching large audiences. Costs in Tanzania have been modest, and there is no reason to think that they need be much higher elsewhere. Mobilizing large groups to action, as was done in the health and food-growing campaigns of 1973 and 1975, does take careful planning and control, which may be difficult to achieve in some countries. This strategy calls for an organized audience, but not one that is of long duration where people lose interest or drop out.

Reviewing all of the cases, we conclude that radio has a generally untapped potential for development communication. There are a large number of cases where this potential has been frustrated by the constraints that operate both within and outside the medium. On the whole, however, we conclude that most countries could more deeply exploit the opportunities radio provides. We hope that the examples of the cases we have cited will challenge countries to greater use of an old resource for accomplishing some of their new development tasks.

NOTE

1. Two other major projects have used educational technology to extend schools—one was also in Mexico (Mayo, McAnany, and Klees, 1975) and the other in Brazil (Arena, Jamison, Oliveira, and Orivel, 1977). Both of these were much more successful than the radio projects we have just discussed; they differed from the radio projects in using television, in teaching secondary rather than primary school students, and in having firmer official commitment to their success.

References

AED. *The basic village education project (programa de educación básica rural) Guatemala.* Third Interim Report, Washington, D.C.: Academy for Educational Development, 1976.

AED. *The basic village education project (programa de educación básica rural) Guatemala. Oriente Region combined report 1973-1976.* Washington, D.C.: Academy for Educational Development, 1977.

AHMED, M. and COOMBS, P. (eds.) *Education for rural development: Case studies for planners.* New York: Praeger, 1975.

ARANA DE SWADESH, E. *Informe sobre la influencia que la radio ejerce en una comunidad indígena: Xoxcotla, Morelos.* Paper presented at the Friedrich Ebert Foundation Seminar on Rural Radio, Mexico City, December 1971.

ARENA, E., JAMISON, D., OLIVEIRA, J., and ORIVEL, F. *Economic analysis of educational television in Maranhao, Brazil.* Paris: UNESCO, 1977.

Asociación Latinoamericana de Educación Radiofónica (ALER). *Que es ALER?* Buenos Aires, 1975.

BARRETT, H. *Tanzania: Planning a national mass adult education campaign.* Paper given at Conference on Communication Policy and Planning for Education and Development, Stanford University, July 1976.

BELTRAN, L. *Social Structure and Rural Development Communication in Latin America: The 'Radiophonic Schools' in Colombia.* Paper presented at the Summer Conference on Communication and Group Transformation for Development, East-West Communications Institute, Hawaii, June 29-July 11, 1975.

BOWMAN, M. M. *Rural people and rural economic development.* Paris: UNESCO International Institute for Educational Planning, 1976.

BRUMBERG, S. "Colombia: A multimedia rural education program." in AHMED, M. and COOMBS, P. (eds.) *Education for rural development: Case studies for planners.* New York: Praeger, 1975.

Bureau of Public Schools (Department of Education and Culture, Republic of the Philippines). "A study on the effectiveness of instructional broadcasts in the teaching of English as a second language in grade 1." Unpublished paper, Manila, 1969.

CABEZAS, E. *Documento Informativo sobre Radio Santa María.* Seminario de Santo Domingo, 3 al 12 de Abril de 1975.

CARNOY, M. and LEVIN, H. "Evaluation of educational media: Some issues." *Instructional Science,* Vol. 4. 1975: 385-406.

CASSIRER, H. "Radio in an African context: A description of Senegal's pilot project." In Spain, P., Jamison, D., and McAnany, E. (eds.), *Radio for education and development: Case studies,* Vol. 2. Washington, D.C.: World Bank, Working Paper 266, 1977.

CEPEDA, L. *Radio Ecca: Centro docente.* Canary Islands: Radio ECCA, 1976.

CHAMBERS, R. *Managing rural development: Ideas and experiences from East Africa.* Uppsala: Scandinavian Institute for African Studies, 1974.

CHU, G. and SCHRAMM, W. *Learning from television: What the research says.* Stanford, California: Institute for Communication Research, 1967.

CLARK, R. "Report on an experimental course in the use of two-way radio in adult education for the Lilongue Land Development Programme." Limbe, Malawi: Univ. of Malawi, Center for Extension Studies, February 1972.

COLCLOUGH, M. and CROWLEY, D. *The people and the plan: A report of the Botswana Government's educational project on the five year national development plan.* Gaverone, Botswana: Univ. of Botswana, Swaziland and Lesotho, Extra-mural Services, 1974.

COLEMAN, W., OPOKU, A. and ABEL, H. *An African experiment in radio forums for rural development: Ghana 1964-65.* Paris: UNESCO Reports and Papers on Mass Communications, No. 51, 1968.

COLIN, R. "L'animation, clef de voute de développement." *Développement et Civilisation,* No. 21. March 1965: 5-10.

COLLE, R. "Cassette, special communication systems." Paper prepared for conference on Nonformal Education and the Rural Poor, Michigan State University, 1976.

COLOMINA DE RIVERA, M. *El Huesped Alienante: un Estudio sobre Audiencia y Effectos de las Radio-telenovelas en Venezuela.* Maracaibo: Universidad de Zuelia, 1968.

CONSTANTINE, M. "Radio in the elementary school." *Science Education.* 1964: 121-132.

COOK, T. and others. *Sesame Street revisited.* New York: Russell Sage Foundation, 1975.

COOKE, T. M. and ROMWEBER, S. T. *Radio nutrition education—A test of the advertising technique: Philippines and Nicaragua.* Washington, D.C.: Manoff International Inc., 1977.

COOMBS, P. and AHMED, M. *Attacking rural poverty: How nonformal education can help.* Baltimore, Md.: Johns Hopkins Univ. Press, 1964.

––– and HALLAK, J. *Managing educational costs.* New York and London: Oxford Univ. Press, 1972.

CROWLEY, D. and R. KIDD. "Radio Learning Group Campaign in Botswana." Paper prepared for International Extension College Distance Teaching and Rural Development Workshop, Devon, U.K.: Dartington Hall, September 1977.

CUCA, R. and PIERCE, C. S. *Experiments in family planning: Lessons from the developing world.* A World Bank Research Publication. Baltimore and London: Johns Hopkins University Press, 1977.

D'ARINOS SILVA, L. "Joao Silva: A telenovela course." *Education Broadcasting International.* March 1975.

DECENA-DILONA, H. "Estudio comparativo del rendimiento de los alumnos de las Escuelas Radiofónicas de Radio Santa María y de educación de adultos oficial." Tesis, Universidad Católica, Santiago, República Dominicana, 1973.

DE KADT, E. *Catholic radicals in Brazil.* London: Oxford, 1970.

DODDS, T. *Multi-media approach to rural education.* London: International Extension College, 1972.

EL HADJ BADGE, M. and ROBERT, J. *Dix ans d'animation radiophonique en milieu rural.* Niamey, Niger: Association des Radio-Clubs du Niger, 1972.

ELLIOT, R. *A study of taped lessons in geography instruction.* Westfield, Mass.: The Abner mmm mmm

ETHERINGTON, A. *Tribal grazing land policy radio learning group consultation campaign: The costs of the campaign.* Gaberone, Botswana: The Government Printer, 1977.

EVANS, D. "Technology in nonformal education: A critical appraisal." *Comparative Education Review,* Vol. 20. 1976: 305-327.

FAGEN, R. *The transformation of political culture in Cuba.* Stanford: Stanford Univ. Press, 1969.

FELSTEHAUSEN, H. "Conceptual limits of development communication theory." *Rural Sociology.* 38. 1973: 39-54.

FISHER, G. *Cost consideration in systems analysis.* Santa Monica: Calif.: RAND Corporation, 1971.

FORSYTHE, R. *Instructional radio: A position paper.* Unpublished paper. Stanford Univ., 1970. (ERIC: ED 004 933).

FOSTER, P. and SHEFFIELD, J. (eds.) *Education and rural development.* New York: World Yearbook of Education, 1974.

GALLEGO, D. "The ECCA system of radio teaching." *Multi-media International.* 1974.

GOLDING, P. "Media role in national development: Critique of a theoretical orthodoxy." *Journal of Communications,* 24: 3. Summer 1974.

GOMEZ, L. and GUTIERREZ, A. *Encuesta sobre radio-fusión entre los campesinos,* Bogotá: Acción Cultural Popular, 1970.

GOODY, J. and WATT, I. "The consequences of literacy." In Goody, J. (ed.), *Literacy in Traditional Societies.* Cambridge, England: Cambridge Univ. Press, 1968: 27-68.

GRANT, S. *An administrative history of out-of-school educational television in the Ivory Coast.* Washington, D.C.: Academy for Educational Development, 1977.

GRUNIG, J. "Communication and the economic decision-making processes of Colombian peasants." *Economic Development and Cultural Change,* 19: 3. July 1971: 580-598.

GUNTER, J. and THEROUX, J. "Open-broadcast educational radio: Three paradigms." In Spain, P., Jamison, D., and McAnany, E. (eds.) *Radio for education and development: Case studies,* Vol. 2. Washington, D.C.: World Bank, Working Paper 266, 1977.

HALL, B. and DODDS, T. "Voices for development: The Tanzanian National Radio Study Campaigns." In Spain, P., Jamison, D., and McAnany, E. (eds.) *Radio for education and development: Case studies,* Vol. 2. Washington, D.C.: World Bank, Working Paper 266, 1977.

HERON, W. and ZIEBARTH, E. "A preliminary experimental comparison of radio and classroom lectures." *Speech Monographs,* 13. 1946: 54-57.

HOLMBERG, B. *Distance learning.* London: Kegan Paul, 1977.

HUDSON, H. "Community use of radio in the Canadian north." In Spain, P., Jamison, D., and McAnany, E. (eds.), *Radio for education and development: Case studies,* Vol. 2. Washington, D.C.: World Bank, Working Paper 266, 1977.

INKELES, A. "The international evaluation of educational achievement." *Proceedings of the National Academy of Education,* 4. 1977: 139-200.

JAMISON, D, "Radio education and student repetition in Nicaragua." Washington, D.C.: World Bank, 1977a.

JAMISON, D. *Cost factors in planning educational technology systems.* Paris: UNESCO International Institute for Educational Planning, Fundamentals of Educational Planning Series, No. 24, 1977b.

––– and KIM, Y. "The cost of instructional radio and television in Korea," In Bates, T. and Robinson, J. (eds.), *Evaluating educational television and radio.* Milton Keynes, England: Open Univ. Press, 1977: 70-78.

JAMISON, D., KLEES, S., and WELLS, S. *The costs of educational media: Guidelines for planning and evaluation.* Beverly Hills and London: Sage Publications, 1978.

JAMISON, D. and LESLIE, J. "Planning radio's use for formal education: Methodology and application to Indonesia." In Spain, P., Jamison, D., and McAnany, E. (eds.), *Radio for education and development: Case studies,* Vol. 1. Washington, D.C.: World Bank, Working Paper 266, 1977.

JAMISON, D., SUPPES, P., and WELLS, S. "The effectiveness of alternative instructional media: A survey." *Review of Educational Research,* 44. 1974: 1-67.

KANOCZ, S. "Part-time higher education using radio—an example from the Federal Republic of Germany." In MacKenzie, N., Postgate, R., and Stephen, J. (eds.), *Open learning.* Paris: UNESCO Press, 1975: 163-181.

KEDI. *Development of the air and correspondence high school in Korea.* Seoul: Korean Educational Development Institute (KEDI), 1976.

KINYANJUI, P. "Training teachers by correspondence." *IEC Broadsheets on distance learning, No. 5.* Cambridge, England: International Extension College, 1974.

––– "In-service training of teachers through radio and correspondence in Kenya." In Spain, P., Jamison, D., and McAnany, E. (eds.), *Radio for education and development: Case studies,* Vol. 1. Washington, D.C.: World Bank, Working Paper 266, 1977.

KLEES, S. *"Instructional technology and its relationship to quality and equality in education in a developing nation: A case study of instructional television in Mexico."* Stanford: unpublished dissertation, Stanford Univ., 1974.

––– and JAMISON, D. *"A cost analysis of instructional television in the Ivory Coast."* Washington, D.C.: Academy for Educational Development, unpublished paper, 1976.

KRAWCEWICZ, S. *The Radio-Television University for teachers in Poland.* Warsaw, Poland: Radio-Television University, Institute of Teachers' Education, 1976.

KREIMER, O. "Interactive radio for health care and education in Alaska." In Spain, P., Jamison, D., and McAnany, E. (eds.), *Radio for education and development: Case studies,* Vol. 2. Washington, D.C.: World Bank, Working Paper 266, 1977.

KRISHNAYYA, J. G. "Regional radio service for rural development." In *Electronics—Information and planning.* New Delhi: Government of India, Department India, Department of Electronics (IPAG), 1976.

KRIVAL, A. *Project Report: Radio/Correspondence Education Project No. 615-11-650-129, USAID/UWEX.* Univ. of Wisconsin, October 1970.

LAIDLAW, B. and LAYARD, R. "Traditional versus Open University teaching methods: A cost comparison." *Higher Education,* 3. 1974: 439-474.

LEFRANC, R. *European university and post-university distance study systems.* Strasbourg, Council of Europe, 1977.

LESLIE, J. "Mass media and nutrition education." Palo Alto, Calif.: EDUTEL, Inc., 1977.

LUMLEY, F. "Rates of speech in radio speaking." *Quarterly Journal of Speech,* 1933.

LUMSDEN, K. and RITCHIE, C. "The Open University: A survey of economic analysis." *Instructional Science,* 4. 1975.

MACKEN, E., van den HEUVEL, R., SUPPES, P. and SUPPES, T. *Home-based education.* Washington, D.C.: National Institute of Education, U.S. Department of Health, Education and Welfare, April 1976.

MacKENZIE, N., POSTGATE, R., and SCUPHAM, J. *Open learning: Systems and problems in post-secondary education.* Paris: UNESCO Press, 1975.

MADDEN, R. "Educational radio bibliography 1954-67." *Educational Broadcasting Review,* 2. 1968: 66-79.

Manoff International Inc. *Mass media and nutrition education.* Progress report. Contract AID/TA-C-1133. September 1975.

MAYO, J., HERM, L., HORNIK, R., JAMISON, D., SAHDEV, N., and SMEE, M. *Development radio for Nepal: Report of the radio feasibility study team.* February 1975.

MAYO, J., HORNIK, R., and McANANY, E. *Education reform with television: The El Salvador experience.* Stanford: Stanford Univ. Press, 1976.

MAYO, J. and MAYO, J. *An administrative history of El Salvador's educational reform.* Stanford: Institute for Communication Research, Stanford University, November 1971.

MAYO, J. McANANY, E., and KLEES, S. "The Mexican telesecundaria: A cost-effectiveness analysis." *Instructional Science,* 4. October 1975: 193-236.

McANANY, E. *Radio's role in development: Five strategies of use.* Washington, D.C.: Information Center on Instructional Technology, Academy for Educational Development, September 1973.

——— "Radio schools in nonformal education: An evaluative perspective." In La Bell, T. (ed.), *Educational alternatives in Latin America: Social change and social stratification.* Los Angeles: UCLA Latin American Center Publications, 1975: 238-254.

——— , HORNIK, R., and MAYO, J. *Studying instructional television: What should be evaluated.* Stanford: Institute for Communication Research, Stanford University, 1973.

MENNE, J. W., KLINGENSCHMIDT, J. E., and NORD, D. L. "The feasibility of using taped lectures to replace class attendance." Paper presented at the American Educational Research Association meeting, Los Angeles, 1969.

MUSTO, S., et al. *Los medios de comunicación social al servicio del desarrollo: Análisis de eficiencia de 'Acción Cultural Popular–Radio Sutatenza,' Colombia.* Bogotá: Acción Cultural Popular, 1971.

NHK. *The effects of educational radio music classroom.* Tokyo: NHK Radio and TV Culture Research Institute, 1956a.

——— *The listening effect of radio English classroom.* Tokyo: NHK Radio and TV Culture Research Institute, 1956b.

NHK. *World Radio and TV 1977.* Tokyo: NHK Radio and TV Culture Research Institute, 1977.

OSAL (Oficina de Servicios para América Latina). *Las escuelas radiofonicas en América Latina.* Bogotá, Colombia: OSAL, 1972.

OXENHAM, J. *Non-formal education approaches to teaching literacy.* Michigan State University Program of Studies in Nonformal Education, Supplementary Paper No. 2, 1975. East Lansing: MSU Institute for International Studies in Education, 1975.

PARKER, E. and LUSIGNAN, B. "Technical and economic considerations in planning radio services." In Spain, P., Jamison, D., and McAnany, E. (eds.), *Radio for education and development: Case studies,* Vol. 2. Washington, D.C.: World Bank, Working Paper 266, 1977.

POPHAM, J. "Tape recorded lectures in the college–II." *Audio-Visual Communication Review,* 10. 1962: 94-101.

RATHJENS, G. W. "Comments on expanding radio and television broadcasting services in Ethiopia." In Butman, R., Rathjens, G., and Warren, C. (eds.), *Technical-economic considerations in public service broadcast communications for developing countries.* Washington, D.C.: Academy for Educational Development, 1973.

ROGERS, E., BROWN, J., and VERMILION, M. "Radio forums: A strategy for rural development." In Spain, P., Jamison, D., and McAnany, E. (eds.), *Radio for education and development: Case studies,* Vol. 2. Washington, D.C.: World Bank, Working Paper 266, 1977.

ROGERS, E. and SHOEMAKER, F. *Communication of innovations: A cross-cultural approach.* New York: Free Press, 1971.

———. "Communication and development: The passing of the dominant paradigm." In Rogers, E. (ed.), *Communication and Development: Critical Perspectives.* Beverly Hills and London: Sage Publications, 1976: 121-148.

ROLING, N. *"Knowledge brokerage for increasing the relevance of agricultural research to African small holders."* Paper presented at the Second General Conference of AAASA, Dakar, March 1975.

RUF (Rundfunk und Fernseh Consulting). *Rural radio in Indonesia: Investigation into possibilities for expansion.* Bonn: West German Federal Ministry for Economic Cooperation, 1974.

SCHMELKES DE SOTELO, S. "The radio schools of the Tarahumara, Mexico: An Evaluation." In Spain, P., Jamison, D., and McAnany, E. (eds.), *Radio for education and development: Case studies,* Vol. 1. Washington, D.C.: World Bank, Working Paper 266, 1977.

SCHNITMAN, J. "Communication, mobilization, and development." Stanford: Institute for Communication Research, Stanford University, 1976.

SCHRAMM, W. *Mass Media and National Development.* Stanford, Calif.: Stanford Univ. Press, 1964.

– – – *Big media, little media.* Beverly Hills and London: Sage Publications, 1977.

– – – , COOMBS, P. H., KAHNERT, F., and LYLE, J. *The new media: Memo to educational planners.* Paris: UNESCO International Institute for Educational Planning, 1967.

SCHULTZ, T. *Investment in human capital.* New York: Free Press, 1971.

SEARLE, B., FRIEND, J., and SUPPES, P. *The radio mathematics project: Nicaragua 1974-1975.* Stanford: Institute for Mathematical Studies in the Social Sciences, Stanford University, 1976.

– – – and TILSON, T. *Application of radio to teaching elementary mathematics in a developing country.* Stanford: Institute for Mathematical Studies in the Social Sciences, Stanford University, June 1976.

SEARLE, B., MATTHEWS, P., SUPPES, P., and FRIEND, J. *Formal evaluation of the radio mathematics instructional program: Nicaragua–grade 1, 1976.* Stanford: Institute for Mathematical Studies in the Social Sciences, Stanford University, 1977.

SEARLE, B., SUPPES, P., and FRIEND, J. "The Nicaraguan radio mathematics project." In Spain, P., Jamison, D., and McAnany, E. (eds.), *Radio for education and development: Case studies,* Vol. 1. Washington, D.C.: World Bank, Working Paper 266, 1977.

SHEFFIELD, J. and DIEJOMAOH, W. *Nonformal education in African development.* New York: African-American Institute, 1972.

SPAIN, P. *A survey of radio listenership in the Davao Province of Mindanao, The Philippines.* Stanford: Institute for Communication Research, Stanford University, September 1971.

– – – "The Mexican radioprimaria project." In Spain, P., Jamison, D., and Mc Anany, E. (eds.), *Radio for education and development: Case studies,* Vol. 1. Washington, D.C.: Education Department of the World Bank, 1977.

– – – , JAMISON, D., and McANANY, E. (eds.), *Radio for education and development: Case studies.* Washington, D.C.: World Bank, Working Paper 266, 1977.

SPECTOR, P. and TORRES, P. *Communication and motivation in community development.* Washington, D.C.: Institute for International Services, 1963.

SUCHMAN, E. *Evaluative research: principles and practice in public service and social action programs.* New York: Russell Sage Foundation, 1967.

TRABELSI, K. *The cost of rural education radio in Senegal.* Working document IIEP/RP/7/-C.S.4F (in French). Paris: UNESCO International Institute for Educational Planning, 1972.

UNICEF. *Zaa na uwatanze (The Kiroboto Show): Listenership and educational impact.* American Technical Assitance Corporation, McLean, VA, U.S.A. and Bureau of Educational Research, University of Nairobi, Kenya, December, 1975.

WARREN, C. "Introductory assessment of the technical aspects of educational communication technologies." In Butman, R., Rathjens, G., and Warren, C. (eds.), *Technical-economic considerations in public service broadcast communications for developing countries.* Washington, D.C.: Academy for Educational Development, 1973.

WHITE, R. *An alternative pattern of basic education: Radio Santa María.* Paris: UNESCO, 1976a.

——— *Mass communications and the popular promotion strategy of rural development in Honduras.* Stanford: Institute for Communication Research, Stanford University, 1976b.

WHITE, R. "Mass communications and the popular promotion strategy of rural development in Honduras." In Spain, P., Jamison, D., and McAnany, E. (eds.), *Radio for education and development: Case studies,* Vol. 2. Washington, D.C.: Workd Bank, Working Paper 266, 1977a.

——— "The use of radio in primary and secondary formal education: the Radio Santa María model in the Dominican Republic." In Spain, P., Jamison, D., and McAnany, E. (eds.), *Radio for education and development: Case studies,* Vol. 1. Washington, D.C.: World Bank, Working Paper 266, 1977b.

WILEY, D. "Another hour, another day: Quantity of schooling, a potent path for policy." Reprinted in M. Guttentag (ed.), *Evaluation studies review annual,* Vol. 2. Beverly Hills and London: Sage Publications, 1977: 434-476.

Wisconsin Research Project in School Broadcasting. *Radio in the classroom.* Madison: Univ. of Wisconsin Press, 1942.

WOELFEL, N. E. and TYLER, I. K. (eds.) *Radio and the school: A guidebook for teachers and administrators.* Yonkers-on-the-Hudson, N.Y.: World Book, 1945.

XOOMSAI, T. and RATANAMANGALA, B. *School broadcast: Its evaluation.* Bangkok: Ministry of Education, 1962.

Appendix A.

As we have indicated in the preface, this volume draws heavily on the material that was prepared for *Radio for Education and Development: Case Studies,* edited by Peter L. Spain, Dean T. Jamison, and Emile G. McAnany. (The case studies volume is published as World Bank Staff Working Paper 266.) In this Appendix we reproduce the contents of that document and provide addresses for the authors of studies in it. Individuals interested in the individual case studies can write to the authors directly; individuals interested in the bound set of case studies can write, for a free copy, to the Office of Professional and Technical Publications, Room N1002, The World Bank, 1818 H Street, N.W., Washington, D.C. 20433, U.S.A.

TITLES OF THE CASE STUDIES

The following is a listing of the titles of the case studies.

VOLUME 1

PART ONE: RADIO FOR IN-SCHOOL EDUCATION

Chapter I — The Nicaraguan Radio Mathematics Project
By Barbara Searle, Patrick Suppes, and Jamesine Friend

149

PART FOUR: RADIO FOR DEVELOPMENT
COMMUNICATIONS

PART FIVE: TECHNICAL AND ECONOMIC
CONSIDERATIONS

ADDRESSES OF THE AUTHORS

JUAN BRAUN is an advisor to a nonformal education group working
with the Ministry of Education of Paraguay.
Address: c/o Jon Gant
Education Office/USAID
U.S. Embassy
Asunción, Paraguay

HENRY CASSIRER is an international consultant for communication
and education.
Address: Les Moulins
74290 Menthon St. Bernard
France

TONY DODDS is a member of the International Extension College and
has worked with the IEC in Tanzania, Mauritius, and Nigeria.
Address: International Extension College
18 Victoria Park Square
Bethnal Green
London, England

JAMESINE FRIEND is the on-site Project Manager for the Radio Mathematics Project in Masaya, Nicaragua.
Address: c/o The Institute for Mathematical Studies in the
Social Sciences
Stanford University
Stanford, California 94305
U.S.A.

JONATHAN GUNTER is the Director of the Clearinghouse on Development Communication (ICIT) in Washington, D.C.
Address: Clearinghouse on Development Communication (ICIT)
The Academy for Educational Development
1412 22nd Street, N.W.
Washington, D.C. 20036
U.S.A.

BUDD L. HALL has been involved in the evaluation of several of the Tanzanian radio campaigns and is currently research officer at the International Council for Adult Education.
Address: The International Council for Adult Education
252 Bloor Street, West
Toronto, Ontario M5S 1V6
Canada

HEATHER HUDSON is a consultant to the Academy for Educational Development.
Address: The Academy for Educational Development
1412 22nd Street, N.W.
Washington, D.C. 20036
U.S.A.

DEAN T. JAMISON is an economist in the Development Economics Department of the World Bank.
Address: The World Bank
1818 H Street, N.W.
Washington, D.C. 20433
U.S.A.

PETER KINYANJUI is the Director of the Institute for Adult Studies at the University of Nairobi.
Address: Institute for Adult Studies
P.O. Box 30688
Nairobi, Kenya

OSVALDO KREIMER is a Specialist in the Division of Educational Affairs of the Organization of American States.
Address: Organization of American States
PAR—924
1725 Eye St., N.W.
Washington, D.C. 20006
U.S.A.

JOANNE LESLIE is a graduate student in the Department of International Health, Johns Hopkins University.
    Address: P.O. Box 141
                 Johns Hopkins School of Hygiene and Public Health
                 615 North Wolfe Street
                 Baltimore, Maryland 21205
                 U.S.A.

BRUCE LUSIGNAN is Associate Professor of Electrical Engineering at Stanford University.
    Address: Department of Electrical Engineering
                 Stanford University
                 Stanford, California 94305
                 U.S.A.

EMILE McANANY is Assistant Professor of Communications, Institute for Communication Research, Stanford University.
    Address: The Institute for Communication Research
                 Stanford University
                 Stanford, California 94305
                 U.S.A.

EDWIN PARKER is Professor of Communications, Institute for Communication Research, Stanford University.
    Address: The Institute for Communication Research
                 Stanford University
                 Stanford, California 94305
                 U.S.A.

EVERETT ROGERS is a Professor of Communications, Institute for Communication Research, Stanford University.
    Address: The Institute for Communication Research
                 Stanford University
                 Stanford, California 94305
                 U.S.A.

SYLVIA SCHMELKES DE SOTELO is a research director with the Centro de Estudios Educativos, Mexico City.
    Address: Centro de Estudios Educativos
                 Avenida Revolución, 1291
                 Mexico 20, D.F.
                 Mexico

BARBARA SEARLE is Senior Research Associate at Stanford University.
Address: The Institute for Mathematical Studies
in the Social Sciences
Stanford University
Stanford, California 94305
U.S.A.

PETER L. SPAIN is Research Associate, Institute for Communication Research, Stanford University.
Address: The Institute for Communication Research
Stanford University
Stanford, California 94305
U.S.A.

PATRICK SUPPES is Professor of Philosophy, Professor of Psychology, Professor of Statistics, and Director, Institute for Mathematical Studies in the Social Sciences, Stanford University.
Address: The Institute for Mathematical Studies
in the Social Sciences
Stanford University
Stanford, California 94305
U.S.A.

JAMES THEROUX is directing research on radio software at the University of Massachusetts.
Address: Nonformal Education Center
University of Massachusetts
Hills House South
Amherst, Massachusetts 01002
U.S.A.

MARK VERMILION is a media consultant in San Francisco.
Address: 1278 Noe Street
San Francisco, California
U.S.A.

ROBERT A. WHITE is a member of the Instituto de Investigaciones Socio-económicas, Tegucigalpa, Honduras.
Address: Instituto de Investigaciones Socio-económicas
Apartado 786
Tegucigalpa, Honduras

Appendix B.

RADIO TRANSMISSION AND
RECEPTION FACILITIES OF THE
COUNTRIES OF THE WORLD

This Appendix contains tables for each of the major regions of the world that show, on a country-by-country basis, the number of radio transmitters the country has, the average power of the transmitters, and the number of radio receivers in the country per 1,000 population. Table B.1 contains data for Africa; B.2 contains data for the Americas; B.3 contains data for Asia and the Middle East; B.4 contains data for Europe; and B.5 contains data for the Pacific. We draw our data from the *UNESCO Statistical Yearbook 1974;* though UNESCO updates these yearbooks annually, the 1975 yearbook has no more recent data on receivers and no data at all on transmitters.

The Radio and TV Culture Research Institute of the Japan Broadcasting Corporation (NHK) has recently published data on the nature and extent of radio and television programming in 156 countries around the world (NHK, 1977); these data provide a valuable complement to the information in the UNESCO yearbooks.

TABLE B.1
Radio Facilities in Africa[a]

Country	Number and power of transmitters[b]		Number of receivers per 1,000 population
	medium-wave (AM)	short-wave	
Algeria	20 (185)	—	46
Angola	—	—	20
Botswana	1 (1)	2 (10)	17*
Burundi	2 (.62)	4 (9.5)	25
Cameron	3 (7.33)	5 (15.2)	36
Cape Verde Islands	—	—	19*
Central African Republic	2 (.75)	3 (44.6)	38
Chad	1 (1)	2 (17.0)	18
Comoro Islands	1 —	1 —	120
Congo	2 (12)	5 (8.2)	75
Dahomey	2 (.55)	2 (17.0)	52*
Egypt	27 (104.29)	16 (129.3)	143
Ethiopia	3 (83.3)	2 (100)	7
French Terr. of the Afars & Issas	2 (4)	1 (4)	99
Gabon	6 (4.01)	4 (33.25)	174
Gambia	2 (.52)	1 (3.5)	122
Ghana	—	16 (62.8)	85*
Guinea	—	—	24
Guinea-Bissau	—	—	7*
Ivory Coast	—	—	18*
Kenya	—	—	41
Lesotho	—	—	11
Liberia	6 (3.05)	9 (11.6)	132*
Libyan Arab Republic	—	—	46
Madagascar	8 (1.75)	8 (23.4)	104
Malasi	7 (2.28)	3 (43.3)	23
Mali	4 (16.25)	10 (32.6)	14
Mauritania	2 (10.5)	2 (17.0)	64
Mauritius	2 (10)	1 (10)	125*
Morocco	26 (65.65)	3 (23.3)	74

TABLE B.1 (Continued)

Country	Number and power of transmitters[b]		Number of receivers per 1,000 population
	medium-wave (AM)	short-wave	
Mozambique	—	—	20
Niger	10 (.275)	3 (12.66)	36*
Nigeria	25 (47.63)	21 (48.14)	49
Reunion	2 (6)	2 (4)	190
Rwanda	—	4 (137.5)	8*
St. Helena	1 (.5)	—	160
Sao Tome and Principe	—	—	96
Senegal	—	—	67
Seychelles	2 (.75)	2 (14)	136*
Sierra Leone	2 (10)	1 (10)	21
Somalia	—	5 (14.2)	22
South Africa	—	—	102*
Rhodesia	—	—	38
Spanish Sahara	4 (16.8)	2 (10)	162
Sudan	2 (80)	5 (66)	80*
Swaziland	1 (10)	—	111
Tanzania, United Republic of	—	—	16
Togo	2 (10.5)	3 (35)	24
Tunisia	4 (200)	3 (83)	50
Uganda	3 (17.6)	3 (6.6)	23
Upper Volta	1 (1)	3 (9.3)	17
Zaire	4 (153)	16 (23.1)	4
Zambia	—	—	22

SOURCE: UNESCO (1974).
a. All figures are for 1973 (most recent available) except those with asterisk.
b. The average power (in kilowatts) of the country's transmitters appears in parentheses after the number of transmitters.

TABLE B.2

Radio Facilities in the Americas[a]

Country	Number and power of transmitters[b]		Number of receivers per 1,000 population
	medium-wave (AM)	short-wave	
North America			
Canada	466	9	865
Mexico	542 (5.59)	28 (1.29)	311
United States	4,306	61	1,752
Central America and Caribbean			
Antigua	2 (3.0)	—	176
Bahamas	4 (5.31)	—	440
Barbados	2 (5.5)	—	477
Belize	4 (5.75)	—	515
Bermuda	5 (1.05)	—	891
Cayman Is.	—		546*
Costa Rica	—		74
Cuba	—		202
Dominican Republic	108 (1.56)	38 (2.46)	41
El Salvador	62	3	95*
Guadeloupe	2 (12.0)		82*
Guatemala	87 (3.17)	2 (7.5)	47
Haiti	—		17
Honduras	79 (2.0)	37 (.82)	56
Jamaica	8 (5.0)	—	320
Martinique	1 (50.0)	3 (4.0)	93
Neth. Antilles	—		556
Nicaragua	—		62
Panama	76 (2.12)	1 (1.0)	162
Puerto Rico	95 (2.29)	—	587
Trinidad and Tobago	5 (6.2)	—	287*

TABLE B.2 (Continued)

Country	Number and power of transmitters[b]		Number of receivers per 1,000 population
	medium-wave (AM)	short-wave	
South America			
Argentina	147 (14.25)	16 (40.65)	425*
Bolivia	54 (1.14)	38 (2.32)	288*
Brazil	913 (2.45)	59 (8.99)	62
Chile	188 (4.48)	41 (.75)	147
Colombia	—	—	120
Ecuador	225 (1.37)	7 (8.93)	279*
Falkland Islands	1 (5.0)	1 (.5)	467
French Guiana	1 (4.0)	2 (2.5)	106*
Guyana	4 (10.0)	3 (7.5)	198
Paraguay	—	—	66
Peru	241 (2.36)	51 (5.6)	134
Surinam	—	—	250
Uruguay	79 (7.60)	16 (6.06)	501
Venezuela	139 (9.45)	78 (4.65)	177

SOURCE: UNESCO (1974).

a. All figures are for 1973 (most recent available) except those with asterisk.
b. The average power (in kilowatts) of the country's transmitters appears in parentheses after the number of transmitters.

TABLE B.3
Radio Facilities in Asia and the Middle East[a]

Country	Number and power of transmitters[b]		Number of receivers per 1,000 population
	medium-wave (AM)	short-wave	
Afghanistan	2 (62.5)	3 (60)	—
Bahrain	3 (11.6)	—	352
Bhutan	—	—	—
Brunei	4 (10.0)	2 (10.0)	110
Burma	2 (50)	3 (50)	21
China	—	—	—
Cyprus	4 (10.6)	—	259
Hong Kong	16 (7.25)	—	240
India	107 (38.48)	25 (20.86)	24
Indonesia	100 —	484 —	49*
Iran	32 (141.2)	4 (200)	229*
Iraq	10 (81.0)	2 (50)	120
Israel	16 (131)	5 (98)	221*
Japan	474 (7.72)	7 (27.14)	658*
Jordan	3 (112.5)	2 (53.7)	211
Khmer Republic	4 (35.5)	3 (38.3)	145
Korea, Republic of	82 (28.0)	5 (25)	127*
Kuwait	7 (353)	—	238
Laos	3 (3.33)	3 (6.33)	32
Lebanon	2 (55)	1 (100)	211*
Macau	—	—	37*
Malaysia	6 (25.6)	31 (41.2)	40
Maldive Islands	1 (10)	4 (15.7)	20
Mongolia	—	—	129*
Nepal	2 (5.12)	3 (36.6)	9*
Pakistan	10 (39.6)	12 (71.6)	16
Philippines	—	—	45
Portugese Timor	—	—	5*
Qatar	2 (30)	2 (50.5)	—
Saudi Arabia	12 (117)	7 (57.1)	11*

TABLE B.3 (Continued)

| Country | Number and power of transmitters[b] | | Number of receivers per 1,000 population |
	medium-wave (AM)	short-wave	
Singapore	5 (166)	7 (26.8)	139
Sri Lanka	11 (24.1)	7 (10)	39*
Syria	8 (156.3)	3 (30)	374*
Thailand	34 (25.3)	5 (36)	76
United Arab Emirates	—	—	240
Viet-Nam, Republic of	18 (33.1)	7 (19.4)	80
Viet-Nam, Democratic Republic of	—	—	23
Yemen	2 (60)	2 (25)	14
Yemen, People's Democratic Republic of	3 (16.6)	1 (7.5)	407*

SOURCE: UNESCO (1974).

a. All figures are for 1973 (most recent available) except those with asterisk.
b. The average power (in kilowatts) of the country's transmitters appears in parentheses after the number of transmitters.

TABLE B.4
Radio Facilities in Europe[a]

| Country | Number and power of transmitters[b] | | Number of receivers per 1,000 population |
	medium-wave (AM)	short-wave	
Albania	—	—	73
Andorra	2 (250)	—	381
Austria	142 (4.9)	—	287
Belgium	16 (43.3)	8 (60)	375
Bulgaria	12 (62.5)	4 (58.8)	263
Cyprus	—	—	259
Czechoslovakia	57 (43.5)	33 (51.2)	260
Denmark	5 (58.4)	1 (50)	333
Faeroe Islands	1 (5)	—	524
Finland	13 (36.5)	5 (29.2)	418
France	56 (81.8)	20 (100)	329*
German Democratic Republic	23 (128)	2 —	358
Germany, Federal Republic of	49 (146)	23 (150)	332
Gibraltar	3 (1)	—	137
Greece	12 (31.9)	2 (67.5)	111*
Greenland	3 (16.6)	5 (4.6)	147
Holy See	3 (151)	12 (53.7)	—
Hungary	12 (67.9)	8 (69.4)	243
Iceland	15 (8.7)	—	311*
Ireland	6 (21.3)	—	266
Italy	128 (21)	10 (55.5)	227
Liechtenstein	—	—	214*
Luxembourg	2 (1150)	2 (125)	503
Malta	1 (5)	—	401
Monaco	2 (800)	4 (65)	300
Netherlands	7 (38.3)	—	284
Norway	37 (13.4)	2 (65)	317
Poland	—	—	176
Portugal	59 (14.4)	35 (96.2)	176
Romania	23 —	19 —	148

TABLE B.4 (Continued)

Country	Number and power of transmitters[b]		Number of receivers per 1,000 population
	medium-wave (AM)	short-wave	
San Marino	—	—	247
Spain	180 (11.32)	17 (244)	230
Sweden	29 (39.1)	—	32
Switzerland	5 (13)	10 (200)	311
Turkey	14 (283)	3 (117)	106
United Kingdom	79 (54.9)	66 (16.6)	697
USSR	—	—	442
Yugoslavia	285 (15)	8 (36.2)	176

SOURCE: UNESCO (1974).

a. All figures are for 1973 (most recent available) except those with asterisk.
b. The average power (in kilowatts) of the country's transmitters appears in parentheses after the number of transmitters.

TABLE B.5

Radio Facilities in the Pacific[a]

Country	Number and power of transmitters[b]		Number of receivers per 1,000 population
	medium-wave (AM)	short-wave	
American Samoa	1 (10)	—	128
Australia	198 (13.3)	21 (73.5)	214
British Solomon Islands	1 (5)	2 (5)	69*
Cook Islands	1 (10)	—	105*
Fiji Islands	—	—	97*
French Polynesia	1 (20)	4 (12)	331*
Gilbert and Ellice Islands	1 (10)	—	214
Guam	3 (3.1)	—	1064
Nauru	1 (.13)	—	557
New Caledonia	1 (20)	2 (20)	303
New Hebrides	2 (1)	2 (2)	117
New Zealand	59 (8.02)	—	911
Niue	1 (.25)	—	140
Norfolk Island	1 (.05)	—	550
Pacific Islands	10 (2.95)	—	645
Tonga	2 (10)	—	99
Western Samoa	1 (10)	—	338*

SOURCE: UNESCO (1974).

a. All figures are for 1973 (most recent available) except those with asterisk.

b. The average power (in kilowatts) of the country's transmitters appears in parentheses after the number of transmitters.

Appendix C.

ANNOTATED BIBLIOGRAPHY

By Peter L. Spain

Assembled in the following annotated bibliography is a great deal of material on radio's use for education and development. Although, due to constraints of time and space, neither the bibliography nor the annotations claim to be exhaustive, they do cover a solid core of the writing and provide a foundation for a reader interested in further exploring a particular aspect of this topic.

An index follows the bibliography. This section is meant as an orientation to the references listed in the bibliography and as a guide to the reader with a specific area in mind. The index lists references first according to geographic locale and then according to major theme or subject area.

For additional material on radio's use in education and development, the reader is referred to *A Sourcebook on Radio's Role in Development,* Information Bulletin Number Seven (The Clearinghouse on Development Communication, 1414 Twenty-Second Street, N.W., Washington, D.C. 20037). As well as providing an annotated bibliography organized somewhat differently from this one, this publication provides the names and addresses of journals and organizations that are possible sources of new information.

AUTHOR'S NOTE: This bibliography was compiled with the help of Miren Etcheverry and Noreene Janus.

ANNOTATED BIBLIOGRAPHY

ABLES, H. A. *Radio farm forum in the Philippines: A proposal for a pilot study,* Research Paper. East Lansing, Michigan State Univ., Department of Communication, 1966.

Academy for Educational Development (AED). *Educational technology and the developing countries: a handbook.* Washington, D.C., 1972. 180 pp.

This handbook presents ideas about educational development, technology, changes, and the improvement of learning. It also includes case studies of educational technology in action, discussing the use of television in El Salvador, Samoa, Singapore, Mexico, and Colombia.

––– *The basic village education project (programa de educación básica rural) Guatemala. Oriente Region combined report 1973-1976.* Washington, D.C.: Academy for Educational Development, 1977.

Acción Cultural Popular (ACPO), Bogotá. *ACPO en cifras: 1947-1962.* Bogotá, Andes, 1963.

––– *Informe al Gobierno Nacional.* Bogotá Acción Cultural Popular, 1964.

––– *Cruzada Cultural Campesina.* Bogotá: ACPO, 1964. (*Peasant Cultural Crusade.*)

––– *What is, what are the objectives of, what does Acción Cultural Popular do?* Bogotá, Andes, 1965. (Also in Spanish)

––– *Escuelas radiofónicas: Informe Anual 1966.* Bogotá, 1966.

––– *Escuelas radiofónicas: Informe Anual 1967.* Bogotá, 1967.

––– *Radio Sutatenza: programación.* Bogotá, 1969: 131 pp.

––– *ACPO: Agencia de desarrollo.* Bogotá, Andes, 1970.

––– *Mensaje de la Dirección General a los colaboradores de la institución; 25 años de servicio a la cultura del pueblo.* Bogotá, 1972: 40 pp.

––– *La industria y el desarrollo social; el caso de la industria privada frente a las entidades fiscalmente exentas o privilegiadas.* Bogotá, 1973: 125 pp.

––– *Conclusions of studies on the effectiveness of radiophonic schools of Acción cultural Popular.* ACPO, December 1972.

ADJANGBA, M. "L'Université Radiophonique de Guitarama." *Interstages* (Brussels), 47, April 1, 1968: 14-19.

This paper describes a program of primary education in Rwanda, an evaluation of current results, and includes a description of MERA, a cooperative using handicapped workers to manufacture radios of the same quality as imported sets but which sell for half the price.

––– "La Radiovision en Républic Centra-africaine." *Interstages* (Brussels), 45, January 1, 1968: 3-7.

"Radiovision" is a program of radio integrated with films or slides on subjects such as agriculture, cattle-raising, health, and hygiene, projected in rural villages by an "animateur" or teacher, who answers questions and leads discussion.

AHMED, M. *Farmer Education Program of the Office of Rural Development in the Republic of Korea.* ICED Case Study No. 5. Essex, Connecticut, July 1972.

In the Republic of Korea, the Office of Rural Development adapted a multimedia approach, using–in addition to extension workers–farm radio broadcasts, films, posters, bulletins, and a farm journal. Though little systematic effort has been made to determine the impact of these media, or even to find about them, such evidence as is available suggests that they have had significant influence.

AHMED, M. and COOMBS, P. (eds.) *Education for Rural Development: Case Studies for Planners*. New York: Praeger, 1975.

Contains studies of media projects, including Brumberg's chapter on ACPO.

AKINTAYO, O. "Schools broadcasting in Nigeria." *Combroad,* 24, July-September, 1974.

ALCALAY, R. "El medio radial; su especificidad y un diagnóstico de, su quehacer en Chile." *Revista EAC Artes de la Communicación* (Chile), No. 3, 1973: 30-55.

This study describes some of the main characteristics of radio and its specific role vis-à-vis other media. It also analyzes the results of a national survey of the owners and directors of radio stations throughout Chile. The survey dealt mainly with problems of audience, financing, programming, and legislation concerning radio in Chile at the time (1971).

ALI-KHAN, A. *Educational Development International,* Vol. 2, No. 4, October 1974: "People's Open University in Pakistan," *Direct* I-2.

The article describes the Open University established by the Pakistani government as an experimental means of nonformal education. Also included is a description of the objectives and functions of the University which teaches through radio and television broadcasts in conjunction with correspondence courses.

ALLEBACK, S., ERRAHMANI, A., and OULDAH, B. *Radio-télévision éducative en Tunisie*. Paris: UNESCO, January 1971.

This is a planning document that outlines some possibilities for Tunisia's use of radio and television for formal and nonformal educational purposes.

ALLEN, C. L. *Communication patterns in Hong Kong*. Chinese Univ. of Hong Kong, 1970: 125 pp.

This book presents data on the media habits of respondents from various social backgrounds. The section on radio and TV contains information on program preference, radio and TV ownership, time spent on both media, the popularity of news broadcasts, and the broadcasting stations.

AMAYA, S. "Radio helps erradicate mass illiteracy in rural Colombia." *Gazette* No. 5, 1969: 403-408.

——— *A Plan for Empirical Testing of the Spaulding Readability Formula for Colombian Agricultural Publications*. Ph.D. dissertation, Univ. of Wisconsin, 1972.

——— *Communication and Policy-Making in Colombian Rural Development: A Survey and Experiment*. Ph.D. dissertation, Univ. of Wisconsin, 1972b.

AMIC annual list of theses: studies on mass communication in Asia, 1971-1973. Asian Mass Communication Research and Information Centre, Singapore.

This compilation of 78 thesis titles on mass communication in Asia represents those that were submitted to colleges and universities in Asia and the United States in 1971. This classified list contains most of the entries, an author and title index, and a list of institutions polled. It is the first of a series of lists of theses scheduled to be published by AMIC annually.

AMIC semiannual index of periodicals, No. 1, 1972. Asian Mass Communication Research and Information Centre. Singapore.

This is a supplement for AMIC's documentation list; it indexes periodicals received regularly by the AMIC documentation unit and selectively lists articles concerning mass communications in Asia. The first issue of this index covers articles published in 1971. Requests for items indexed on this list can be met on an exchange basis or at cost.

––– *Communication and change in rural Asia: A Select Bibliography.* Asian Mass Communication Research and Information Centre. Singapore, 1973: 50 pp.

Compiled as a background paper to AMIC's Regional Conference on Communication and Change in Rural Asia (Bangalore, August 1973), this annotated bibliography is based on the materials. published and unpublished, available in AMIC's collection. The entries are classified under nine broad subject headings, and cover all aspects of communication in rural development and change.

––– *Broadcasting in Asia: An Annotated Bibliography.* Singapore, Asian Mass Communication Research and Information Centre. Singapore, 1974: 92 pp.

This is the second in a very useful series of bibliographies. This one was prepared for the joint AMIC/Asian Broadcasting Union seminar on "Broadcasting in the National Interest," held in Singapore in November 1974.

ANATOL, K. W. and BITTNER, J. R. *Southeast Asian Broadcasting: The Emergence of Thailand.* Long Beach: California State College; Lafayette, Indiana: Purdue University, Department of Communication, April 1971. Paper presented at the International Communication Association Annual Conference, Phoenix, Arizona. 7 pp.

ARANA DE SWADESH, E. *Informe sobre la influencia que la radio ejerce en una comunidad indígena: Xoxcotla, Morelos.* Friedrich Ebert Foundation Seminar on Rural Radio, Mexico: December 1971.

This survey of an Indian village in the State of Morelos, Mexico shows radio listening patterns to local and Mexico City stations. It concludes that local audiences pay little heed to educational/informational programs and a great deal to entertainment, more to Mexico City than to local radio.

ARENA, E., JAMISON, D., OLIVEIRA, J., and ORIVEL, F. *Economic analysis of educational television in Maranhao, Brazil.* Paris: UNESCO, 1977.

AREVALO, M. and ALBA ROBAYO, V. "Análisis de la investigación en comunicaciones agropecuarias." Bogotá, Instituto Colombiano Agropecuario, 1974: 89 pp. *(Boletín de investigación,* No. 8).

This article analyzes some studies on agricultural information, carried out in Colombia during the period 1972-1973, to determine what elements of the communication process had been studied and the methods used.

ARMSEY, J. W. and DAHL, N. C. *An Inquiry Into the Uses of Instructional Technology: A Ford Foundation Report.* New York: Ford Foundation, 1973: 113 pp. 00385 LNNO/0072 840 1972.

ARNOVE, R. F. "Education and Political Participation in Rural Areas of Latin America." *Comparative Education Review,* 17. 1973: 198-215.

By focusing on a narrow but dramatic issue—rural education in Latin America—this paper explores the more general theme of the relationship between schooling and political development.

ASBU Review. "Educational Broadcast of Radio Pakistan." January 1975.

This study is meant to give an overview of the educational uses of radio in Pakistan.

Associación Latinoamericana de Educación Radiofónica (ALER). *Que es ALER?* Buenos Aires, 1975.

ASPINALL, R. *Radio programme production.* Paris: UNESCO, 1971.

This manual/handbook discusses how to produce radio programmes, but not particularly for education.

ASSMAN, H. *Evaluación de algunos estudios latinoamericanos sobre communicación masiva; con especial referencia a los escritos de Armand Mattelart.* San José, Costa Rica, Escuela de Ciencias de la Comunicación Colectiva, Univ. de Costa Rica, 1974: 43 pp.

Australian Broadcasting Commission/British Broadcasting Corporation. *Using radio and television in the classroom.* Sydney, 1973: 15 pp.

This is an instructional booklet on the teacher's role, classroom use, listening and viewing conditions, equipment maintenance, and using recorded broadcasts, if the best results are to be achieved in viewing ETV films.

AWASTHY, G. *Broadcasting in India.* Bombay, Allied Publishers, 1965: 268 pp.

The author, a former employee of All India Radio, calls this book a "critical narrative of AIR, its programmes, its policies, its ambitions, and its failures since 1946."

AXINN, G. H. and N. W. "Communication Among the Nukka Igbo: A Folk-Village Society." *Journalism Quarterly,* 46, Summer 1969: 320-324, 406.

The researchers use observer-diarists to analyze communications behavior in Nigeria. The article throws doubt on assumptions about the ubiquity of radio.

AZIZ, S. "The Chinese approach to rural development." *Ideas Action Bulletin,* 98, 1974: 16-23.

BAHIA HORTA, J. S. "Historico do radio educativo no Brasil (1927-70)." In *Cadernos da pub,* no. 10/72, Univ. Catolica, Rio de Janeiro.

This article gives the history of educational radio with detailed data on different projects and an analysis of their political, organizational, and philosophical backing.

BAKER, F. J. *Community Development in Northeast Thailand: A Descriptive Study of Radio Station 909, Sakon Nakorn, as an Educational Vehicle for Change.* East Lansing: Michigan State Univ., Ph.D. dissertation, 1973.

BALL, J.C.H. "Beginning Science: a radio series for primary schools in Africa." *Educational Broadcasting International,* Vol. 5, 2, June 1971: 79-82.

This adaptation of a British primary school radio series for use in Kenya was written by the director of the project.

— — — "Using sound effects in school's broadcasting." *Educational Broadcasting International,* Vol. 5, 3, September 1971: 208-214.

"We know very little about the use of sound effects in school's radio in the context described in this report—a context by no means peculiar to Kenya. Until we do know more we should think very carefully before we use any sound effect in a school's broadcast."

——— "School Radio: the future. Part 1: Radiovision and Tape Recorder." *Educational Broadcasting International,* Vol. 7, 1, March 1974.

The author, experienced in educational broadcasting in Kenya, deals with the question: What role can radiovision and tape recorders play in a classroom? He gives the advantages and disadvantages of use in developing countries. He defines the role of educational broadcasting on open circuits versus taping programs that can be replayed.

——— "School Radio: the future. Part 2: Producing Programmes for school children (with special reference to the African scene)." *Educational broadcasting International,* Vol. 7, 2, June 1974: 101-106.

Here, Ball looks at some of the techniques and methods of producing radio programmes for school children. He includes sections on radio reception, dramatization, analogies, pronunciation and vocabulary, sound effects, and programme structure.

——— "School Radio: the future. Part 3: In the classroom and aspects of training." *Educational Broadcasting International,* Vol. 7, 3, September 1974: 137-141.

"It is time now that school broadcasters rethought their role in the educational system, particularly with reference to print and the tape recorder. This rethinking must be based on an overall comprehensive plan of research. We can no longer afford to waste time, money, and manpower on guessing and hoping. We must know the necessary programme conditions, in terms of content, format, amount of actuality, level of difficulty, and rate of presentation to whom we are broadcasting."

——— and MAY, J. P. "Health education radio lessons for primary schools: some further problems." *Educational Broadcasting International,* Vol. 5, 4, December 1971: 233-237.

This article describes a series of tests on the form and value of health education radio lessons. While not conclusive, the results highlight important questions, especially: are these teaching aids suitable for use in the area and for the students concerned?

BARRETT, H. "MTU NI AFYA—Health Education by Radio in Tanzania." *Combroad* (London), 21, October-December, 1973: 37-38.

——— *"Tanzania: Planning a national mass adult education campaign."* Paper given at Conference on Communication Policy and Planning for Education and Development, Stanford Univ., July 1976.

BELTRAN, L. *Communication and Modernization: the Case of Latin America.* New Delhi: Eleventh World Conference of the Society for International Development.

——— "Radio Forums and Radio Schools in Rural Mass Education for National Development." East Lansing, Michigan: Michigan State University, Communications Department, 1968. (mimeo).

–– "The Determinants of Change in Society: Communication, A Crucial Non-Economic Factor in National Development." Lansing, Michigan: Lansing Community College, 1969.

––– "Radio forum y radio escuelas rurales en la educación para el desarrollo." *IICA: Materiales de Ensenanza de Comunicación,* 25, 1971: 58 pp.

––– "Comunicación y desarrollo económico." *Chasqui,* 2, 1973: 50-72.

This article analyzes how far communication can go in the service of development, and focuses on Latin America. It notes the uneven distribution of the media in Latin America and the fact that most media are consumed by the cities.

––– "Communication Research in Latin America; The Blindfolded Inquiry?" Paper submitted to the International Scientific Conference on Mass Communication and Social Consciousness in a Changing World held in Leipzig, September 17-20, 1974, under the auspices of the International Association for Mass Communication Research.

Most valuable as a bibliography, this article is based on several hundred other articles and books.

––– "Rural development and social communication; relationship and strategies." In *International Symposium on Communication Strategies for Rural Development,* Cali, Colombia, 1974. Proceedings. Cali, Cornell University-CIAT, 1974, pp. 11-27.

––– *Alien premises, objects, and methods in Latin American communication research; a critical perspective in light of U.S. influences.* Bogotá, 1975: 41 pp.

A paper prepared for the special issue of *Communication Research,* an international quarterly on communication and development.

––– *Social Structure and Rural Development Communication in Latin America: The 'Radiophonic Schools' in Colombia.* Paper presented at the Summer Conference on Communication and Group Transformation for Development, East-West Communications Institute, Hawaii, June 29-July 11, 1975.

Benson's media information, 1971. A collection of articles on media published in *Benson's Media Information* during 1971. Bombay: Oglivy, Benson, & Mather, 1972: 95 pp.

This collection includes a discussion of the commercial radio in India, a survey to find out the listenership profile and popularity rating of programmes broadcast over the radio in the Bombay-Poona-Nagpur region, and radio coverage in Gujerat and Mysore.

BENVENISTE, A. "Rapport d'évaluation," Private circulation, May 1974. Available from Stanford Univ., Institute for Communication Research, Stanford, California 94305.

The author presents descriptions of television viewing groups in villages in the Ivory Coast. She points out some of the problems encountered, particularly the lack of involvement in village life on the part of the village teacher. He is an outsider who remains so, and is unable to contribute his services as animator of the viewing group.

BERLO, D. K. *Mass Communication and the Development of Nations.* East Lansing: Michigan State Univ., International Communication Institution Monograph, 1968.

BERNAL, A. H.*"Effectiveness of Radio Schools of "Acción Cultural Popular"
of Colombia Promoting the Adoption of Innovation."* Unpublished MS thesis,
Univ. of Wisconsin, 1967.

— — — "Educación fundamental integral y medios de comunicación social; el uso
sistemático de los medios de comunicación en programas de desarrollo."
Bogotá, Acción Cultural Popular, 1971. 103 pp.

— — — *Ideas sobre el tema "comunicación social y desarrollo."* October 1972.

— — — *Análisis Estructural de las Escuelas Radiofónicas.* Buenos Aires: Boletin de
la Educación Radiofónicas Latinoamericana. Año 1, n. 2. pp. 25-40. Spanish.

— — — and NIETO, M. E. *Diseño de una investigación, "Participación campesina
en la producción de materiales educativos escritos, utilizando un equipo
movil de comunicaciones."* February 1975.

— — — and PALACIO, Q. *La Operación Antioquia de Acción Cultural Popular.*
Bogotá: Acción Cultural Popular (ACPO), Documento de Trabajo No. 7,
1968. 97 pp. Spanish.

BERRIGAN, F. "Communication, Family Planning, and Development." *Educational Broadcasting International,* 8, 1975: 79-86.

The author discusses the role of media to teach underdeveloped nations
about birth control methods.

BESIROGLU, A. "Forty-Eight Years of Broadcasting Services in Turkey." *EBU
Review.* Vol. 25, 4, July 1974: pp. 23-25.

Failure to account for the cost and depreciation of capital leads to suboptimal investments in education, specifically to excessively capital-intensive
instructional technologies. This type of error, which is particularly serious
when planning for developing countries, can be easily avoided.

BHATT, B., KRISHAMOORTHY, P., MARATHY, R., and BOURGEOIS, M.
Radio broadcasting serves rural development. Paris: UNESCO, Reports and
papers on Mass Communications, No. 48, 1965.

BISHOP, G. D. "Réalisme et Diversité: un Nouvel Enseignement pour les îles du
Pacifique Sud." *Informations Unesco,* No. 600, April 1974. *Direct* VI-84.

The project undertaken in 1970 by UNESCO has developed programs and
teaching aids for the islands of the South Pacific. The contents are adaptable
to the different geographies, climates, and economies of the societies on the
different islands. Instruction by correspondence would be followed up by
broadcast courses.

BLACKBURN, P. P. *Communications and National Development in Burma,
Malaysia, and Thailand: A comparative Systematic Analysis.* Washington,
D.C.: The American Univ., 1971.

The mass media of Burma, Malaysia, and Thailand are examined as comparative national system reflecting both the spread of communications media and
the use made of such resources by the respective countries as of approximately 1970. The study examines official information budgets and organizations and then proceeds to a description of newspapers, periodicals, radio,
television, and motion pictures from the perspective of communications hardware, imported materials, government regulatory activiey, and local media
content.

BLED, C. "Review of Audience Research in Some Developing Countries in Africa." *Journal of Broadcasting,* 13, 2, Spring 1969: 167-180.

This article synthesizes information from research conducted by African broadcasting organizations, and is based on a larger document prepared by the author for the C.B.C.

BLONDIN, M. "Animación Social: Una Filosofía para la Acción." *Educación Popular para el Desarrollo,* 1, 4, October 1970: 41-48.

BOCK, J. and PAPAGIANNIS, G. The demystification of nonformal education. Amherst: Center for International Education, Univ. of Massachusetts, 1976.

BOISSCHOT, H. "African Radio and Television Production Center, Tele-Star: Description." Kinshasa, Zaire, April 1969.

This document briefly describes the beginning of a private television-production center in Kinshasa since taken over by the government. Also some reference is made to the earlier Radio-Star, a private radio-production center.

Boletín Informativo Centro, Año II, No. 1 "Federación Guatemalteca de Escuelas Radiofónicas." pp. 3-5.

This document summarizes two seminars sponsored by FGER on evaluation and planning. It describes the roles of radio teachers and radio monitors.

"Acción Cultural Popular Hondurena." pp. 6-7.

This general, brief introduction to the radio schools of Honduras focuses on the effects on adult education.

Boletín Informativo Centro, Año II, No. 3 "Escuelas Radiofónicas de Nicaragua." pp. 4-5.

This document is a very short sketch of the Nicaraguan radio schools following the 1972 Managua earthquake.

Bolivia. Ministerio de Educación. *Escuelas radiofónicas.* La Paz, ERBOL. Colección Nuevos Caminos, No. 5, 1970: 31 pp.

Bolivia. Escuelas Radiofónicas. *Evaluación de las escuelas radiofónicas de Bolivia.* La Paz, ERBOL, 1973: 7 pp.

BONILLA, F. D., et al. *"Causa popular, ciencia popular, una metodología del conocimiento científico a través de la acción."* Bogotá: Rosca, 1972: 78 pp. (Serie: *Por ahí es la cosa* No. 2).

BOWMAN, M. J. *Rural people and rural economic development,* Paris: UNESCO International Institute for Educational Planning, 1976.

BOX, L. de la R. *Organization of Educational Broadcasting in Brazil.* Ph.D. dissertation. New York: Columbia Univ., 1973.

The author analyzes the reasons for success and failure of educational broadcasting organizations and projects.

BOYD, D. "The Story of Radio in Saudi Arabia." *Public Telecommunications Review,* Vol. 1, 2, October 1973: pp. 53-60.

BRAUN, J. "Educational Technology and Rural Change." Paper presented at the International Workshop "Non-formal Education: New Strategies for Developing an Old Resource." East Lansing: Michigan State Univ., 1974.

––– "Los Medios Masivos y las Redes de Comunicación Interpersonal en la Difusión de Innovaciones Agropecuarias y de Control de la Natalidad." Inter-American Research Workshop sponsored by the Center of Educational Studies of Mexico City and the Institute for Communication Research of Stanford University. Oaxtapec, Mexico, 1975.

———"Communication, non-formal education, and national development: the Colombian radio schools." Unpublished Ph.D. dissertation. East Lansing: Michigan State Univ. 1975. 153 pp.

BREMBECK, C. and THOMPSON, T. New Strategies for Educational Development: The Cross-Cultural Search for Nonformal Alternatives. New York: D.C. Heath, 1973.

BROCKHALL, F. "Radio as an agricultural extension aid in Papua, New Guinea." South Pacific Bulletin, Third Quarter 1970.

BROWNE, E. "Radio in Africa: Problems and Prospects." NAEB Journal, November-December 1963.

This is a general article on the outlook for African radio at that time.

BRUMBERG, S. Educación no formal para el desarrollo rural. Bogotá, Acción Cultural Popular. Departamento de Sociología. Documento de Trabajo, 17, 1972: 16 pp.

———Acción Cultural Popular: mass media in the service of Colombian rural development. New York: International Council for Education Development. Case study no. 1, 1972.

———Los medios masivos de comunicación al servicio del desarrollo rural en Colombia. January 1974.

———"Colombia: a Multimedia Rural Education Program." in Education for Rural Development: Case Studies for Planners, Manzoor Ahmed and Philip Coombs (eds.). New York: Praeger, 1975.

This case study of ACPO gives information on its organization, goals, accomplishments, and costs at the time of the study (1971).

BUENO, P. B., et al. Rural broadcasting: syllabus on radio. Prepared by P. B. Bueno, P. M. de la Paz, and F. Lebrero. Department of Agricultural Communication College of Agriculture, Univ. of the Phillipines, Laguna, 1972: 37 pp.

To help the broadcasting student understand the rudiments of rural educational broadcasting, this syllabus covers some theoretical aspects of broadcasting, extension education, radio journalism, production and programming for rural audiences, and a report on DZLB, the rural education radio station of the University of the Philippines at Los Baños.

Bureau of Public Schools (Department of Education and Culture, Republic of the Philippines). "A study on the effectiveness of instructional broadcasts in the teaching of English as a second language in grade 1." Unpublished paper, Manila, 1969.

CABEZAS, E. A. Documento Informativo Sobre Radio Santa María. Santo Domingo, Dominican Republic, 1975.

CAMUS, J. and BAEZA, O. La radio en la escuela, método audiovisual de enseñanza. Lo Barnechea, Chile: Centro de Perfeccionamiento, Experimentación, e Investigaciones Pedagógicas (CPEIP), 1974: 83 pp. Spanish. (Abstract−8.)

CARNOY, M. and LENIN, H. "Evaluation of education media: Some issues." Instructional Science, Vol. 4, 1975: 385-406.

CARPENTER, C. R. "The Application of Less Complex Instructional Technologies," in *Quality in Instructional Television,* Wilbur Schramm (Ed.) Univ. of Hawaii, 1972.

––– *Public Telecommunications Review,* Vol. 2, 2, April 1974. "Intercultural Broadcasting: A Preface to Development." *Direct* VI-97.

This article discusses the prerequisites for the production and broadcasting of intercultural educational radio and TV programs. It includes suggestions based on research in programmed instruction. It suggests a world standard for research labs in social and behavioral sciences using communications methods, a world standard for library laboratories where audio-visual materials are collected and distributed, and a new international standard for combining large public and commercial stations with small educational stations.

––– "International Broadcasting: A Preface to Development." *Public Telecommunications Review,* Vol. 2, 2, April 1974.

CASSIRER, H. R. "Two-way Radio in Rural Senegal." *Educational Television International* (now called *Educational Broadcasting International*), 4, 2, June, 1970; 148-149.

This article is a short description of an important type of radio technology for rural areas.

––– "Radio in an African context: A description of Senegal's pilot project." In Spain, P., Jamison, D., and McAnany, E. (eds.) *Radio for education and development: Case studies,* Vol. 2. Washington, D.C.: The World Bank, Working Paper 266, 1977.

CAZENEUVE, J. "Niveau de culture et audition de la radio à Madagascar." *Cahiers Internationaux de Sociologie* (Paris) 43, July-December, 1968: 85-98.

Results of a study of the habits of radio listeners in Tananarive, shows two types of audience–traditionalist and modern. This influences program content.

Center for Educational Development Overseas (CEDO), Commonwealth Secretariat. *New Media in Education in the Commonwealth.* London, Commonwealth Secretariat, 1974: 292 pp.

Center for International Education. *Nonformal Education in Ecuador 1971-1975.* Amherst: Univ. of Massachusetts.

CEPEDA, L. *Radio Ecca: Centro docente.* Canary Islands: Radio ECCA, 1976.

CHAMBERS, R. *Managing rural development: Ideas and experiences from East Africa.* Uppsala: Scandinavian Institute for African Studies, 1974.

CHARCONNET, M. "L'Ecole Radiophonique au Maroc." *Interstages* (Brussels), February 15, 1966: 17-19.

CHU, G., and SCHRAMM, W. *Learning from television: What the research says.* Stanford, California: Institute for Communication Research, 1967.

CLARKE, R. *Report on an Experimental Course in the Use of Two-way Radio in Adult Education for the Lilangwe Land Development Programme.* Limbe, Malawi: Univ. of Malawi, Center for Extension Studies, January 1972.

This is a description of an experiment with two-way radio for teaching English in a number of sites outside the capital city of Malawi.

CLIPPINGER, J. *Who Gains by Communications Development? Studies of Information Technologies in Developing Countries. Working Paper 76-1.* Harvard Univ.: Cambridge, Massachusetts, Program on Information Technologies and Public Policy.

To identify the distribution of benefits that accrue from introducing communications technology in developing societies, two case studies were undertaken. The first case looks at telecommunications development in Algeria where telecommunications systems are being rapidly introduced to speed up industrialization and where a satellite system is in use to promote regional development. The second case study is of educational television in El Salvador. In both cases, it was found that the government was the primary beneficiary. The introduction of the new technology led to a greater concentration of power, increased centralization, and a growing technocratic elite, but in neither case did the technology have a salutary effect on the problems of undereducation, underproduction, or national strife.

COEHLO DOS REIS, T. *Teleducaçao Brasil, 1958/70.* Rio de Janeiro, 1972.

This document details the history of educational broadcasting during the period 1958-70, particularly rich on legal aspects.

COLCLOUGH, M. and CROWLEY, D. "The People and the Plan: A Report of the Botswana Government's Educational Project on the Five-Year National Development Plan, 1973-1978." Univ. of Botswana, Lesotho, and Swaziland; Division of Extramural Services.

This document describes a radio campaign designed to acquaint the people of Botswana with the development plan of the government. The campaign used radio in combination with a trained group leader and flip charts. The group leader is supplied with study guides to direct the discussion; he also reports on the questions that the groups want answered and forwards them to the program producers. Later programs respond to these questions.

The group leader also had a radio provided by the government. He organizes the group (5-20 members), arranges a meeting place, and guides the group through the programs and discussion.

This project is influenced by the radio discussion campaigns in Tanzania.

COLEMAN, W. F., OPOKU, A. A., and ABELL, H. C. *An African Experiment in Radio Forums for Rural Development: Ghana, 1964-1965.* Paris: UNESCO, Reports and Papers on Mass Communications, No. 51, 1968.

This publication contains reports of a major UNESCO project which set a standard for certain types of rural programming.

COLIN, R. L'animation, clef de voute de développement. *Développement et civilisation,* No. 21, March 1965: 5-10.

COLLE, R. *Informe Preliminar Sobre Escuelas Radiofonicas Populares del Ecuador.* Santiago: Secretariado de Comunicación Social (SEDECOS), 1974. Spanish.

––– Cassette, special communication systems. Paper prepared for conference on Nonformal Education and the Rural Poor, Michigan State Univ., 1976.

COLOMINA DE RIVERA, M. *El huesped alienante: un estudio sobre audiencia y effectos de las radio-telenovelas en Venezuela.* Maracaibo: Universidad del Zulia, Facultad de Humanidades y Educación, 1968: 150 pp.

This is one of the few empirical studies of broadcasting effects in a developing nation. The author finds a positive relation between identification with, believing in, and consumption of televised and radio novelas, and lower socio-economic-educational status.

CONATEH, S. "Radio Gambia: Cooperation with Radio Senegal." *Combroad,* 22, January-March 1974. *Direct* V-79.

The cooperation between Senegal and Gambia during the last five years has led to the exchange of broadcasting materials between the two countries. The two populations are from the same ethnic group and speak the same language (even though the official language of Senegal is French and of Gambia is English). The two countries collaborate, exchange, and coproduce programs, especially cultural programs. The cooperation extends to the area of educational broadcasting with the broadcasting of Senegal's DISSOO in Gambia.

CONDON, J. C. "Some guidelines for mass communication research in East Africa." Gazette (Deventer) 14, 2, 1968: 141-151.

Conferencia Nacional de Obispos del Brasil. Area B, Norte I de Manaus. "Radio difusao rural educativa para Amazonia." In *Reuniao de Planejamiento de um Programa de Radio Difusao Rural Educativa para Amazonia, Manuas, Brasil, 1970.* Documentos. Manaus, 1970.

CONSTANTINE, M. "Radio in the elementary school." *Science Education,* 48, 1964: 121-132.

COOMBS, P. *Non-formal Education for Rural Development: Strengthening Learning Opportunities for Children and Youth.* Essex, Connecticut: International Council for Educational Development, January 1973.

――― and AHMED, M. *Attacking rural poverty: How nonformal education can help.* Baltimore, Md.: Johns Hopkins Univ. Press, 1964.

COOMBS, P. and HALLAK, J. *Managing educational costs.* New York and London: Oxford Univ. Press, 1972.

CORTES, O. *Movimiento de Educación de Base.* Sutatenza, 1972: 26 pp. Spanish.

CORTEZ, C. *Movimiento de Educación de Base (MEB).* Rio de Janeiro, MEB 1972: 25 pp. Spanish.

COWLAN, B. "Educational Satellites over Africa: an Unlikely Scenario." *Educational Broadcasting International,* Vol. 7, 3, September 1974. *Direct* IX-149.

The possible effects of using a system of telecommunications via satellite for Africa are discussed here. The report is directed to concerns of researchers, politicians, economists, planners, educators, and technicians.

CUSACK, M. A. "New Media in Africa: Trends and Strategies." *Educational Broadcasting Review,* 4, 5, October 1970: 23-30.

CUTTER, C. H. *Nation-Building in Mali: Art, Radio, and Leadership in a Preliterate Society.* Univ. of California at Los Angeles, Ph.D. dissertation, 1971.

DANEY, C. and MADRE, J. "The Role of Radio and Television in Teaching in France." *Programmed Learning and Educational Technology,* Vol. 11, September 1974. *Direct* I-1.

This article describes the role of OFRATEME (Office Français des Techniques Modernes d'Education) in the production and distribution of educational programs for radio. The authors give their views of the advantages of specific uses of radio broadcasting in teaching.

D'ARINOS SILVA, L. "Joao Silva: A telenovela course." *Education Broadcasting International.* March 1975.

DAS, G. "People playing their part in AIR's programmes." *ABU Newsletter,* 106, July 1974: 14-16.

DAVIGNON, C. P. *A History of the Radio Schools of Peru (at Puno) from 1961 to 1969 and Their Contribution to Present and Future Education in Peru.* Washington, D.C.: The Catholic Univ. of America, Ph.D. dissertation, 1973.

DAVIS, G. "The Challenge of Educational TEchnology in Underdeveloped Countries." *Audiovisual Instruction,* 15, March 1970: 64-67.

DECENA-DILONA, H. Estudio comparativo del rendimiento de los alumnos de las Escuelas Radiofónicas de Radio Santa María y de educación de adultos oficial. Tesis, Univ. Católica, Santiago, República Dominicana, 1973.

Deemar Co. Ltd. *Deemar media index final report, 1972.* Southern region (urgan areas). Bangkok, 1972.

This survey, conducted among a representative cross-section sample of the population 15 years of age and above in the urban areas of Thailand, provides general information on the size and composition of various mass media audiences. A profile of radio and TV viewers is given together with data on the frequency and recency of TV viewing and radio listening.

DEFEVER, A. "La radiovisión agricola." In Seminario Nacional de Radiodifusión Rural, Bogotá, 29 de Noviembre a 11 de Diciembre de 1971. Informe preliminar. Bogotá, FAO, Ministerio de Agricultura, 1971. 6 pp. (Documento C-17).

DE KADT, E. *Catholic radicals in Brazil.* London: Oxford, 1970.

DIALLO, S. Y. "Une radiodiffusion equipée par souscription (Mali)." *Journalisme* (Strasbourg), 30 1968: 96-97. English translation on p. 98.

DIAZ BORDENAVE, J. "Communication and adoption of agricultural innovations in Latin America." In *International Symposium on Communication Strategies for Rural Development,* Cali, Colombia, 1974. Proceedings. Cali, Cornell University-CIAT, 1974: 205-217.

DIEUZEIDE, H. "La radio-télévision au service de l'éducation en Europe Occidentale. Quelques remarques sur son état présent et ses perspectives." *Revue U.E.R. Programmes, administration, droit.* Vol. xxv, 2, March 1974. *Direct* VI-89.

DINAH, J. and PEERALLY, S. "La radiovision: nouveau médium audiovisuel." *Journal of Mauritian Education,* 3, July 1973, *Direct* I-3.

Twenty primary-level schools on the island of Mauritius have used radiovision since September 1972. The method consists of a prerecorded commentary lasting about 20 minutes, supplemented by black and white photos shown to the class during the lecture.

Direct III-42. "Radio's Role in Instruction—Report and Recommendations of the Instructional Radio Task Force." Paris, March 1974: 42, French.

Following a study undertaken in 1972 of the uses of educational radio in the United States, the task force recommended that radio be considered as a

means of specific education. They suggested a planned national standard be applied to the production, acquisition, reproduction, and broadcasting of educational radio programs. They consider a study based on use of radio in the United States and Great Britain in the framework of the Open University.
Direct IV-25. "Plaidoyer pour régionalisation administrative."

Availability of television in Belgium is due to its geographic location, giving viewers a choice of 11 channels broadcasting in several languages, and in color since 1971.

The country has two major stations, La Radio-Télévision Belge (1960), better known as RTB, and la Belgische Radio-Televisie (BRT). Their division is due to the bilingual character of the country. Stations are charged with three goals—information, advertisement, and education. The educational function has been developing since 1962 with the aid of the Ministry of Education.
Direct V-60. "Le Vocabulaire de la Radio." Paris, May 1974: p. 6. French.

This review of vocabulary of broadcasting by the International Council of French language was published by Hachette in 1972. The lexicon is a good means for a nonspecialist to penetrate one of the most abstruse of universal linguistics. It contains translations and explanations of "slang" which differ in meaning from use in current French, technical words, words taken from foreign languages, professional abbreviations, and so forth.
Direct V-76. "C.B.C.'s Maison de Radio-Canada."

This article refers to the articles on "Maison de Radio-Canada" in *Combroad* for 1974 describing the modern broadcasting and television installation. This is one of the first to use a satellite for broadcasting of programs.
Direct V-79. "Co-opération entre Etablissements Publics et Privés." Paris, May 1974: p. 79, French.

The Indiana Higher Education Telecommunications System promotes the cooperation of public and private institutions for higher education. They share in the costs, equipment, and materials in broadcasting to five cities with the objective to combine and serve all institutes of higher learning in the state.
Direct V-158. "Un moyen de communication universel." Paris, 1974: p. 158, French.

This article comments on the universality of radio. There are 20,000 transmitting stations and 650-million receivers worldwide. Considering a world population of 4 billion, there is nearly one radio for every seven people. The figures are distorted by the affluence of North America with some 6,900 transmitters and 310 million receivers. UNESCO statistics of 1971 show 50 million receivers in the Third World countries of South Asia and Africa, averaging one for every 20 in Africa.

The effects of television on radio listening are described here. Third World organization of media is altogether different. Television is still unknown by some countries, while in others it is reserved for urban populations and then only to those persons or groups with the means of financing the broadcasting and reception. UNESCO shows 1 TV for every 300 people in Africa, 1 for 400 in Asia, 1 for 3 in North America, and 1 for 4 in Europe.

The article proposes radio as excellent means of communication and education because of lack of printed matter, literacy, and electricity.

Direct VI-65. "Le développement rural: la part des media." Paris, June 1974: p. 65, French.

The modern techniques in communications can be a great help to rural development—first, because radio and TV can bring together a dispersed audience, and second, because teaching can be directed to adults who are engaged in agriculture. The programs do not use principles of formal education; rather emphasize learning by doing. Third, since communications between authorities and rural people are often difficult, radio can permit such communication, and communication among the people themselves.

Direct VI-69. "Techniques visuelles dans le développement." Paris, June 1974: p. 69, French.

The use of visual aids helps understanding of spoken words. That is why some countries engaged in rural development are using visual techniques. Radiovision is a combination of black and white photographs shown with a radio broadcast. The pictures are produced and sent out by the station. The broadcast commentary gives signals when it is time to change the picture. Radiovision has been used for 10 years in Central Africa to teach reading and writing. Another technique is television, as in India, Senegal, Tunisia, and the Ivory Coast. Film is less appropriate for rural development.

Direct VI-70. "La tribune radiophonique rurale de Dahomey." Paris, June 1974: p. 70, French.

This article describes the radio forums in Dahomey. Begun in 1968, by 1972 they were in one third of the villages. Its contents deal with understanding the modern techniques, health and hygiene, and the national plan. One 30-minute broadcast per week (in 10 languages) forms the basis for discussions in each village directed by an animateur.

Direct VI-72. "Le développement rural de l'Inde." Paris, June 1976: p. 72, French.

This article contains reflections on the politics and strategies of rural development in India. It describes the beginning of the radio forums in 1956—biweekly broadcasts to 144 villages where groups of about 20 gathered to hear programs on agriculture, health, and domestic economy. In 1959, it was decided to spread the project over all of India. Extending the forums was slow and difficult, due to 100 different dialects among the 550,000 villages.

Now the authorities of India have chosen to accelerate rural development by using a satellite for communications. The Satellite Instructional Television Experiment (SITE) began in 1975, with an American satellite. Special antennas were installed in villages, and villagers received programs on family planning, new methods in agriculture, integration of different linguistic communities, and acceleration of social evaluation. The one-year experiment is confined to pilot areas, and will be evaluated for future direction.

Direct VI-75. "L'extrascolaire en Côte d'Ivoire." Paris, 1974: p. 75, French.

Television for formal in-school education has been implemented on a large scale in the Ivory Coast. But efforts have also been made to use TV for the nonschool population. Directed mainly to the rural areas and using school receivers in the evening hours, the programs deal with nutrition and hygiene. Still experimental, however, this out-of-school effort has not yet dealt fully with the language difference found in the rural areas.

Direct VI-76. "La vulgarisation agricole en Tunisie." Paris, June 1974: p. 76, French.

After experimenting with radio and television for agricultural education, Tunisia is now using videocassettes. This medium has adapted well to the needs of the rural sectors with its flexibility.

Direct VII-113. "La Nouvelle Maison de Radio-Canada à Montréal."

This is a reference to *Revue de L'U.E.R.-Technique* (April 1974), article describing the Maison de Radio-Canada, established in December 1973 by the Société Radio-Canada. The article describes the setup of the station including the equipment and procedures used.

Direct VIII-130. "Programming for French Canada." *Combroad,* 24, July-September 1974.

Raymond David, vice-president and general director of the French broadcasting on the Société Radio-Canada, wrote an article describing how the coming of television in Canada in 1952 has accelerated the sociological, political, religious, and especially the cultural development of French Canada. That article is reviewed here.

Direct X-80. "La Radio au service du développement en Afrique." Paris, October 1974: p. 80, French.

The article describes rural educational radio (DISSOO) in Senegal, begun in 1968. Broadcasts are made to rural areas three evenings a week. Most people gather in public places after their work to hear broadcast and follow-up discussion among themselves. Of TV, films, and radio, radio is the most successful and adaptable to the needs of Senegal, particularly the rural areas.

Direct X-164. "L'Utilisation des ondes pour véhiculer les sons." Paris, October 1974: p. 164, French.

The article discusses acoustical phenomenon in radio transmission of sound by sound waves. The reader is referred to Direct (No. 5 and No. 8) for full explanation of transmitting sounds by radio-electric or electromagnetic sound waves. This is a technical explanation of formation, transmission, and reception of sound by sound waves.

Direct X-172. "La Radioprimaria experimentale." Paris, October 1974: p. 172, French.

This article summarizes the work in Mexico using radio as a supplement to rural primary schools—the radioprimaria experiment.

Direct X-173. "La radiovision." Paris, October 1974: p. 173, French.

The mixing of radio and multi-media makes it possible for different senses of the individual to be involved. Radio can be mixed with television and film. Radiovision, a technique uniting images and sound, uses black and white photos accompanying radio broadcast pictures. OFRATEME (L'office français des techniques modernes d'education) has promoted this technique since 1961. It is used generally in elementary education.

In 1974, radiovision was revived in France. It is used experimentally on the island of Mauritius in 1973 and 1974, and in Africa for adult education. The article concludes with a description of radiovision services available from OFRATEME.

The following references to *Direct* are for the calendar year 1975. The numbering system follows that for the previous references for 1974 – that is, *Direct* I-1 refers to page one of the January edition, and so forth.

Direct I-1. "La Teleducación en la República Federal de Alemania."

This general description of the radio and television networks in German includes a detailed description of the main stations broadcasting educational programs. Síntesis Quincenal, *Revue du Cedal,* No. 19, 15 Octubre 1974.

Direct I-3. "Los medios de información en un contexto Africano: evaluación del proyecto piloto del Senegal."

This article presents the development of the project in Senegal organized by UNESCO in 1964 to produce audio-visual materials for education. (The Senegal project has been described in other *Direct* volumes.) Sintesis Quincenal, *Revue du Cedal,* No. 18, 30 Septiembre 1974.

Direct III-42. "Telecommunications Services for Rural Educational Development." Paris, March 1975: p. 420, French.

The satellite ATS-6 is being used in the Rocky Mountain region to meet specific educational needs in the rural zones of the United States. This report points out the obstacles to having an effective rural educational system and it describes the telecommunication systems that exist and are being used in education in the United States. Included in the report is an inventory describing the educational uses of existing telecommunications systems (including radio, television, cable, video, and so on).

Direct I-1. "La nécessité d'une approche systématique." Paris, January 1975: p. 1, French.

During its first year of publication, *Direct* has tried to examine specific media in an attempt to clarify concepts associated with each and to explore the potential uses of each medium. It is now the time to examine various media in relation to each other and the pedagogical effectiveness of combining several media. It is shown that the combined use of visual, audio-visual, and acoustic media with written material produces better results in learning that the use of a single medium. This article deals with the selection of a multimedia package that will have the greatest success for instruction. Many kinds of media are discussed including television, radio, film, sound tracks, transparencies, lectures, and written materials. Statements are made on the effectiveness of the various media in different situations. Guidelines are given for the selection of a multimedia system according to specific needs. Various authors are cited to support viewpoints in this article.

Direct I-6. "Quelques règles élémentaires d'establissement d'un système multimedia." Paris, January 1975: p. 6, French.

This article presents some criteria for the selection of one or more media to be used for instructional purposes. It is recognized that multimedia kits cannot be used effectively in all areas as may be claimed by manufacturing agencies. Careful selection must be made after extensive analysis. It is recommended that the chosen media should adapt themselves to the instructional process. The media should contain qualities determined as necessary to obtain the educational objectives.

Included at the end of the article is a table categorizing and rating media for use in various circumstances and different kinds of learning.

Direct I-9. "Les Principles de l'Éducation à Distance." Paris, January 1975: p. 9, French.

This is a description of the characteristics of the Open University and its advantages for education today. This type of education does not limit itself to specific locations such as classrooms and certain times and ages. The article presents the development of the Open University which provides a very flexible system available to a large number of people. It is pointed out that this method provides the means for true individualized instruction that can be tailored for many specific needs.

Direct I-11. "L'Open University Britannique." Paris, January 1975: p. 11, French.

As the most famous example, the Open University of Great Britain is pre-presented in this article. The description includes the admission requirements, its areas of study, and its various methods of instruction utilizing many different media, and the division of courses and requirements for course credits. Included is a description of the methods of instruction of the Open University and the relationship between the media and their effectiveness. Much emphasis is placed on radio broadcasting because of its flexibility and the ability to integrate it with other instructional materials.

Direct I-14. "Les Systèmes Multi-média Utilisés pour L'Education des Adultes." Paris, January 1975: p. 14, French.

To have an educational system that could meet the changing needs of the people of Quebec, reforms were suggested and instituted throughout the 1960s. The TELVEC project was begun in 1967 to provide adult education by means of closed-circuit television. This article describes the establishment and working of the project. This pilot project ended in 1969, to be followed by the Multimedia Program for Adult Education. The second part of the article is concerned with that program as established in Quebec in 1971. The evaluation of this project is to be made during the summer of 1975.

Direct I-22. "Les Systèmes Multi-média dans le Tiers-Monde." Paris, January 1975: p. 22, French.

This is a presentation of the difficulties with the use of multimedia packages in Third World countries. The presentation is made in view of the financial costs, and the human and technical requirements.

One question explored is the applicability of the open university concept in developing nations. The conditions necessary for success of the open university are presented along with the potential financial impact on a country.

As examples of education in Third World countries, the article describes several existing programs. The University of Malawi has established in 1969 an extension studies program to try to meet the needs of the rural sections. Pakistan, which has a high illiteracy rate, has instituted programs for adult education. The predominant means is through educational television. Examples are also given of the use of media for education in the Ivory Coast.

Direct II-25. "Une Disponibilité Limitée." Paris, February 1975: p. 25, French.

The article starts by referring to the book *Big Media, Little Media,* by Wilbur Schramm, to point out the difficulty of evaluating the quality of education. Recognizing that different media are more effective in different circumstances, it is impossible to create a hierarchy of instructional media. The inadequacy of standardized tests to measure the effectiveness of media is due partly to the fact that education cannot be measured by amounts of knowledge learned or required time. It is rather a transformation of a person who will subsequently interact in society. This result cannot be easily measured or evaluated.

The article discusses various media and their probable benefits for classroom use based on the way they can be adapted to the ongoing instruction. Availability of materials is a large factor in choosing media. Problems arise when teachers do not receive their "first choice" of films, for example, or they cannot preview a television broadcast, or insufficient information is available from existing resources, and so forth. Other factors such as costs are also considered.

Direct I-1. "Co-existence des Systèmes Multi-média et de l'Enseignement formel."

This article describes Radio Television Scolaire (RTS), which was established in France in 1963, for adult education and later extended to other ages. RTS exercise books are available for students; the books accurately review the material presented in the broadcasts. Records and slides are also available in some cases to provide material for more formal instruction in groups. The article continues with more information about audio-visual programs for instruction.

Another example is ICAV set up in 1966 by Le Centre Régionale de Documentation Pédagogigue de Bordeaux (CBDP). Its purpose was to explore further uses of audio-visual means of communication in education.

A multimedia operation called 'Acquaintance to the Present' was begun in 1971 by OFRATEME. This project was directed towards multimedia usage in elementary school.

A third program cited in the article is also established in Bordeaux—this is the audio-visual center at Tivoli College where they use closed-circuit television. The center was strated in 1971 to encourage use of audio-visual media by students as well as teachers. This center is a multimedia center utilizing not only television, but films, slides, and so forth. Materials are used and created by students or teachers.

Direct III-19. "Quand les auxiliaries audiovisuels participent au développement rural." Paris, March 1975: p. 19, French.

This article points out the benefits audio-visual instruction can bring to rural development. Using Senegal as an example, and considering its agricultural situation and the development of its national products, the article shows that rural people can be helped to use new technologies by audiovisual instruction.

DODDS, T. *Multi-media approach to rural education.* London: International Extension College, 1972.

DOUGLASS, J. *Notas sobre radiodifusión agricola.* Roma, FAO, 1965: 59 pp.

DUBLY, A. *Evaluación de las Escuelas Radiofónicas Populares de Riobamba.* Quito: Instituto Ecuatoriano de Desarrollo Económico y Social (INEDES), 1973: 70 pp., Spanish.

EAPEN, K. F. *Communication and Development: A Case Study of Indonesia.* Leicester: Centre for Mass Communication Research, Univ. of Leicester, 1973: 25 pp.
   This paper attempts first to trace the research trend dealing with the problem of national development and mass communication in Indonesia. It then examines the mass-media system dealing specifically with radio broadcasting and radio farm forums.

EDINGTON, A. B. "The dream that hasn't come true." In *Educational Broadcasting International,* Vol. 7, 3, September 1974. *Direct* IX-141.
   This article analyzes the last ten years since television has been officially connected with education. It focuses on the treatment of the objectives and results of various developments in educational television. It refers to research in the historical development of educational television and discusses the influence of technological progress on new educational systems using television.

EGLY, M., McANANY, E., and MARGOLIN, J. *Alternatives for Application of Communication Technology to the Educational Needs of the Democratic Republic of the Congo (Zaire).* Washington, D.C.: Agency for International Development, May 1971.
   This report stresses the development of radio as a useful immediate means of support for innovation and expansion of education in Zaire.

EL HADJ BADGE, M. and ROBERT, J. *Dix ans d'animation radiophonique en milieu rural.* Niamey, Niger: Association des Radio-Clubs du Niger, 1972.
   This article summarizes the first ten years of the experiences of one of the oldest rural radio projects in Africa. Its method of getting rural people's input for the programming is original and has spread to other projects.

ELLIOT, R. *A study of taped lessons in geography instruction.* Westfield, Mass.: The Abner Gibbs Schools, 1948.

ELY, D. P. "Beyond Our Borders: The Educational Technologist Abroad." *Audiovisual Instruction,* 21. 1976: 8-11.
   The article includes a discussion of educational technology in the international setting based on several short-term international assignments filled by the author in Latin America and the Far East.

EMERY, W. B. *National and International Systems of Broadcasting: Their History, Operation, and Control.* East Lansing: Michigan State Univ. Press, 1969.

ENCALADA R., M. *Contribución de la radiodifusión al desarrollo de Ecuador: un estudio del contenido de la programación radiofónica ecuatoriana.* Quito, 1974: 114 pp.
   This document studied the function of radio in Ecuador and the way radio has a part in the development—economic, social, and cultural—of the country. A random sampling method was used. Through a content analysis of the programming, the author concludes that radio does not really take part

in any development process nationally, because one radio network does not exist by itself, the stations are not adapted to the audiences, the stations do not have enough power to cover the great rural segment of the population, and because the advertising used may alienate the masses of people who live only a marginal existence in terms of the processes of the nation.

ESMAN, M. "Popular participation and feedback systems in rural development." In *International Symposium on Communication Strategies for Rural Development,* Cali, Colombia, 1974. Cali, Cornell Univ.-CIAT, 1974: pp. 70-78.

ETHERINGTON, A. *The costs of the campaign.* Botswana: Ministry of Local Government and Lands, November 1977: 12 pp.

ETI (Educational Television International), 4, 1, March 1970. "Literacy through Radio and Television in Jamaica." (By the Literacy Section of the Social Development Commission).

    This description of the Literacy program covers its early stages before an evaluation unit was formed.

EVANS, D. Technology in nonformal education: A critical appraisal. *Comparative Education Review.* Vol. 20, 1976: 305-327.

FAGEN, R. *The transformation of political culture in Cuba.* Stanford: Stanford Univ. Press, 1969.

FANON, F. "This is the Voice of Algeria." In *Studies in a Dying Colonialism,* Ch. 2. New York: Monthly Review Press, 1965.

    Valuable insight on the role radio played in the Algerian war of Independence.

FARIS, R. L. *Adult Education for Social Action or Enlightenment: An Assessment of the Development of the Canadian Association for Adult Education and its Radio from 1935-1952.* Toronto: Univ. of Toronto, Ph.D. dissertation, 1971.

FAULKNER, S. H. "In defense of the C.B.C." *Combroad,* 24, July-September 1974. *Direct* VIII-130.

    This article is a reprint of the speech delivered by the Secretary of State of Canada in February 1974 outlining the principles of the Public Broadcast Television of Canada. It traces the history of the société Radio-Canada and the creation of the Canadian Broadcasting Commission in 1938.

FELSTEHAUSEN, H. "Conceptual limits of development communication theory." *Rural Sociology,* 38, 1973: 39-54.

FERRER, M. S. *Muestra piloto de las escuelas radiofónicas rurales,* ACPO. Bogotá, UNESCO, 1958-1959.

– – – *Acción Cultural Popular, Escuelas Radiofónicas de Sutatenza, Colombia; estudio y evaluación de la obra.* Bogotá, UNESCO, 1959.

– – – *Historia de las escuelas radiofónicas.* Bogotá, Acción Cultural Popular, 1959.

FEWSTER, J. "Radio farm forums: The development of this technique and its use today in developing countries." Madison: Univ. of Wisconsin, Department of Agricultural Journalism, 1965.

FIERRO, G., HUMBERTO, L., and ROBAYO, A. *Datos básicos sobre radiodifusión agropecuaria en Colombia.* Bogotá, Instituto Colombiano Agropecuario. Programa de Comunicación de Masas, 1974: 41 pp.

FISHER, G. *Cost consideration in systems analysis.* Santa Monica, California: the RAND Corporation, 1971.

FONTAN, J. *Communication in Sutatenza Radio Schools, Colombia.* East Lansing: Michigan State Univ., Department of Communications, 1965.

FORSYTHE, R. *Instructional Radio: a Position Paper.* Stanford: ERIC, Stanford Univ., 1970.

FOSTER, P. and SHEFFIELD, J. (eds.) *Education and rural development.* New York: The World Yearbook of Education, 1974.

The author describes a number of instructional radio projects, with a view to showing the nature, scope, and functions of radio as they relate to instructional applications.

Fundaçao Movimento Brasileiro de Alfabetizacao (MOBRAL). *Gerencia Pedagogica. Projeto de Trainamento de Alfabetizadores pelo Radio.* Rio de Janeiro, 1974: 74 pp.

FUNDACAO, P. A. Editora Abril, Instituto de Pesguisas Espaciais. Madureza Ginasial—Avaliaçao de Resultados, Sao Paulo, 1971.

This document is an evaluation of the results of a radio course for adults broadcast in Sao Paulo.

GALLEGO, D. The ECCA system of radio teaching. *Multi-media International,* 1974.

General Learning Corporation. *Cost study of educational media systems and their equipment components.* 3 vols. Washington: GLC, 1968.

GERBNER, G., GROSS, L., and MELODY, W. (eds.) *Communication technology and social policy: understanding the new "cultural revolution".* New York: John Wiley, 1973.

This useful volume contains an interesting section on intercultural communication: Articles by Schiller, Guback, Mattelart, and Smythe among many others.

GOLDING, P. "Media role in national development: Critique of a theoretical orthodoxy." *Journal of Communications,* 24:3, Summer 1974.

GOMEZ, A. "Federación Guatemalteca de Escuelas Radiofónicas (FEGER)." Mexico, D.F. Friedrich Ebert Foundation Seminar on Rural Radio, 1971.

GOMEZ POSADA, L. *Opinión de los lideres sobre el functionamiento de las escuelas radiofónicas en Colombia.* Bogotá, ACPO, 1967.

——— *Influencia previa de los elementos de acción de Acción Cultural Popular sobre los jóvenes campesinos que asisten a la primera promoción de los institutos en 1968.* Bogotá, ACPO, 1968.

——— and GUTIERREZ, A. *Encuesta sobre radiodifusión entre los campesinos.* Bogotá, Acción Cultural Popular, 1970: 84 pp.

GOMEZ POSADA, L. et al. *La audiencia campesina de Radio Sutatenza.* Bogotá, Acción Cultural Popular. Departamento de Sociología. Documento de Trabajo, no. 10. 1970: 40 pp.

GOONASEKERA, S. *Radio listenership behavior in relation to occupation and urbanization in Sri Lanka*. Colombo: Department of Information, 1972: 12 pp.

This document discusses the difference in listenership behavior between rural and urban people and between people of different occupations in Sri Lanka based on media consumption survey. Specifically, it deals with the types of programs listened to, the most preferred channels, the reasons for listening to radio, and whether radio has affected people's attitudes toward certain things.

GRATTAN, D. "Les Cinquante Premières Années." *Revue de L'U.E.R., Adm./droit,* Vol. XXV, 6, November 1974. *Direct* I-6.

The subtitle of this article is "Reflections on the past, present, and future of the First World service of educational radio broadcasting." It is essentially a retrospective and prospective study of the role of the PBC in educational radio.

GRISE, P., et al. *Educational Radio: A review of the Literature*. Florida State Univ., Tallahassee: Center for Educational Technology, 1974.

Radio has been used for educational purposes since its beginning in the early 1920s; the application of radio to the educational problems of the developing nations is not a new concept by any means. Among the uses of educational radio are foreign radio schools, classroom radio uses, "Acción Cultural Popular" (ACPO), and correspondence radio courses. Educational radio for classroom presentation has been demonstrated as effective as television, slide/tape presentations, and other media, and to be cost effective.

GRUNDIG, J. "Communication and the economic decision-making processes of Colombian peasants." *Economic Development and Cultural Change,* 19, 3, July 1971: 580-598.

GRUNIG, J. "The structuralist approach to rural communication is outlined." *New directions for research in communications and international development; from the study of individuals to the study of formal organizations*. Montreal: International Communication Association, 1973.

GUEULETTE, D. G. "The Mass Media in Adult Education in Developing Countries: a Literature Review." *Mass Media/Adult Education,* 34, August-November 1971: 1-9.

GUNTER, J. (ed.) *A Sourcebook on Radio's Role in Development*. Washington, D.C.: The Academy for Educational Development, 1976.

This bibliography has over 600 entries, and is divided into fifteen categories, including audience, cost, open broadcast, instruction, farm forums, radio schools, and animation.

--- and THEROUX, J. Open-broadcast educational radio: Three paradigms. In Spain, P., Jamison, D., and McAnany, E. (eds.) *Radio for education and development: Case studies*. Vol. 2. Washington, D.C.: World Bank, Working Paper 266, 1977.

GUTIERREZ, A. *Marginalidad rural y desarrollo en Colombia*. Bogotá, ACPO, January 1971.

--- *Ideas sobre planeación y programación*. Bogotá: ACPO, February 1971.

GUTIERREZ DE ZARATE, M. C. *El liderazgo de opinión*. Bogotá, ACPO, December 1973.

HACHTEN, W. A. *Mass Communication in Africa: An Annotated Bibliography*. Madison: Center for International Communications Studies, Univ. of Wisconsin, 1972.
This useful listing is not restricted to items about education. It contains many references to the press in the African nations.

HALL, B. "Provision for the Poorly Educated Rural Areas." *Adult Education*, 46, 4, November 1973: 254-259.
Traditional university adult education is seen as catering to elite in contrast with the university radio study-group campaign which proved far more effective in reaching less well educated and financially insecure rural inhabitants in Tanzania.

– – – *Who Participates in the University Adult Education?* Dar es Salaam Univ., Institute of Adult Education, 1973.
In Tanzania, adult education is seen as going beyond increasing skill levels to raising political consciousness. If it is desired to narrow the gap between the educated and uneducated, the role of the University adult education evening classes as an agent of increased social stratification must be examined. Mass radio study groups may be one means of reducing educational inequalities while still affording the educational elite participation opportunities. A study of the radio discussion-group participants revealed that more men than women took part, the age group ranged from 12 to 80, and the intended rural audience was reached.

– – – "Mtu ni Afya! Tanzania's Mass Health Education Campaign." *Convergence*. Vol. VII, 1, 1974.

– – – "Revolution in Rural Education: Health Education in Tanzania." *Community Development Journal*, 9, 1974: 133-139.
Based upon the success of three smaller radio study campaigns, a program for a preventive health campaign was planned to directly improve the lives of Tanzania's rural inhabitants. Elements in the campaign included: a national coordinating committee, radio programs, printed materials, trained study-group leaders, leader's manuals, and supervision.

– – – "Development Campaigns in Rural Tanzania." *Rural Africana*, June 1975.

– – – "The 'Man is Health' Mass Study Campaign." *Literacy Discussion*, 6, 1, Spring 1975: 95-108.
This paper, based on the evaluation of the Tanzanian education campaign "Man is Health," reviews the genesis of the campaign, objectives and organization, training system, examples of groups at work, preliminary findings, and other significant aspects of the total effort.

HALL, B. and DODDS, T. *Voices for Development: the Tanzanian National Radio Study Campaigns*. International Extension College, Broadsheets on Distance Learning, Cambridge, 1974.
This article contains an historical account of the development of the strategy of organized group-listening to radio study campaigns in Tanzania, culminating in 1973 in a massive nationwide campaign on Health Education.

––– "Voices for development: The Tanzanian National Radio Study Campaigns."
In Spain, P., Jamison, D. and McAnany, E. (eds.) *Radio for education and de-
velopment: Case studies,* Vol. 2. Washington, D.C.: World Bank, Working
Paper 266, 1977.

HALL, B. and ZIKAMBONA, C. *An Evaluation of the 1973 Mass Health Education Campaign in Tanzania (Studies in Adult Education, No. 12).* Dar es
Salaam: Institute of Adult Education, 1974.

HANCOCK, A. "Mass Media and National Development." *Educational Broadcasting International,* Vol. 7, 2, June 1974. *Direct* VII-105.

This paper offers a new look at the work of W. Schramm, *Mass Media and
National Development,* originally done in 1964. Schramm discusses the prerequisites for developing a functional communications system. His proposi-
tions include: planning the system–a theoretical model; applying the theories;
combining media technology with existing local means of communication;
finally, developing standards primarily for an educational system through
international exchange and cooperation.

HAWKRIDGE, D. G. *The Open University in the Third World.* 1973. Available
from ERIC.

The British Open University is described in the first section of this paper
as a multimedia system for teaching at a distance. Details are provided on the
texts and other materials mailed to the students, on the radio and television
broadcasts provided by the BBC, and on the auxiliary sources of assistance
offered to the students. The following section of the report presents data on
the Open University's cost-effectiveness. The concluding portion discusses
the possibility of transplanting both the concept and the actuality of the
Open University as an institution to the Third World. Five conditions necessary for the successful functioning of an Open University are specified and
five kinds of assistance which the British Open University provides to Third
World educators are reviewed.

HEAD, S. *Broadcasting in Africa: A Continental Survey of Radio and Television.*
Philadelphia: Temple Univ. Press, 1974. 454 pp.

This is a book with rich information about radio and television's development in each African country. It includes a number of substantive chapters
on international broadcasting, foreign aid in African media, teaching problems,
educational uses of media and research, among others, as well as a lengthly
bibliography at the end of the book.

––– and BECK, L. *The Bibliography of African Broadcasting: An Annotated
Guide.* Philadelphia: Temple Univ., School of Communications and Theater,
1974.

HEAD, S. and GORDON, T. *World Broadcasting: a Statistical Analysis.* Report 6.
Philadelphia: Temple Univ., School of Communications and Theater, April
1975.

HERON, W. and ZIEBARTH, E. "'A preliminary experimental comparison of
radio and classroom lectures." *Speech Monographs,* 13. 1946: 54-57.

HERZOG, W. A., Jr. *The utilization of radio and television for adult education in Brazil.* East Lansing: Michigan State Univ., Department of Communications, 1967.

––– and BRAUN, J. *Radiophonic schools as instruments for diffusion of innovations.* East Lansing: Michigan State Univ., 1975, 15 pp.

HILBRINK, A. and LOHMANN, M. "Are rural radio forums dying in Indonesia?" *Media Asia,* Vol. 1, 3, 1974: 37-40.

A discussion of problems found in Indonesia. The result of the research of a German study team.

HIMMEL, E. and BOHM, M. T. *Proyecto de Evaluación de la Radiovisión Educativa.* Santiago: Univ. de Chile, Instituto de Investigaciones Estadísticas, 1975: 17 pp., Spanish.

HOFFMAN, M. "Mass Communication for Mass Development." *Ceres,* Vol. 5, 1, January-February 1972: pp. 40-43.

Hoffman views the problem of development as one of popularizing as efficiently and rapidly as possible new techniques, and of persuading people to adopt them. He feels that the new communication media should provide the answer but are not doing so. He describes a research project carried out in Upper Volta to test the results of the first nationwide agricultural modernization project using radio, films, posters, pamphlets, and so forth.

HOLEC, H. "Une experience de formation à distance." *Mélanges Pédagogigues du CRAPEL.* 1973. *Direct* II-35.

This articles discusses research in the process of forming professors of living languages. The experiment was multilingual, multinational, and included several media. The experiment was done in the framework of a European project: Centre de Recherches at d'Applications en Langue, le CRAPEL.

HOLMBERG, B. *Distance learning.* London: Kogan Paul, 1977.

HOOPER, R. "Education and the Mass Media." *Educational Development International,* Vol. 2, 2, April 1974. *Direct* VII-116.

This article discusses the technical, economic, and ideological obstacles that restrain the use of mass media in education. It treats specifically the role of radio and television in education and discusses the resistance to change and refusal to accept mass communications in the classroom.

HOWSE, H. R. "A Pioneering Venture in English Teaching." Linguistic Reporter, 17, 2, February 1975: 11-12.

The author reports on six innovative English-language teaching projects for developing nations, including a film series and radio series.

HUDSON, H. "Community use of radio in the Canadian north." In Spain, P., Jamison, D. and McAnany, E. (eds.) *Radio for education and development: Case Studies,* Vol. 2. Washington, D.C.: World Bank, Working Paper 266, 1977.

HUDSON, H. E. and PARKER, E. B. "Medical Communication in Alaska by Satellite." *New England Journal of Medicine,* December 1973.

An experimental communication satellite has been used since later summer of 1971 to provide daily two-way radio contact between native health aides in remote Alaskan communities and a Public Health Service doctor.

––– "Telecommunication Planning for Rural Development." *IEEE Transaction on Communications* 23, 10, October 1975: 1177-1185.

In many parts of the world, basic communication capabilities, such as telephone services and radio and television broadcasting, do not exist. In these areas, development planners are faced with the decision of ordering equipment priorities and determining how to achieve them.

HULSEN, A. L. "Radio Education in Korea." *Educational Broadcasting Review,* 1, 2, December 1967: 43-46.

This article describes efforts in South Korea where instructional radio has been encouraged for all schools.

HUPE, H. "An Education Satellite: Costs and Effects on the Educational System." *Educational Technology,* XIV, 10, October 1974. *Direct* II-28.

HURST, P. "Educational Technology and Innovation in the Third World." *Educational Broadcasting International,* 8, 4, December 1975: 160-165.

INGLE, H. T. *Communication Media and Technology: a look at their role in nonformal education programs.* Washington, D.C.: The Academy for Educational Development, 1974.

The author sketches the state of the art, citing many projects and pointing out the scarcity of hard evaluation data. He provides a wide range in his citations, making this a very usable booklet.

INGUAI, S. *The Application of Radio in Community Education in Ethiopia.* Columbus: Ohio State Univ., Ph.D. dissertation, 1963.

INKELES, A. "The International evaluation of educational achievement." *Proceedings* of the National Academy of Education, 1977: 139-200.

INRAVISION. "Fondo de Capacitación Popular–'INRAVISION'–hacia un modelo de educación a distancia. 1974: 15 pp. *Direct* II-19.

This brochure published by the 'Fondo de Capacitacion Popular' describes an educational program developed to meet the needs of adult education. The proposed model uses radio, television, and correspondence courses as the means for social communication. The presentation covers the philosophy of the project, the means of communication, and the organization of studies for the educational system.

Institute of Adult Education, Dar es Salaam. *Adult Education Handbook.* Tanzania Publishing House, Dar es Salaam, 1971.

The chapter on adult education by radio is a simple guide to Tanzanian extension workers and adult educators on how to make use of radio in their programs.

Instituto de Cultura Popular (INCUPO). *Estudio de Audiencias: Provincias de Santa Fe y Corrientes.* Reconquista: INCUPO, 1973. Spanish. (Abstract–8.)

Instituto de Planejamento Económico Social. *Diagnóstico de Radio Educativa.* Rio de Janeiro, 1973.

Instituto de Radio Difusão Educativa de Bahia (IRDEB). *Difusao Cultural.* Salvador, 1975: 5 pp., Portuguese.

Instituto de Radio Difusão Educativa de Bahia (IRDEB). Salvador, 1975: 13 pp., Portuguese.

The state of the art in Brazil in 1970/1971 is discussed in this document.

International Broadcast Institute. *Programme on cultural heritage; the report of the meeting of the ad hoc group on the cultural heritage project which met in Bali, 13-16 September, 1972.* London, 1972: 17 pp.

This paper discusses the two directions in the wake of the present cultural imbalances. The two directions are 1) to concentrate on the relationship between the modern media and traditional forms of cultural expression; 2) to find out the impact of modern communication media in non-Western societies. It also contains concrete proposals for action.

Internationales Zentralinstitüt für das Jugend- und Bildungs Fernsehen. *Multimedia Systems in Adult Education–12 Projects in 9 Countries.* Munich, 1971.

This book contains a collection of case studies on educational projects in Europe, Japan, and America in some of which radio was linked to printed materials and study groups to form the basis of multimedia teaching systems.

JAIN, N. C. *Some Social-psychological Factors Related to the Effectiveness of Radio Forums.* East Lansing: Michigan States Univ., Department of Communication, 1968.

– – – *An Experimental Investigation of the Effectiveness of Group Listening, Discussion, Decision, Commitment, and Consensus in Indian Radio Forums.* East Lansing, Michigan: Michigan State University, Ph.D. dissertation, 1969a.

– – – "The influence of group radio listening, discussion, decision, and commitment on attitude change in Radio forums." Paper (summarizing a doctoral dissertation) for International Communications Division, Association for Education in Journalism, Berkeley, California, August 22-25, 1969b.

The general finding is that the theoretical concept of radio forums and the predicted role of group discussion, group decision, and public commitment is rather well supported by the data.

JAMISON, D. *The Cost of Instructional Radio in Nicaragua: An Early Assessment.* Revista de Tecnología Educativa, No. 3, Vol. 2, 1976. Organisación de los Estados Americanos.

This paper gives an assessment of what the costs of the Radio Mathematics Project of Nicaragua have been and can be expected to be. The author shows that until now the costs per student have been high but can be lowered by making the programs available to a larger audience.

– – – *Cost factors in planning educational technology systems.* Paris: UNESCO International Institute for Educational Planning, Fundamentals of Educational Planning Series, No. 24, 1977. (Available in English and French.)

This booklet summarizes the rationale for using educational media in low-income countries and presents evidence on their cost. A technical appendix describes methods for cost analysis.

JAMISON, D. "Radio education and student repetition in Nicaragua." Washington, D.C.: The World Bank, mimeographed. 1977.

This paper examines the impact of the Nicaragua Radio Mathematics Project on the propensity of students to repeat grades; it concludes that, because of the radio's effect on increasing student achievement, students exposed to radio are less likely to fail.

――― and KIM, Y. T. "The Cost of Instructional Radio and Television in Korea." In Bates, T. and Robinson, J. (eds.) *Evaluating Educational Television and Radio.* Proceedings of the International Conference on Evaluation and Research in Television and Radio, The Open University, United Kingdom, 70-versity, United Kingdom, 70-78, April 1976.

The authors discuss the cost of educational television and radio within the Korean Education Reform at a time when the first phase of activities—initial planning for and try outs of the new instructional approaches—is nearing completion and the second phase—demonstration of the project in 45 schools—is about to begin.

JAMISON, D., KLEES, S., and WELLS, S. *The costs of educational media: Guidelines for planning and evaluation.* Beverly Hills and London: Sage Publications, 1978.

This book describes the methodology for undertaking cost analyses of projects, with particular emphasis on projects involving instructional radio and television. It then presents nine cost-analysis case studies and summarizes findings concerning the cost of educational media.

JAMISON, D. and LESLIE, J. "Planning radio's use for formal education: Methodology and application to Indonesia." In Spain, P., Jamison, D. and McAnany, E. (eds.) *Radio for education and development: Case studies,* Vol. 1. Washington, D.C.: World Bank, Working Paper 266, 1977.

JAMISON, D., SUPPES, P., and WELLS, S. "The Effectiveness of Alternative Instructional Media: A Survey." *Review of Educational Research,* 44, 1.

This paper surveys available literature on the effectiveness of variants of traditional education methods, of instructional radio and television, and of computer-assisted and computer-managed instruction.

JAYAWEERA, N. *Radio listening and readership.* Sri Lanka Centre for Development Studies. Lectures of Sinhala translation programme, Marga Library Readership Survey. Colombo, 1973.

JEFFREY, P. "Research into the effectiveness of a radio and loudspeaker comgination for schools in Papua, New Guinea." Papua, New Guinea: Univ. of Papua, Teaching Methods and Materials Centre, 1972: 15 pp.

JENGO, E. "Educational Technology: Its Place in the Process of Lifelong Education in Tanzania." *Programmed Learning and Educational Technology,* 12, 1975: 270-273.

JHA, P. N. and KATIYAR, S. K. "Radio Listening Behavior and Preferences of Farmers—A Panoramic Analysis." *Indian Journal of Adult Education,* 35, 12, December 1974: 101-105.

JIMENEZ ACOSTA, L. *Diálogos con los líderes.* Bogotá, ACPO, April 1974.

KAPOOCZ, S. "Part-time higher education using radio—an example from the Federal Republic of Germany." In MacKenzie, N., Postgate, R., and Stephen, J. (eds.) *Open learning.* Paris: The UNESCO Press, 1975, pp. 163-181.

KASSAM, Y. O. "Towards Mass Adult Education in Tanzania: The Rationale for Radio Study Group Campaigns." *Literacy Discussion,* 6, 1, Spring 1975: 79-94.

This article examines the suitability and effectiveness of radio study-group campaigns. Ideological and pedagogical rationales, educational impact, coordination of resources, cost, and success with illiteracy are discussed.

KEDI. *Development of the air and correspondence high school in Korea.* Seoul: Korean Educational Development Institute (KEDI), 1976.

KHAN, A. *Functional relevance of local and central radio broadcasts of agricultural information in India.* Unpublished Ph.D. dissertation, Univ. of Wisconsin, 1972.

KIMMEL, P., KIES, N., and LYLE, J. *ITV and education of children: Cross-cultural comparisons of international uses of media.* Washington: The American Univ., January 1971.

KINCAID, R. T. "Some Application of Television and Radio to the Teaching of English as a Second Language in Northern Nigeria." Washington, D.C.: Agency for International Development, November 1, 1967.

The author presents a description of activities, accomplishments, host-government contributions, problems, and recommendations made concerning two-year project in which television and radio were used as media for teaching English as a second language in Northern Nigeria. He also used teachers' notes and guides, weekly time tables, and visual aids. There is an emphasis on pupil participation in this project.

KINROSS, F. "An experiment in teaching English by radio in primary schools in Ghana." *Teacher Education,* 3, 1961: 36-43.

Radio was found successful in this limited experiment.

KINYANJUI, P. "Radio correspondence courses in Kenya: an evaluation." *Educational Broadcasting International,* 6, 4, December 1973: 180-187.

An earlier version of the material by Mr. Kinyanjui is expanded and updated in this volume.

– – – "Training teachers by correspondence." *IEC Broadsheets on distance learning, No. 5.* Cambridge, England: International Extension College, 1974.

– – – "In-service training of teachers through radio and correspondence in Kenya." In Spain, P., Jamison, D., and McAnany, E. (eds.) *Radio for education and development: Case studies,* Vol. 1. Washington, D.C.: World Bank, Working Paper 266, 1977.

KIYLIN, J. E., et al. "Communication in India: Experiments in Introducing Change." Also available from: The Department of Communication, Michigan State Univ., East Lansing, 48823. May 1968: 61 pp.

KLAVER, F. "Communication-Satellites and International Copyright." *Gazette,* XXI, 3, 1975: 125-135.

The article contains a discussion of the political background for the international disagreement on the control of direct broadcast satellites.

KLEES, S. "The Costs of Radioprimaria" in P. L. Spain, *A Report on the System of Radioprimaria in the State of San Luís Potosí, Mexico.* Stanford, California: Stanford Univ. Institute for Communication Research, 1973.

This short chapter compares the costs of traditional direct teaching with radio and concludes that the Radioprimaria system costs less per student than traditional teaching systems.

— —*"Instructional technology and its relationship to quality and equality in education in a developing nation: A case study of instructional television in Mexico."* Stanford, California: Unpublished dissertation, Stanford Univ., 1974.

— — and JAMISON, D. *"A cost analysis of instructional television in the Ivory Coast."* Washington, D.C.: Academy for Educational Development. Unpublished paper, 1976.

KLONGAN, G. "Radio Listening Groups in Malawi, Africa." Ames: Iowa State Univ., Rural Sociology Department, Report 70, 1967.

KRAWCEWICZ, S. *The Radio-Television University for teachers in Poland.* Warsaw, Poland: The Radio-Television Univ., Institute of Teachers' Education, 1976.

KREIMER, O. (ed.) "Sistemas de radio educación: prioridades de investigación y de desarrollo de metologías." *Revista del Centro de Estudios Educativos.* Mexico, D.F. Second quarter 1975.

This article is a resume of the proposals drafted by directors, researchers, and evaluators of radio education systems in Latin America at the Oaxtepec Seminar held February 17-21, 1975. The recommendations refer to evaluation priorities for radio education systems in the following areas: ties with the national system of development; social impact and effects of change; institutional analysis; content of the educational messages; the functioning process of radio schools; and audience participation.

— — "Interactive radio for health care and education in Alaska." In Spain, P., Jamison, D., and McAnany, E. (eds.) *Radio for education and development: Case studies,* Vol. 2. Washington, D.C.: World Bank, Working Paper 266, 1977.

KRISHNAYYA, J. G. "Regional radio service for rural development." In *Electronics—Information and planning.* New Delhi: Government of India, Department India, Department of Electronics (IPAG), 1976.

KRIVAL, A. *Project Report: Radio/Correspondence Education Project No. 615-11-650-129, USAID/UWEX.* Univ. of Wisconsin, October 1970.

— — , et al. *Project Report: radio/correspondence education project. No. 615-11-650-129, USAID/UWEX* (Kenya). Part I: Administration (Krival); Part II: Evaluation (Thiede). Madison: Univ. of Wisconsin, Extension Division, 1970-1971.

The American chief of party reports on the Kenya radio correspondence project.

LAIDLAW, B. and LAYARD, R. "Traditional versus Open University teaching methods: A cost comparison." *Higher Education,* 3, 1974: 439-474.

LEE, T. C. "A survey of radio audiences in Taiwan." *National Chengchi University Graduate School Journal of Mass Communication Research,* 11, 1973: 227-294, Chinese.

This 1970 survey of radio audiences in Taiwan contains data such as the number of radio-receiving sets, listening habits, listeners' options of radio programs, and radio commercials. The effects of television on radio listeners and the credibility of radio news are also examined together with listeners' suggestions on the improvement of the broadcasting service.

LEFRANC, R. *European university and post-university distance study systems.* Strasbourg, Council of Europe, 1977.

LENT, J. A. *Philippine Mass Communications Bibliography.* Dumaguete City: Silliman Univ. Press, 1966, 110 pp.

——— "Philippine Radio–History and Problems," *Asian Studies* (Philippines), April 1968: 37-52.

——— "Influences of Transistor Radio in the Philippines," *EBU Review.* May 1968: 39-40.

——— "Philippine Media and Nation-Building: an overview," *Gazette,* XVI, 1, 1970: 2-12.

——— "Mass Media in the Netherlands Antilles," *Gazette,* XVII, 1/2, 1971: 51-73.

——— *Philippine Mass Communications: Before 1811: After 1966.* Manila: Philippine Press Institute, 1971.

——— "Commonwealth Caribbean Mass Media: History and Development." *Gazette,* XX, 3, 1974: 170-179.

——— "Malaysia's Guided Media," *Index on Censorship,* Winter 1974: 65-74.

——— "Cultural Confusion and Media Infusion Leave Few Options for the Commonwealth Caribbean," *Journal of Communication,* Spring 1975: 114-117.

——— *Asian Mass Communications: A Comprehensive Bibliography.* Philadelphia: Temple Univ., School of Communications and Theater, 1975: 708 pp.

   This is the most complete list of sources on Asian mass communications: over 15,000 items. It includes numerous citations on mass media and development, radio, and educational broadcasting.

——— "Asian Mass Communication: Selected Information Sources." *Journal of Broadcasting,* 19, 3, 1975: 321-340.

   The material in this article is drawn from the volume *Asian Mass Communication,* also cited here.

——— *Broadcasting in Asia and the Pacific.* Philadelphia: Temple Univ. Press, forthcoming.

   This book contains thirty-four chapters covering broadcasting in most Asian nations including one chapter on educational television in Asia.

LESLIE, J. *"Instructional Radio for Developing Countries."* Unpublished paper. Stanford, California: Stanford Univ., Institute for Mathematical Studies in the Social Sciences, 1971.

   The paper summarizes a number of cases where radio has been used for school instruction and makes suggestions for future use.

——— "Mass media and nutrition education." Palo Alto, California: EDUTEL, Inc., 1977.

LEWIS, H. "Communication barriers between educated and uneducated persons." *Literacy Work,* 3, 4, April 1974: 29-38.

Literacy Work, 4, 1975: 1-28. "Literacy from the Sky."

   This article is a brief review of the uses of the ATS-F satellite and the part it could play over Asia for literacy education, beginning with India's SITE project. A bibliography is included.

LIU, A.P.L. *Radio broadcasting in Communist China.* Cambridge: Massachusetts Institute of Technology, Center for International Studies, 1964.

LOWRY, D. "Radio, TV, and Literacy in Mexico." *Journal of Broadcasting,* XIV, 2, Spring 1970: pp. 239 ff.

   The author describes Mexico's literacy project, with some results indicating gains made.

LOZANO JIMENEZ, B., et al. "Experimentacion de la cartilla de alfabetizacion radiofonica para adultos." Mexico, D.F., Laboratorio de Pedagogia, Instituto Nacional de Pedagogia, 1966.

LUMLEY, F. "Rates of speech in radio speaking." *Quarterly Journal of Speech,* 1933.

LUMSDEN, K. and RITCHIE, C. "The Open University: A survey of economic analysis." *Instructional Science,* 4, 1975.

LUNDGREN, R. "Grandes questions et avenir de la radio-diffusion éducatif." *Revue de L'U.E.R.,* No. 5, September 1973. *Direct* I-9.

   This article describes problems to be considered in developing educational broadcasts: the collaboration between educational radio-broadcasting and the world of education, the cost of educational radio-broadcasting, problems involved in introducing new procedures.

McANANY, E. G. "Radio Clubs of Niger: September 1972." Stanford Univ.: Institute for Communication Research, 1972.

   This brief report on the radio clubs was written after the author visited them in 1972.

--- "Radio Clubs of Dahomey: September 1972." Stanford Univ.: Institute for Communication Research, 1972.

--- *Radio's role in development: five strategies for use.* Washington, D.C.: Information Center on Instructional Technology, Information Bulletin No. 4, 1973, 28 pp.

   This booklet focuses on radio in the rural setting of developing countries where it seems to have the greatest potential for aiding human growth and development. The review arranges projects into five types of uses for radio: open broadcasting, instructional radio, radio farm forums, radio schools, and animation.

--- "African Rural Development and Communication: Five Radio-based Projects." *Rural Africana: Current Research in the Social Sciences.* Spring 1975.

McLEISH, R.W.M. "Some Notes on Public Service Radio in a Developing Country." *World Development,* Vol. 2, 2, February 1974: pp. 57-59.

   The author discusses the ways in which the government can foster trust between the government, the broadcasters, and the listeners. The advantages and disadvantages of various methods of financing broadcasting are also discussed, as is the question of program control.

MacKAY, I. K. "Dual broadcasting in Papua New Guinea." *Combroad,* 20, July-September 1973: 27-31.

   The author gives an outline of the problems encountered in setting up the broadcasting service in Papua, New Guinea as well as an account of the development of the two broadcasting services, the New Guinea Service of the Australian Commission and the Government Broadcasting Service.

––– "Broadcasting in Papua New Guinea." *ABU Newsletter,* 102, March 1974: 5-7.

This article outlines the policy, legislation, and programming plans of the newly established National Broadcasting Commission in Papua, New Guinea.

MacKENZIE, N., POSTGATE, R., and SCUPHAM, J. *Open learning: Systems and problems in post-secondary education.* Paris: UNESCO Press, 1975.

MACKEN, E., VAN DEN HEUVEL, R., SUPPES, P., and SUPPES, T. *Home-based education.* Washington, D.C.: The National Institute of Education, U.S. Department of Health, Education and Welfare, April 1976.

MACKIE, W. E. *Radio Broadcasting in Malawi: A Search for Identity and Service.* Columbia: Univ. of Missouri, 1971.

MADDEN, R. "Educational Radio Bibliography," *Educational Broadcasting Review,* 5, October 1968: 66-79.

This broadly based bibliography, without annotations, contains a topical index which lists forty-nine entries on educational radio in foreign countries.

MADDISON, J. *Radio and Television in Literacy: a survey of the use of the broadcasting media in combating illiteracy among adults.* Paris: UNESCO, Reports and Papers on Mass Communication, 62, 1971: 82 pp.

This study is based on data compiled through a questionnaire survey conducted by UNESCO in 1969 covering forty nations supplemented by information from other published sources. The study includes a brief country summary of the use of radio and television in adult literacy work, followed by an analysis of the world situation, recommendations for future development, and the questionnaire that was sent out.

MANDULEY, J. C. "Teacher Utilization of Instructional Radio–Part I." *Educational Broadcasting,* March/April 1976: 41-46.

––– "Teacher Utilization of Instructional Radio–Part I." Educational Broadcasting, May/June 1976: 25-27.

Manoff International, Inc. *Mass media and nutrition education.* Progress report. Contract AID/TA-C-1133. September 1975.

MANSFIELD, N. "School Broadcasting in Teaching English as a Second Language." *Educational Broadcasting International,* 5, December 1971: 265-268.

The author cites suitable and unsuitable items for radio teaching based on experience in Fiji.

MARATHEY, R. *Togo: Radio Educative.* Paris: UNESCO, April 1965.

MARQUEZ, F. T. "The Relationship of Advertising and Culture in the Philippines." *Journalism Quarterly,* 52, 3, 1975: 436-442.

This study of print media finds that advertisements reflect Western rather than indigenous culture.

MARSTEN, R. B. and ROGERS, D. P. "ATS Alaska Telemedicine Experiment," in *Telecommunications Research in the United States and Selected Foreign Countries: a Preliminary Survey,* Vol. 2. National Technical Information Service, U.S. Department of Commerce: Springfield, Virginia, 1973.

This document briefly describes the Alaska project where radio linked rural native health aides to doctors. It contains technical information on the equipment involved.

MARTIN, P.E.G. *Jamaica: educational broadcasting.* Paris: UNESCO, 1972, 25 pp. (Serial no. 2586/RMD.RD.MC.)

MARTING, B. and DE CASTILO, M. *Evaluación de los Dirigentes-Institutos Campesinos de Acción Cultural Popular,* ACPO. Bogotá, Colombia, 1974.

MATHUR, J. C. and NEURATH, P. *An Indian experiment in farm radio forums.* Paris: UNESCO, 1959.

This document contains a good description of the early Indian experience showing the possibilities of media that have organizational support.

MATIKO, J.M.M. "Communication Policy and Planning for Education and Development: The Tanzania Radio Campaigns." Paper presented at the Conference on Communication Policy and Planning for Education and Development. Stanford Univ., July 11-15, 1976.

The Tanzania Radio Campaigns are described within the context of Tanzania's approach to Education for Self-Reliance. The author begins by looking at the history, planning, and implementation (including problems) and evaluation of the campaigns. He concludes by describing one recent campaign—the "Food is Life" campaign.

Mauritius, Ministry of Education and Cultural Affairs. *Report on Educational Developments, 1971-1973.* Port Louis: 1973, 5 p., English.

MAYO, J., HERM, L., HORNIK, R., JAMISON, D., SAHDEVE, N., and SMEE, M. *Development radio for Nepal: Report of the radio feasibility study team.* February 1975.

MAYO, J., HORNIK, R., and McANANY, E. *Education with television: The El Salvador experience.* Stanford, California: Stanford Univ. Press, 1976.

MAYO, J., McANANY, E., and KLEES, S. "The Mexican telesecundaria: A cost-effectiveness analysis." *Instructional Science,* 4, October 1975: 193-236.

MAYO, J. and MAYO, J. *An administrative history of El Salvador's educational reform.* Stanford: Institute for Communication Research, Stanford Univ., November 1971.

MEDARD, B. "Teaching French by Radio." *South Pacific Bulletin,* April 1962: 28-30.

MEENE, J. W., KLINGENSCHMIDT, J. E., and NORD, D. L. "The feasibility of using taped lectures to replace class attendance." Paper presented at the American Educational Research Association meeting, Los Angeles, 1969.

MERINO UTRERAS, J. "La investigación científica de la comunicación en America Latina." *Chasqui* (Ecuador), 1974: 81-103.

MEYER, G. "Science by Radio and Television in a developing country—Mauritius: a Case Study." Australian *Science Teachers Journal,* August 1970: 21-27.

MEYER, R. "Educational Broadcasting in Thailand: A Microcosm of Asia." *Educational Broadcasting Review,* 5, February 1971: 30-34.

This survey of the Asian scene—with Thailand as the main focus—calls for more external aid for Asian educational broadcasting.

MILLS, A. "Radiovision in the Central African Republic."

"Rural Radio in Upper Volta."

"Senegal: Radio Dissoo."

Unpublished reports. Stanford Univ.: Institute for Communication Reresarch, 1972.

These publications are based on visits to projects in Central and West Africa.

MITCHELL, J. L. and KIM, J. H. "Sociological survey: Korea; a survey of mass communication in Korea 1968." Seoul: Sogang College, Department of Mass Communication, 1968, 352 pp.

The authors report on the status of the mass media in South Korea including print and electronic media and commercial advertising based on a survey. They also discuss the nature and the interest of the radio listening audience, mass communications activities at educational institutions, and evaluation. The report also contains a summary and conclusions, sources and bibliography.

MONTEIRO, H. *Research in Agricultural Communications in Brazil: Descriptive Report of Selected Studies.* MS dissertation, Univ. of Wisconsin, 1972.

Movimiento de Educación de Base, Rio de Janeiro. *MEB: Relatorio Anual.* Rio de Janeiro, 1972.

MUELANZAMBI, B. "Quelques problèmes des émissions de Radio TV Scolaire au Zaire." *Interstages,* 102, 1975.

This study of educational media in Zaire gives particular emphasis to its problems in expansion.

MUJAHID, S. A. "Mass Media in Pakistan (1947-1971)," in *Conference on Communication Research Needs: Urbanization and Communication.* Honolulu: East-West Center, 1973.

This article discusses the history, development, and problems of the press and broadcasting media in Pakistan. It contains a section on the electronic media, which traces the development of the television service in Pakistan, giving an outline of its objectives, coverage, programming, and problems. It also discusses the development of radio in West and East Pakistan (now Bangladesh), the disparity of broadcasting facilities and service in the two territories, as well as the various radio networks, audience, programming, finance, governmental pressures, and influence on the media. It concludes with an examination of Radio Pakistan in its role in nation building.

MUSTO, S. *Escuelas radiofónicas. Modernisación, innovatividad, y grado de desarrollo regional.* Bogotá, Acción Cultural Popular. Departamento de Sociología. Documento de Trabajo, no. 11. 1970: 32 pp.

――― *Communication Media for Rural Development. The Colombia Model Radio Sutatenza.* Bogotá: Acción Cultural Popular (ACPO), conclusions of some studies on the effectiveness of the radiophonic schools of Acción Cultural Popular, working document 20, 1972: pp. 19-59, English.

――― et al. *Los Medios de Communicación Social al Servicio del Desarrollo: Análisis de Eficiencia de "Acción Cultural Popular"–Radio Sutatenza, Colombia.* Bogotá: Acción Cultural Popular, June 1971.

This is a Spanish translation of a critical report on ACPO published in German in 1969. The present version includes in the text (though set off in bold face) ACPO's responses to the criticisms. Based on a German team's evaluation of ACPO.

National Iranian Radio-television. Teheran, NIRT Publication Department, 1972.

This report includes information on the coverage of NIRT, the findings of its audience research, rural TV clubs in Iran, and the NIRT news agency. It also gives information on various institutions affiliated to NIRT, e.g., the Institute for Cinema and TV, which is a training center for TV broadcasting, the Theater Workshop, the Music Workshop, and the Centre for the Presentation and Propagation of Traditional Music. Articles of the 1971 legislation which established the National Iranian Radio and TV Organization are included.

NEURATH, P. M. "Radio Farm Forums as a Tool of Change in Indian Villages," *Economic Development and Cultural Change,* 10, 1962: 275-283.

This article describes a field experiment, comparing the knowledge increase among peasants who lived in (a) villages in which radio forums were established, (b) those in which radios were present, but no forums, or (c) those with neither radio nor forums. Forum villages had much greater gain in knowledge than the others.

NHK. *The effects of educational radio music classroom.* Tokyo: NHK Radio and TV Culture Research Institute, 1956a.

––– *The listening effect of radio English classroom.* Tokyo: NHK Radio-Culture Research Institute, 1956b.

––– *World Radio and TV 1977.* Tokyo: NHK Radio and TV Culture Research Institute, 1977.

NICHOLS, J. C. "Aspects de la Radiodiffusion Directe par Satellite." *Revue de L'U.E.R.,* Vol. XXV, 3, May 1974. *Direct* VII-110.

This article analyzes the potential advantages of direct radio broadcasting via satellite, with one of the most interesting applications being in education. It describes the various satellite projects in different countries and discusses the international exchange of programs and free access to satellites.

NICOL, J., SHEA, A., SIMMINS, G., and SIM, F. (ed.) *Canada's Farm Radio Forum.* Paris: UNESCO, 1954.

Canada originated farm forums, and also first showed the benefits of organized radio-listening. This is one of the earliest reports on those forums.

NIEMI, J. and BLUNT, A. "The Raven Brings Tidings." *Educational Technology International,* 4, April 1971: 15-17.

This article describes developmental radio among the Indians of British Columbia.

NIÑO, A. J. *Evaluación de la Operación Antioquia de Acción Cultural Popular.* Bogotá: ACPO, May 1968.

NISHIMOTO, M. *Modernization of education and educational broadcasting.* Tokyo: NHK Publications Association, 1966, 324 pp., Japanese.

This is a study of the role and profile of the teacher in the electronic media age. It describes also the history of educational broadcasting in Japan as well as the correspondence education through radio and TV. Comparative studies are done on Japanese educational broadcasting and that of other countries. It includes a discussion of how the broadcasting media should contribute to the development of education in this rapidly changing era of science and technology.

––– *The Development of Educational Broadcasting in Japan.* Rutland, Vermont: Charles E. Tuttle, 1969, 287 pp.

NOORANI, H. *Hello TV! goodbye radio? (Wanted: A Mass Media Policy for India).* Bombay, 1973: 5 pp.

This paper discussed the possibilities of the elimination of the most available mass medium—radio—in India due to the introduction of rural television via satellite. The problems (e.g., cost of software, rural infrastructure for TV) of making TV effective are also discussed.

NORDENSTRENG, K., NURMINEN, A., and SUHONEN, P. *Methods of Studying the Size and Composition of Radio and Television Audience: A Comparison.* Stanford Univ.: Institute for Communication Research, 1969, 22 pp., English. (Author File. RECORD No. 44.)

NORDICOM. Bibliography of Works on Mass Communication Published by Scandinavian Scholars in English. Published in March 1975 by NORDICOM, the Nordic Documentation Center for Mass Communication Research, P.O. Box 607, Univ. of Tampere, SF-33101, Tampere 10, Finland.

This document includes data on research and researchers from all the Scandinavian countries.

Oficina de Servicios para América Latina (OSAL). *Las Escuelas Radiofónicas en América Latina: El Seminario de Directores de Escuelas Radiofónicas de América Latina.* Bogotá, Colombia: OSAL, 1972.

This is a summary of activities of many Latin American radio schools submitted at a conference in 1972. Original OSAL group has been superseded by ALER (Asociación Latinoamericano de Escuelas Radiofónicas) but summary information is best available until ALER issues an updated version.

OHLIGER, J. *Listening Groups: Mass Media in Adult Education.* Centre for the Study of Liberal Education for Adults: Boston, 1967.

This is a somewhat pessimistic account of the impermanence of organized group listening to radio series, mainly in North America.

OLIVIERA, J. "ETV Maranhao: An effective case of endogenous growth." In Bates, T. and Robinson, J. (eds.), *Evaluating Educational Television and Radio.* Milton Keynes, England: The Open Univ. Press, 1977, pp. 249-254.

ORLIK, P. B. "South African Radio." *Educational Broadcasting Review,* 3, 4, August 1969: 36-44.

OSAL (Oficina de Servicios para América Latina). *Las escuelas radiofónicas en América Latina.* Bogotá, Colombia: OSAL, 1972.

OXENHAM, J. *Non-formal education approaches to teaching literacy.* Michigan State Univ. Program of Studies in Nonformal Education, Supplementary Paper No. 2, 1975. East Lansing: MSU Institute for International Studies in Education, 1975.

PARKER, E. *Utilization of Satellite Radio for Medical Communication.* Stanford, California: Stanford Univ., Institute for Communication Research, December 1972.

––– and LUSIGNAN, B. "Technical and economic considerations in planning radio services." In Spain, P., Jamison, D., and McAnany, E. (eds.) *Radio for education and development: Case studies,* Vol. 2. Washington, D.C.: World Bank, Working Paper 266, 1977.

PARKER, L. A. "Educational Telephone Network and Subsidiary Communications Authorization: Educational Media for Continuing Education in Wisconsin." *Educational Technology,* Vol. XIV, 2, February 1974. *Direct* V-71.

This article shows the use of radio and telephone for continuing education established at the University of Wisconsin in 1965. It describes the configuration of the system, the program contents, the project function, and an evaluation of the project.

PICKSTOCK, M. "Radiodiffusion rurale–puissance de l'éducation." *Forum Development,* No. 11, June 1974. *Direct* VII-108.

Can education counterbalance the disastrous effect of a too rapid demographic growth? Can the use of mass media, especially radio, solve the problems in education? These questions are discussed in this article, which deals with rural broadcasting in particular. It cites reasons for radio broadcasting being rejected and underestimated by governments. Effectiveness depends on the quality of the people involved in the production of programs as well as the planning and definition of objectives.

––– "Why the rural audiences often stay out of reach." *Media Asia,* 1, 7, July 1974: 19.

POLCYN, K. A. *An Educator's Guide to Communication Satellite Technology.* Washington, D.C.: Academy for Educational Development, September 1973, 99 pp.

This guide deals with the general nature, the basic economics, the evolution and development of communication satellites from Echo I to Intelsat IV. It also covers the present and future satellite educational experimentation which includes a discussion of the Indian experiment in the use of satellite broadcasting for educational purposes. Appended are a bibliography and a glossary of abbreviations.

POPHAM, J. "Tape recorded lectures in the college–II." *Audio-Visual Communication Review,* 10, 1962: 94-102.

PRIMROSE, V. "*Study of the Effectiveness of the Educational Programs of the Radiophonic Schools of Sutatenza on the Life of the Colombian Peasant Farmer.*"St. Louis: St. Louis Univ., unpublished Ph.D. thesis, 1965.

The recommendations offered at the completion of this research for the further development of Radio Sutatenza and its effectiveness are: (1) a wider distribution of cheap radios; (2) literary materials written on the level of the students;, (3) updating of pedagogical techniques for a mass communication program; (4) better testing techniques; (5) more lay leaders to direct the schools; (6) a social-scientific study of the people in the different areas.

QUEBRAL, Nora C. *Development communication: Status and trends, the time is now.* SEARCA Monograph Series No. 1. Philippines, 1976: 23 pp.

––– , and GOMEZ, Ely D. *Development communication primer.* Laguna, Philippines: University of the Philippines at los Baños, College, 1977: 14 pp.

RACHMADI, F. "Communication in rural community." *Communicator,* 10, 5, July 1974: 35-36.

Radio Nepal. *Report on the radio listener analysis survey.* Kathmandu, Radio Nepal, 1969: 8 pp.

This document is the report and conclusions of a survey to provide background information on the radio listening habits of Nepalese and to "permit experimentation with survey techniques as an adjunct to programme operations."

Radio Nepal. *Programme schedule.* Kathmandu, Department of Broadcasting, 1973: 4 pp.

This document contains background historical notes on Radio Nepal, and an outline of its broadcasting times, frequencies, and program content.

Radio Santa María. *La Experiencia Radio Santa María.* La Vega, 1975: 39 pp., Spanish.

Radio Talivishen Malaysia. Kuala Lampur, Ministry of Information and Culture, 1970: 76 pp., Malay/English.

Illustrated information brochures on radio and TV in Malaysia give an outline of its history and development in West Malaysia, Sarawak, and Sabah. They deal also with the program content, coverage, transmission stations, rural broadcasting service, engineering facilities, earth satellite station, news division, design, and staging service of TV Malaysia.

Radio Television Singapore. *Television Singapore—Tenth Anniversary 1963-73.* Singapore, 1973.

RAL, L. D. *Mass Communication: its progress and plan in Nepal.* Kathmandu, 1971: 8 pp.

The author stresses the need for setting up a communication ministry in Nepal for better utilization of the media in national development. The proposed ministry should encompass all aspects of mass media including telecommunications, postal services, as well as other semigovernment corporations.

RAMIREZ PARDO, F. *El determinante comercial en la programación de radionovela de Radio Sutatenza.* Thesis (Licenciado en Comunicación Social), Bogotá: Pontificia Univ. Javeriana. Facultad de Comunicación Social, 1975.

RAMOS FALCONI, R. "Medios de comunicación de masas; mito y realidad." *Textual* (Peru), No. 8. 1973: 67-69.

RATANAMUNGALA, B. *Instructional Radio: A Decade of Thai Experience.* Bangkok: Ministry of Education, 1972.

RATHJENS, G. W. "Comments on expanding radio and television broadcasting services in Ethiopia." In Butman, R., Rathjens, G., and Warren, C., *Technical-economic considerations in public service broadcast communications for developing countries.* Washington, D.C.: Academy for Educational Development, 1973.

RATHJENS, G. W., BUTMAN, R., and RAMESH, V. *Radio Broadcasting and Telecommunications in Nepal.* Massachusetts Institute of Technology: Center for International Studies, January 1975: 24 pp.

This discussion of problems and possibilities in the case of Nepal considers three aspects: radio broadcast services, radio for education in school, and two-way telecommunications. The authors also project some alternate courses of development and their costs.

RESTREPO, M. *Evaluación curso progresivo, primera parte.* Bogotá: ACPO, February 1973.

——— and DE CASTILLO, L. M. *Evaluación curso progresivo, segunda parte.* Bogotá: ACPO, June 1974.

RHOADS, W. G. and PIPER, A. C. *Use of radiophonic teaching in fundamental education.* The Roper Public Opinion Research Center, Williams Cooperative Research Project, No. 1648, 1963.

Early efforts in El Salvador and Honduras are described. It is a useful perspective.

RIBIERO, O. and DIAZ BORDANAVE, J. *Estudio comparativo de la radio y su combinación con discusión de grupo y recursos visuales en el aprendizaje de una práctica agricola.* In Seminario Nacional de Radiodifusión Rural, 10, Bogotá, 29 de Noviembre al 11 de Diciembre de 1971. Informe preliminar. Bogotá, FAO–Ministerio de Agricultura, 1971: 17 pp. (Documento C-22).

RIITHO, V. "Radio in Family Planning in Africa." *Educational Broadcasting International,* 4, 4, December 1971: 243-245.

The author sees radio to be useful for distribution of family-planning information, but has no data on the actual effects of radio for this purpose in Kenya.

ROBOCK, L. I. *Radio reception and listening habits in six provinces of Northeast Thailand: a report.* Bangkok: United States Information Service, 1964: 115 pp.

This 1964 study of medium-wave broadcasting conditions in six provinces in Northeast Thailand was conducted to determine the importance of radio as a psychological weapon in these provinces considered most vulnerable to subversion and infiltration. The study was conducted to obtain information on the listening habits of the villagers, their likes and dislikes, and to assess the strength of the Communist radio signals and the popularity of their programs with local population.

ROBSON, J. S. "Radio in Education." *Programmed Learning and Educational Technology,* Vol. 11, 5, September 1974. *Direct* I-1.

Based on the example of the BBC, the article reviewed presents the role of radio broadcasting as an integral part of the educational system. The 'system' includes all schools, adult education centers, and teacher education. The last part of the study points out problems to be resolved to allow full use of educational radio.

ROBSÓN, M. J. "Question time: a radio science series for African primary schools evaluated." Educational Broadcasting International, 6, 1, March 1973: 10-16.

The article illustrates a teaching method, used with radio, to elicit greater student response.

ROGERS, E. and SHOEMAKER, 'F. *Communication of innovations: A cross-cultural approach.* New York: Free Press, 1971.

ROGERS, E., BROWN, J., and VERMILION, M. "Radio forums: A strategy for rural development." In Spain, P., Jamison, D., and McAnany, E. (eds.) *Radio for education and development: Case studies,* Vol. 2. Washington, D.C.: World Bank, Working Paper 266, 1977.

ROGERS, E. and SOLOMON, D. *Radio Forums for Development.* East Lansing: Michigan State Univ., Department of Communication, June 1972.

ROLING, N. *Knowledge brokerage for increasing the relevance of agricultural research to African small holders.* Paper presented at the Second General Conference of AAASA, Dakar, March 1975.

ROQUETTE PINTO, E. *Seixon Rolados.* Rio de Janeiro, 1927.
This early vision of the potentialities of the utilization of educational radio in Brazil is a plea for action.

ROY, F. B., WAISANEN, E., and ROGERS, E. *The impact of communication on rural development: an investigation in Costa Rica and India.* Paris: UNESCO, 1969.

ROZSA, G. "The Great Illusion." *CERES,* 8, 1975: 35-38.
The author describes pitfalls which developing nations must avoid in the creation of an information system.

RUIZ, A. A. "Radio ECCA–A Spanish Contribution to Educational Broadcasting." *EBU Review,* 25, 1974: 22-24.
This is a description of educational radio on the Canary Islands.

Rundfunk and Fernseh Consulting. "Rural Radio in Indonesia: Investigations into Possibilities for Expansion." *Africa Asian Bureau,* Cologne, 1974.
The article recommends a national system of rural forums with more than agricultural content only.

RYAN, J. W. "Problems of Recruitment in Literacy and Adult Education Programmes." *Literacy Work,* 4, 1975: 59-65.
A University of Massachusetts program, "Model to Recruit Illiterate Adults to Adult Basic Education Programmes," is described, with the potential and requirements of radio and television publicity examined. Fundamental problems involved with the stigma of illiteracy are discussed as they are experienced in the United States and in developing countries.

SALGADO, A. *A radiodifusao educativa no Brasil.* Rio de Janeiro, 1946.
This is a plea for the utilization of radio as a factor of development.

SCHENKEL, P. *La estructura del poder de los medios de comunicación en cinco países latinoamericanos.* Santiago de Chile: Instituto Latinoamericano de Investigaciones Sociales, 1973, 104 pp. (ILDIS, Estudios y Documentos, no. 21).

SCHILLER, H. "The Appearance of National Communication Policies: A New Arena for Social Struggle," *Gazette,* XXI, 2, 1975: 65-81.
In the major industrialized capitalist nations of Western Europe, in North America and Japan, a new element has entered the worker-capitalist confrontation. The thorough utilization by the dominating class of an enormously expanded and totally penetrative informational apparatus has been experienced in full measure in recent decades.

SCHMELKES, S. *Estudio de Evaluación Aproximativa de las Escuelas Radiofónicas de la Tarahumara.* Mexico: Revista del Centro de Estudios Educativos, Vol. 2, 2, 1972: 11-36, Spanish.

SCHMUECKER, M. *Feedback techniques at educational television service.* Bangkok Municipality, Bangkok ETV Project, 1972: 7 pp.

This article discusses the feedback techniques in the light of the past efforts, the developments that followed, and the present approach. It contains also the summary of these techniques and the background information on the Educational Television Service, Bangkok municipality.

SCHNITMAN, J. "Communication, mobilization, and development." Stanford: Institute for Communication Research, STanford Univ., 1976.

SCHRAMM, W. *Mass Media and National Development.* Stanford: Stanford Univ. Press, 1964.

This is Schramm's key book containing the seminal ideas for the following decade in the field of international communication research.

––– *Peru's Puno-based Educational Radio Project.* Stanford: Institute for Communication Research, 1969.

––– *The INTE Project: Peru's Mass Media Development Project.* Stanford: Institute for Communication Research, 1969b.

––– *Radio San José, La Voz Cultural de la Amazonia.* Stanford: Institute for Communication Research, 1969c.

––– "Communication in Family Planning." *Reports on Population/Family Planning,* 7, 1971: 1-43.

––– *Television reconsidered.* Singapore: Asian Mass Communication Research and Information Centre, 1972, 16 pp. (AMIC occasional paper No. 1).

The author presents the potential of TV teaching and stresses the need for careful reconsideration as to how people are using TV and how it can benefit them most.

––– *Big Media, Little Media.* Stanford: Institute for Communication Research, March 1973.

Media for instruction can be characterized as big (expensive) or little (inexpensive), but research evidence suggests that whether a student learns more from one medium than another depends at least as much on how the medium is used as on what medium is used. Thus, this report discusses not only example programs and their results, but also considerations involved in choices among the different possible media. One conclusion that is reached, however, is that the inexpensive media have often been neglected because of the glamour of the expensive media.

––– et al. *New educational media in action–Case studies,* 3 vols. Paris: UNESCO, 1967.

This document includes radio projects in Thailand, India, Japan, Australia, Togo, Niger, New Zealand, Honduras. It is a standard collection.

SCHUMACHER, E. F. *Small is Beautiful, Economics As If People Mattered.* New York: Harper and Row, 1973.

This book is an argument for intermediate technologies, particularly in developing areas, showing the futility of purely economic criteria. It is a different, but common sense, point of view that puts many development theories into a new light. Communication technologies, some of the largest scale innovations, are challenged.

SEAGO, J. A. "The Use of Media in Non-Formal Education for Rural Development: a Report on British Experience." Paper prepared for the International Council for Education Development in cooperation with the Overseas Development Administration. Reading, England: Agricultural Extension and Rural Development Centre, Univ. of Reading, May 1972.

SEARLE, B. "Site Selection Process: Radio Mathematics Project." Stanford, California: Institute for Mathematical Studies in the Social Sciences. February 8, 1974.

The author recounts visits to twelve countries by a team of researchers. They were looking for a site "to conduct research in the teaching of primary school mathematics by radio in a developing country." This report "describes the criteria in making a final site selection, compares the characteristics of the countries visited—as observed by site selection teams—and makes recommendations."

——— "Instructional Radio: the Nicaraguan Connection." Stanford Univ.: Institute for Mathematical Studies in the Social Sciences. Paper presented at the Fiftieth Convention of the National Association of Educational Broadcasters, Las Vegas, Nevada. November 19, 1974.

——— *Application of Radio to Teaching Elementary Mathematics in a Developing Country. First Annual Report.* Stanford, California: Stanford Univ., Institute for Mathematical Studies in Social Science, 1974.

This pilot project has as its goals: to investigate the use of radio for elementary mathematics instruction in underdeveloped countries, to evaluate a prototype system, to develop a methodology for producing radio instructional materials, and to foster in the host country the ability to self-sustain the project. Toward these goals the report cites accomplishment to date: selection of a host country (Nicaragua-Department of Masaya), the steps involved in establishing and sustaining the project in its initial period, and formation of a schedule for 1974 activities. In addition, the general research plans for the project are outlined. Several related researches in the United States, development of mental arithmetic tests, pilot testing lessons, experiment on digit writing time, and a textbook survey are described.

——— , FRIEND, J., and SUPPES, P. *The radio mathematics project: Nicaragua, 1974-1975.* Stanford: Institute for Mathematical Studies in the Social Sciences, Stanford Univ., 1976.

——— , and TILSON, T. *Application of radio to teaching elementary mathematics in a developing country.* Stanford: Institute for Mathematical Studies in the Social Sciences, Stanford Univ., June 1976.

SEARLE, B., MATTHEWS, P., SUPPES, P., and FRIEND, J. *Formal evaluation of the radio mathematics instructional program: Nicaragua – grade 1, 1976.* Stanford: Institute for Mathematical Studies in the Social Sciences, Stanford Univ., 1977 (draft).

SEARLE, B. and SUPPES, P. "The Nicaragua Radio Mathematics Project." *Educational Broadcasting International,* Vol. 8, 3, 1975: 117-120.

This article discusses the background and location of the radio mathematics project. The authors then go on to describe the actual operation of the project including psychological principles of instruction, educational materials, curriculum structure, and project evaluation.

– – – , and FRIEND, J. "The Nicaraguan radio mathematics project." In Spain, P., Jamison, D., and McAnany, E. (eds.) *Radio for education and development: Case studies,* Vol. 1. Washington, D.C.: World Bank, Working Paper 266, 1977.

Secretaria de Educaco e Cultura da Bahia. Instituto de Radio Difusao Educativa da Bahia (IRDEB). *Programação 1975.* Salvador, 1975, Portuguese.

Secretariado de Comunicación Social (SEDECOS). *Problemas de la Educación Radiofónica en América Latina.* Santiago: SEDECOS, 1974, 11 pp., Spanish.

SHEFFIELD, J. and DIEJOMAOH, W. *Nonformal education in African development.* New York: African-American Institute, 1972.

SINGH, K. N. "What research says about communicating with rural people." *Media Asia,* 1, 3, 1974: 41-47.

SITARAM, K. S. *The Experimental Study of the Effects of Radio upon the Rural Indian Audience.* Eugene: the Univ. of Oregon, Ph.D. dissertation, 1969.

SKORNIA, H. J. "Broadcast Media in Cuba." *Educational Broadcasting,* 6, 5 (September-October, 1973): pp. 24 ff.

   The author cites many technical and economic problems affecting Cuban television accounting for limited coverage. TV does not reach the masses. Radio is more widespread and vital, particularly short-wave radio.

SOCK, B. "A la radio Sénégalaise, Les ruraux parlent aus ruraux." *Informations de l'Unesco,* No. 654. *Direct* 1-7.

   The national Radio-Senegal channel has broadcast education programs in Wolof for four years. The rural people gather in groups to listen and discuss actions of the administration. This program, DISSOO, also has written documents containing listeners' reactions and state agent response. Since 1972, broadcasting has included other languages too.

SOIFER, J. "Radio para o desenvolvimento." *Revista Brasileira de Teleducacao,* December 1973.

   The article lists the techniques available particularly for the poor North and Northeast regions in Brazil.

– – – "50 Años de Teleducaçao no Brasil." Associaçao Brasileira de Teleducaçao, Garanhuna, 1973.

   The author analyzes the reasons of success and failures on educational broadcasting projects in the period 1922-1972 ("some success during 20 years," "pioneers," "the legislation," "success of SENAC and MEB," "SIRENA and other projects," "the reasons for success," "10 years of hope," "the new laws," "some case studies," "main reasons for success and failures," "the present situation: case studies").

SOIFER, J. *Manual de Teleducação.* SUDAM, Manaus, 1974.

   The author explains how to plan, organize, produce, and evaluate educational radio. The main chapters are: why educational broadcasting?; surveys, planning, and evaluation; mass media—pros and cons; the effects of educational broadcasting; techniques of learning, communication and learning through mass media; techniques for learning through radio and to keep listeners participating; radio program forms; sound sources and equipment; radio script, preparing and directing programs.

——— *Attitudes and Utilization of Mass Media in Rio de Janeiro.* Initial report, Manaus, 1975 (in press).

This document is a survey of daytime hours/week and kind of programs consumed by population of complete junior high school education in Rio de Janeiro. Their attitudes toward radio, TV, newspapers, and schools using a semantic differential scale are validated by Dr. Pfromm Netto in Sao Paulo.

——— *Teleducación y cambio social.* Instituto de Solidaridad Internacional, Lima 1975 (in press).

The author lists the problems arising when one wants to make a summative evaluation of educational broadcasting for development.

Somalia Ministry of Information. *The Development of Broadcasting in Somalia* (compiled by Suleiman Mohammed Adam). Mogadishu: Government Printing Press, 1968.

This document is one of the very few broadcasting studies done by an African on the scene.

SPAIN, P. *A Survey of Listenership in the Davao Provinces of Mindanao, the Philippines.* Eric: Ed. 105858. September 1971.

This report is a listenership study in a remote area showing the penetration of radio in eastern Mindanao. It shows the opportunities open to broadcasters even in such inaccessible places. The number of stations in the area has been reduced since the imposition of martial law.

——— *A Study of the System of Radioprimaria in the State of San Luís Potosi, Mexico.* Stanford Univ.: Department of Communication Research, March 1973.

This is the first report on the project described more fully in this volume.

——— The Mexican radioprimaria project. In Spain, P., Jamison, D., and McAnany, E. (eds.) *Radio for education and development: Case studies,* Vol. 1. Washington, D.C.: Education Department of the World Bank, 1977.

———, JAMISON, D., and McANANY, E. (eds.) *Radio for education and development: Case studies.* Washington, D.C.: World Bank, Working Paper 266, 1977.

SPARKS, K. R. *A bibliography of doctoral dissertations in television and radio.* Syracuse, New York: Newhouse Communications Center, School of Journalism, Syracuse Univ., 119 pp.

This compilation contains 900 dissertation titles completed at American universities and grouped into 12 categories. One section is devoted to international broadcasting.

SPECTOR, P. and TORRES, P. *Communication and motivation in community development.* Washington, D.C.: Institute for International Services, 1963.

SUCHMAN, E. *Evaluative research: principles and practice in public service and social action programs.* New York: Russell Sage Foundation, 1967.

TATTENBACH, F. *Análisis de los Intereses del Auditorio de un Programa de Educación Radiofónica.* (El case de la "Escuela para Todos" de Costa Rica.) Mexico: Revista del Centro de Estudios Educativos, Vol. 4, 4, 1974, pp. 67-94.

TEVOEDJRE, T. "An Educational Campaign by Radio in Dahomey, First Progress Report." *European Broadcasting Review,* March 1969.

After one year on the air, the director of Radio-Dahomey's Educational Broadcasting comments on the development so far and the hopes for the future of radio.

THEROUX, J. "The Quiz Show: A New Tool for Education." *Educational Technology,* Vol. XV, 1, January 1975. *Direct* III-54.

This article explores the uses of radio and television quiz shows for education. The author describes formal criteria and regulations for the production of such educational radio and TV games. Finally, the author describes one use of radio games in a university course in elementary hygiene at the University of Massachusetts.

– – – "A New Context for Radio Broadcaster Training." *Educational Broadcasting International,* December 1976.

– – – "Quality in Instructional Radio." *Public Telecommunications Review,* December 1976.

– – – *Education by radio: an experiment in rural group-listening for adults in Uganda.* Kampala, Uganda: Makerere College, Makerere Adult Studies Center. Occasional Paper No. 6, n.d.

TORRES, C. and CORREDOR, B. *Las escuelas radiofónicas de Sutatenza, Colombia.* Bogotá: Centro de Investigaciones Sociales, 1961.

This article presents Camilo Torres in his social science work before he became involved in the political efforts for which he is most renowned.

TRABELSI, K. *The cost of rural education radio in Senegal.* Working document IIEP/RP/7/-C.S.4F (in French). Paris: UNESCO International Institute for Educational Planning, 1972.

UNESCO. *Mass Media in the Developing Countries:* A UNESCO Report to the United Nations. Reports and Papers on Mass Communication, Number 33. Paris: UNESCO, 1961. Also available from: Mass Communication Clearing House, UNESCO, Place de Fontenoy, Paris-7e, France; and UNESCO Publications Center, P.O. Box 433, 317 E. 34th Street, New York, N,Y. 10016. 47 pp. ED 031 079.

– – – *Radio and Television in Literacy, A Survey of the Use of the Broadcasting Media in Combating Illiteracy Among Adults.* Reports and Papers on Mass Communication, No. 62. Paris 1971.

– – – "Radios' Predominant Role in Literacy Drive." *Literacy Work,* Vol. 4, 1, July/September 1974: 1-32.

– – – *Planning Out-of-School Education for Development. An IIEP Seminar.* Paris: UNESCO, International Institute for Educational Planning, 1972.

the seminar on out-of-school education. The papers include both general treatments of the subject and analyses of particular case studies.

– – – *New Trends in the Utilization of Educational Technology for Science Education.* Paris: UNIPUB, 1974.

This document contains a series of state-of-the-art papers prepared concerning computer-based science education, programmed learning in science education, the use of television and radio, theory and selection of learning media, integrated multimedia systems, and educational technology applied to the learning of science in developing countries.

––– Regional Office for Education in Latin America and the Caribbean. MOR-RAL: *The Brazilian Adult Literacy Experiments.* Paris: The UNESCO Press, 1975, 70 pp. English, French, Spanish.

UNICEF. *Zaa pa uwatanze (The Kiroboto Show): Listenership and educational impact.* American Technical Assistance Corporation, McLean, Va., U.S.A. and Bureau of Educational Research, Univ. of Nairobi, Kenya, December 1975.

USIS Research Office. *Northeast media survey, 1964; a survey in Northeast Thailand of radio listening, film attendance, and newspaper reading habits.* Bangkok: United States Information Service, 1964, 101 pp.

This study develops a profile of media habits in rural and municipal areas of Northeast Thailand in terms of the population at large, and in terms of particular target audiences such as teachers, government officials, priests, farmers, and so forth. It contains fairly detailed information describing the kinds of audiences being reached by mass communications and the habits and preferences of these audiences.

VAN BOL, J. M. and FAKHFAKH, A. *The use of mass media in the developing countries.* Brussels: International Centre for African Social and Economic Documentation, 1971, 751 pp., French/English.

This book is a compilation of over 2,500 entries of published works and periodical articles written in French, English, Dutch, German, Italian, Spanish, and Portuguese on the use of mass media in developing countries in Africa, Asia, and the other regions. The bibliography is laid out according to an analytical plan arranged under the broad subject headings of general theory, press, radio, cinema, television, and miscellaneous. It contains annotations in both French and English.

VEGA, E. and KEELER, H. *Evaluation of the Radio Schools Program for Basic Literacy in Tabacundo, Province of Pichancha, Ecuador.* Quito, Ecuador: Centro de Motivación y Asesoría (CEMA), December 1971.

VERNIER, P. "L'Educacion par la Radio au Gabon." *Interstages* (Brussels), 28, November 15, 1965: 18-20.

With the help of UNESCO, Radio Gabon began a concerted effort to educate villagers in areas such as health and agriculture.

VERNON, E. "Ideología y comunicación de masas; la semantización de la violación política." In Vern, Eliseo et al., *Lenguaje y comunicación social.* Buenos Aires, Nueva Vision, 1969: 133-191.

WAJSMAN, P. "Una historia de fantasmas; a propósito del libro de Ariel Dorfman y Armand Mattelart, para leer el Pato Donald." *Lenguajes* (Argentina). 1974: 127-131.

WANIEWICZ, I. *Broadcasting for adult education: a guidebook to worldwide experience.* Paris: UNESCO, 1972, 132 pp.

This document purports to provide practical advice and guidance on the use of radio and television broadcasting in adult education. It is addressed to educational planner and administrators, educators responsible for curriculum development, and teaching methodology, field-work organizers, as well as broadcasting administrators and producers. It will be of great interest to the readers of those countries where use of radio and TV in adult education is still in its infancy.

– – – "Educational Potentialities and Limitations of Radio and Television." *Indian Journal of Adult Education,* 36. 1975: 2-7.

EJ132168

WARREN, C. "Introductory assessment of the technical aspects of educational communication technologies." In Butman, R., Rathjens, G., and Warren, C. *Technical-economic considerations in public service broadcast communications for developing countries.* Washington, D.C.: Academy for Educational Development, 1973.

WELSH, B. (ed.) *A handbook for scriptwriters of adult education,* 2 vols. Bonn: Friedrich-Ebert-Stiftung, 1973.

AMIC 003433

This book contains information on the nature of radio, radio program forms, program content, radio talks, interviews, discussions, radio magazine programs, radio features, and drama. It includes also additional study material consisting of specimen broadcast scripts as well as a glossary of radio technology and test exercises.

– – – "Kits for Educational Radio Training." *Educational Broadcasting International,* Vol. 6, 3, September 1973: 124-128.

EJ087895

The author looks at the use of educational radio in several developing countries.

WHITE, R. *The Adult Education Program of Acción Cultural Popular Hondurena: An Evaluation of the Rural Development Potential of the Radio School Movement in Honduras,* 2 vols. St. Louis: St. Louis Univ., Department of Anthropology and Sociology, October 1972.

This represents a more lengthy report on some of the material described by White in this volume. It is based on earlier data without the thorough analysis that has been done since.

– – – *An alternative pattern of basic education: Radio Santa María.* Paris: UNESCO, 1976(a).

– – – "The Uses of Radio in Primary and Secondary Formal Education: The Santa María Model in the Dominican Republic." Paper presented at the Conference on Communication Policy and Planning for Education and Development. Stanford Univ., July 11-15, 1976(b).

This paper describes the general objectives of Radio Santa María, the educational methodologies employed, the costs compared to conventional classroom methods, and the outcomes of the project.

– – – "Mass communications and the popular promotion strategy of rural development in Honduras." In Spain, P., Jamison, D., and McAnany, E. (eds.) *Radio for education and development: Case studies,* Vol. 2. Washington, D.C.: World Bank, Working Paper 266, 1977.

WILEY, D. "Another hour, another day: Quantity of schooling, a potent path for policy." Reprinted in Guttentag, M. (ed.) *Evaluation Studies Review Annual, Vol. 2.* Beverly Hills and London: Sage Publications, 1977, pp. 434-476.

Wisconsin Research Project in School Broadcasting. *Radio in the classroom.* Madison: Univ. of Wisconsin Press, 1942.

WOELFEL, N. E. and TYLER, I. K. (eds.) *Radio and the school: A guidebook for teachers and administrators.* Yonkers-on-the-Hudson, N.Y.: World Book, 1945.

XOOMSAI, T. and RATANAMANGALA, B. *School broadcast: Its evaluation.* Bangkok: Ministry of Education, 1962.

YOUSIF, A. M. "Requirements for Radio and Television Broadcasting in the Context of an Arab Space Communication Network." *ASBU Review,* 3, 1974. *Direct* III-51.

This study presents the possibilities of a telecommunications (satellite) system for use by the Arab countries. This preliminary study covers the following points:

– examination of the socioeconomic situation of the people and their needs;

– possibilities for broadcasting programs through a regional network;

– possible beginnings of permanent radio and television stations;

– examination of different modes of programming.

ZULOAGA, A. *Audience reaction to a rural instructional series in Central Mexico.* M.S. dissertation. Madison: Univ. of Wisconsin, 1972.

INDEX TO THE BIBLIOGRAPHY

Ecuador–C.I.E. (n.d.); Colle (1974); Dubly (1973), Encalada (1974); Vega and Keeler (1963).

El Salvador–Academy for Educational Development (1972); Clippinger (1976); Mayo and Mayo (1971); Mayo, et al. (1976); Rhoads and Piper (1963).

England–*Direct* I-11; Grattan (1974); Robson (1974); Seago (1972).

Ethiopia–Luguai (1963); Rathjens (1973).

Fiji–Mansfield (1971).

France–Daney and Madre (1974); *Direct* X-173; *Direct* I-1.

Gabon–Vernier (1965).

Gambia–Conateh (1965).

Germany, Federal Republic of–*Direct* I-1; Kanocz (1975).

Ghana–Kinross (1961).

Guatemala–AED (1976); *Boletín Informativo Centro,* Ano II.

Honduras–*Boletín Informativo Centro,* Año II; Rhoads and Piper (1963); Schramm, et al. (1967); White (1972, 1977).

Hong Kong–Allen (1970).

India–Awasthy (1965); Benson's (1971); Bhatt, et al. (1965); Das (1974); *Direct* VI-69; *Direct* VI-72; Jain (1968, 1969a, 1969b); Jha and Katiyar (1974); Khan (1972); Kivlin, et al. (1968); Mathur and Neurath (1959); Neurath (1962); Noorani (1973); Polcyn (1973); Roy, et al. (1969); Schramm, et al. (1967); Sitaram (1969).

Indonesia–Eapen (1973); Hilbrink and Lohman (1974); Jamison and Leslie (1977); Rundfunk and Fernsen (1974).

Iran–NIRT (1972).

Italy–Schramm, et al. (1964).

Ivory Coast–Benveniste, 1974; *Direct* VI-69; *Direct* VI-75; *Direct* I-22; Klees and Jamison (1976); Schramm, et al. (1967).

Jamaica–Educational Television International (1970); Martin (1972).

Japan–Internationales Zentralinstitüt (1971); Nishimoto (1966, 1969); Schiller (1975); Schramm, et al. (1967).

Kenya–Ball (1971a, 1971b, 1974a, 1974b, 1974c); Kinyanjui (1973, 1977); Krival (1970-1971); Riitho (1971); UNICEF (1975).

Korea, South–Ahmed (1972); Hulsen (1967); Jamison and Kim (1976); KEDI (1976); Mitchell and Kim (1968).

Laos–Lent (1947a).

Malagasy Republic–Cazeneuve (1968).

Malawi–Clarke (1972); *Direct* I-22; Klongon (1967); Mackie (1971).

Malaysai–Balckburn (1971); Lent (1974b); Radio Talivishen Malaysia (1970).

Mali–Cutter (1971); Diallo (1968).

Mauritius–Dinah and Swaleh (1973); *Direct* X-173; Meyer, G. (1970); Ministry of Education and Cultural Affairs (1973).

Mexico–Academy for International Development, 1972; Arana de Swadesh, 1971; *Direct* X-172; Klees (1973, 1974); Lowry (1970); Lozano Jimenez, et al. (1966); Mayo, et al. (1975); Schmelkes (1972); Spain (1973); Spain, et al. (1977); Zuloaga (1972).

Morocco—Charconnet (1966).

Nepal—Mayo, et al. (1975); Radio Nepal (1969, 1973); Ral (1971); Rathjens, et al. (1975).

New Guinea—Brockhall (1970); Jeffrey (1972); MacKay (1973, 1974).

New Zealand—Schramm, et al. (1967).

Nicaragua—*Boletín Informativo Centro,* Año II; Jamison (1976); Jamison (1977a); Searle (1974a, 1974b, 1974c); Searle and Suppes (1975); Searle, et al. (all dates).

Niger—El Hadj Badge and Robert (1972); McAnany (1972a); Schramm, et al. (1967).

Nigeria—Akintayo (1974); Axinn and Nancy (1969); Kincaid (1967); Schramm, et al. (1967).

Pacific Islands—Bishop (1974); Mansfield (1971); Medard (1962).

Pakistan—Ali-Khan (1974); *ASBU Review* (1975); *Direct* I-22; Mujahid (1973).

Peru-Davignon (1973); Ramos Falconi (1973); Schramm, et al. (1967); Schramm (1969a, 1969b).

Philippines—Ables (1966); Lent (1966, 1968a, 1968b, 1970, 1971b); Marquez (1975); Spain (1971).

Poland—Krawcewicz (1976).

Rwanda—Abjangba, 1968a.

Samoa—Academy for Educational Development (1972); Schramm, et al. (1967).

Saudi Arabia—Boyd (1973).

Senegal—Cassirer (1970); Sock (n.d.); Conateh (1974); *Direct* VI-69; *Direct* X-80; *Direct* I-3; *Direct* III-19; Mills (1972).

Singapore—Academy for Educational Development (1972); Radio Television Singapore (1973).

Somalia—Somalia Ministry of Information (1968).

South Africa—Orlik, 1969.

Sri Lanka—Coonasekera, 1972; Jayaweera, 1973.

Tanzania—Barrett (1973, 1976); Hall (1973a, 1973b, 1974b, 1975); Hall and Dodds (1974, 1977); Hall and Zikambona (1974); Institute of Adult Education (1971); Jengo (1975); Kassam (1975); Matiko (1976).

Thailand—Anatol and Bittner (1971); Baker (1973); Blackburn (1971); Deemer Co. Ltd. (1972); Meyer, R. (1971); Tatanamungala (1972); Robock (1964); Schmueker (1972); Schramm, et al. (1967); USIS Research Office (1964).

Togo—Marathey (1965); Schramm, et al. (1967).

Tunisia—Alleback, et al. (1971); *Direct* VI-76.

Turkey—Besiroglu (1974).

Uganda—Theroux (n.d.).

Upper Volta—Hoffman (1972); Mills (1972).

Venezuela—Colomina de Rivera (1968).

Zaire—Boisschot (1969); Egly, et al. (1971); Muelanzambi (1975).

SUBJECT

Acción Cultural Popular–Acción Cultural Popular (all dates); Ahmed and Coombs (1975); Beltran (1975); Bernal (1967a, 1967b, 1968, 1970, 1971, 1972); Bernal and Palacio Londono (1968); Bernal and Nieto (1975); Braun (1975b); Brumberg (1972, 1974, 1975); Ferrer Martin (1958-1959), 1959a, 1959b); Fierro, et al. (1964); Fontan (1965); Gomez Posada (1967, 1968, 1970a, 1970b); Grise (1974); Gutierrez, A. (1971a, 1971b); Gutierrez, M. (1973); Jimenez Acosta (1974); Marting and de Castillo (1974); Musto (1970); Musto, et al. (1971); Nino (1968); Primrose (1965); Ramirez Pardo (1975); Restrepo (1973); Restrepo and de Castillo (1974); Schramm, et al. (1967); Torres and Corredor (1961).

Agricultural information–Acción Cultural Popular (all dates); Adjangba (1968a, 1968b); Ahmed (1972); Ahmed and Coombs, Brockhall (1970); Bueno (1972); Cortes (1972); Cortez (1972); Defever (1971); Diaz Bordanave (1974); *Direct* VI-72; *Direct* VI-76; *Direct* III-19; Douglass (1965); Fierro, et al. (1974); Hoffman (1972); Khan (1972); Mathur and Neurath (1959); Monteiro (1972); Neurath (1962); Nicl, et al. (1954); Ribeiro and Diaz Bordanave (1971); Roling (1975); Roy, et al. (1969); Rundfunk and Fernseh (1974); Schramm, et al. (1967); Seago (1972); Vernier (1965); White (1972).

Bibliographies–AMIC list of theses; AMIC list of periodicals; AMIC (1973, 1974); Beltran (1974); Benson's (1972); Forsythe (1970); Grise (1974); Guelette (1976); Gunter (1976); Hachten (1972); Head (1974); Head and Beck (1974); Ingle (1974); Jamison, et al. (1973); Lent (1966, 1975b, 1975c); Literacy Work (1975); McAnany (1973); Madden (1968); Mitchell and Kim (1968); Nordicom (1975); Polcyn (1973); Rahim (1976); Schramm (1973); Schramm, et al. (1967); Sparks (n.d.); Van Bol and Fakhfakh (1971).

Costs–Bezeau (1975); Coombs and Hallack (1972); Etherington (1977); Fisher (1971); General Learning Corporation (1968); Grise (1974); Hooper (1974); Hupe (1974); Jamison (1976, 1977b); Jamison and Kim (1976); Jamison, Klees and Wells (1978); Klees (1973); Klees and Jamison (1976); Mayo, et al. (1975); Schramm, et al. (1967); Trabelsi (1972).

Distance Learning–Ali Khan (1974); C.I.E. (n.d.); Cortés (1972); Cortéz (1972); *Direct* III-42; *Direct* I-9; *Direct* I-II; *Direct* I-22; Hawkridge (1973); Holmberg (1977); Kinyanjui (1974); Laidlaw and Layard (1974); LeFranc (1977); Lumsden and Ritchie (1975); Mackenzie, et al. (1975); Nordenstreng, et al. (1969).

Family Planning–Adjangba (1968); Ball and May (1971); Barrett (1973); Berrigan (1975); Braun (1975a); *Direct* VI-70; *Direct* VI-72; *Direct* VI-75; Hall (1974a, 1974b); Hall and Zikambona (1974); Hudson and Parker (1973); Marsten and Rogers (1973); Matiko (1976); Parker (1972); Parker and Lisignan (1977); Riitho (1971); Schramm (1971); Schramm, et al. (1967); Vernier (1965).

Farm Forums–Ables (1966); Ahmed (1972); Beltran (1968, 1971); Coleman, et al. (1968); *Direct* VI-70; *Direct* VI-72; *Direct* X-80; *Direct* I-3; Eapen (1973); Fewster (1965); Hilbrink and Lohmann (1974); Klongan (1967); McAnany (1972a, 1972b, 1973); Mathur and Neurath (1959); NIRT (1972);

Neurath (1962); Nicol, et al. (1954); Ohliger (1967); Primrose (1965); Ribeiro and Diaz Bordanave (1971); Rogers and Solomon (1972); Rundfunk and Fernseh (1974); Schramm, et al. (1967); Theroux (n.d.); cf. radio schools.

Health—Adjangba (1968b); Ball and May (1971); Barrett (1973); Berrigan (1975); Braun (1975a); *Direct* VI-70; *Direct* VI-72; *Direct* VI-75; Hall (1974a, 1974b); Hall and Zikambona (1974); Hudson and Parker (1973); Kreimer (1977); Marsten and Rogers (1973); Matiko (1976); Parker (1972); Riitho (1971); Schramm (1971); Schramm, et al. (1967); Vernier (1965); cf. family planning, nutrition.

In-school radio—Adjangba (1968a); Akintayo (1974); Alleback, et al. (1971); Australian Broadcasting Commission/British Broadcasting Corporation (1973); Ball (1971a, 1971b, 1974a, 1974b, 1974c); Daney and Madre (1974); *Direct* X-172; Egly, et al. (1971); Gallego (1974); Grise (1974); Hooper (1974); Hulsen (1967); Jamison, et al. (1973); Jeffrey (1972); Leslie (1971); Manduley (1976a, 1976b); Mansfield (1971); MOBRAL (1974); NHK (1956a, 1956b); Nishimoto (1966); Robson, J. (1974); Robson, M. (1973); Schramm, et al. (1967); Searle (1974a, 1974b, 1974c); Searle and Suppes (1975); Spain (1973); Wisconsin Research Project in School Broadcasting (1942); Woelfel and Tyler (1945); Xoomsau and Ratanamangala (1962).

Literacy—AED (1976); Allen (1970); Educational Television International (1970); Kassam (1975); Lowry (1970); Lozano Jimenez, et al. (166); Maddison (1971); Mobral (1974); Oxenham (1975); Rhoads and Piper (1963); Ryan (1975); Schramm, et al. (1967); UNESCO (1971); Vega and Keeler (1971); Waniewicz (1972).

Nutrition—Leslie (1977); Manoff International, Inc. (1975); cf. health.

Radio Schools—Adangba (1968b); ALER (1975); Beltran (1968, 1971, 1975); Bernal (1967a, 1967b, 1968); *Boletín Informativo Centro,* Año II; Bolivia (1970, 1973); Braun (1975b); Brumberg (1972a, 1972b, 1975); Cabezas Esteban (1975); Camus and Baeza (1974); Charconnet (1966); Colle (1974); Davignon (1973); Decena-Dilona (1973); Ferrer Martin (1958-1959, 1959a, 1959b); Fierro, et al. (1974); Fontan (1965); Gomez (1971); Gomez Posada (1967, 1968, 1970a, 1970b); Herzog and Braun (1975); Kassam (1975); Kreimer (1975); McAnany (1973); Marting and de Castillo (1974); Musto (1970); Musto, et al. (1971); OSAL (1972); Primrose (1965); Schmelkes (1972); Schramm, et al. (1967); Schramm (1969a); Torres and Corredor (1961); Vega and Keeler (1971); White (1972, 1976) cf. farm forums.

Radiovision—Adjangba (1968); Ball (1974a); Defever (1971); Dinah and Swaleh (1973); *Direct* VI-69; *Direct* X-173; Mills (1972); Schramm, et al. (1967).

Satellites—Clippinger (1976): Cowlan (1974); *Direct* III-42; *Direct* V-76; *Direct* VI-72; Hudson and Parker (1973); Hupe (1974); Jamison (1968); Klaver (1975); *Literacy Work* (1975); Marsten and Rogers (1973); Nichols (1974); Noorani (1973); Parker (1972); Polcyn (1973); Radio Talivishen Malaysia (1970); Yousif (1974).

Television—Academy for Educational Development (1972); Alleback, et al. (1971); Allen (1970); Arena, et al. (1977); Australian Broadcasting Commission/British Broadcasting Corporation (1973); Benveniste (1974); Boisschot (1969); Carpenter (1972, 1974); CEDO (1974); Chu and Schramm (1967);

Clippinger (1976); Colomina de Rivera (1968); D'Arinos Silva (1975); Dieu-zeide (1974); *Direct* IV-25; *Direct* V-76; *Direct* VI-69; *Direct* VI-72; *Direct* VI-75; *Direct* VI-76; *Direct* VIII-130; *Direct* III-42; *Direct* I-14; *Direct* I-1; Edington (1974); Educational Television International (1970); Faulkner (1974); Head (1974); Herzog (1967); Inravision (1974); Jamison, et al. (1973); Kincaid (1967); Klees (1974); Klees and Jamison (1974); *Literacy Work* (1974); Lowry (1970); Maddison (1971); Mayo, et al. (1976); Meyer, G. (1970); Muelanzambi (1975); Mujanid (1973); NHK (1977); NIRT (1972); Nishimoto (1966); Noorani (1973); Oliviera (1977); Radio Talivishen Malaysia (1970); Ryan (1975); Schmuecker (1972); Schramm (1969b, 1972, 1973); Schramm, et al. (1967); Soifer (1975a); Sparks (n.d.); Speagle (1972); UNESCO (1971); Waniewicz (1972, 1975); Yousif (1974).
Two-way radio–Cassirer (1970); Clarke (1972); Hudson and Parker (1973, 1975); Marsten and Rogers (1973); Parker (1972).

About
the Authors

DEAN T. JAMISON is a member of the Development Economics Department of the World Bank where he undertakes research on the role of education and communication in development. He holds degrees in philosophy and engineering from Stanford University, and he completed his Ph.D. in economics at Harvard in 1970. After leaving Harvard, he returned for four years to Stanford, where he taught economics, decision theory, and education. Then, prior to joining the World Bank, he spent several years as chairman of the Economics and Educational Planning Group at the Educational Testing Service.

EMILE G. McANANY has worked in the field of development communications for the last ten years. He is presently an assistant professor in the Institute for Communication Research at Stanford University. He is the author, editor, and translator of four books, *The Filmviewers Handbook* (with R. Williams, Paulist, 1965), *Political Psalms* by Cardenal (Herder, 1972), *Educational Reform with Television: The El Salvador Experience* (with J. Mayo and R. Hornik, Stanford University Press, 1976), and *Radio for Education and*

Development: Case Studies, Vol. I and II (edited with P. Spain and D. Jamison, World Bank, 1977). He has also published articles, monographs, and reports in the areas of development communication, educational technology, and evaluation.